Judging the Image

Art, value, law – the links between these three terms mark a history of struggle in the cultural scene. Studies of contemporary culture have thus increasingly turned to the image as central to the production of legitimacy, aesthetics and order. *Judging the Image* extends the cultural turn in legal and criminological studies by interrogating our responses to the image. This book provides a space to think through problems of ethics, social authority and the legal imagination. Concepts of memory and interpretation, violence and aesthetic, authority and legitimacy are considered in a diverse range of sites, including:

- body, performance and regulation
- judgment, censorship and controversial artworks
- graffiti and the aesthetics of public space
- HIV and the art of the disappearing body
- witnessing, ethics and the performance of suffering
- memorial images – art in the wake of disaster.

This book will be fascinating reading for students and academics working at the crossroads of aesthetics, crime, law and culture.

Alison Young is Associate Professor of Criminology at the University of Melbourne.

Transformations: Thinking Through Feminism
Edited by
Maureen McNeil, *Institute of Women's Studies, Lancaster University*
Lynne Pearce, *Department of English, Lancaster University*
Beverley Skeggs, *Department of Sociology, Manchester University*

Books in the series include:

Transformations
Thinking through feminism
*Edited by Sarah Ahmed, Jane Kilby, Celia Lury, Maureen McNeil
and Beverley Skeggs*

Thinking Through the Skin
Edited by Sara Ahmed and Jackie Stacey

Strange Encounters
Embodied others in post-coloniality
Sara Ahmed

Feminism and Autobiography
Texts, theories, methods
Edited by Tess Cosslett, Celia Lury and Penny Summerfield

Advertising and Consumer Citizenship
Gender, images and rights
Anne M. Cronin

Mothering the Self
Mothers, daughters, subjects
Stephanie Lawler

When Women Kill
Questions of agency and subjectivity
Belinda Morrissey

Class, Self, Culture
Beverley Skeggs

Haunted Nations
The colonial dimensions of multiculturalisms
Sneja Gunew

The Rhetorics of Feminism
Readings in contemporary cultural theory and the popular press
Lynne Pearce

Women and the Irish Diaspora
Breda Gray

Jacques Lacan and Feminist Epistemology
Kirsten Campbell

Judging the Image
Art, value, law
Alison Young

Judging the Image

Art, value, law

Alison Young

Routledge
Taylor & Francis Group

LONDON AND NEW YORK

First published 2005
by Routledge
2 Park Square, Milton Park, Abingdon, Oxon OX14 4RN

Simultaneously published in the USA and Canada
by Routledge
270 Madison Ave, New York, NY 10016

Routledge is an imprint of the Taylor & Francis Group

© 2005 Alison Young

Typeset in Times by
BOOK NOW Ltd
Printed and bound in Great Britain by
TJ International Ltd, Padstow, Cornwall

British Library Cataloguing in Publication Data
A catalogue record for this book is available from the British Library

Library of Congress Cataloging in Publication Data
Young, Alison, 1962–
    Judging the image: art, value, law / Alison Young.– 1st ed.
        p. cm.
    Includes bibliographical references and index.
    1. Art, Modern–20th century–Themes, motives. 2. Art, Modern–21st
century–Themes, motives. 3. Art and morals. 4. Culture and law. I. Title.
    N6490.Y68 2004
    701′.03′09045–dc22   2004017565

ISBN 0–415–30183–1 (hbk)
ISBN 0–415–30184–X (pbk)

Contents

List of figures   vii
Acknowledgements   ix

1 The capture of the subject   1

2 Aesthetic vertigo: disgust and the illegitimate touchings
   of art   20

   viewing (de)position
   hidings   45

3 Written on the skin of the city   50

   viewing (de)position
   'where do you live?'   75

4 Disappearing images and the laws of appearance   78

   viewing (de)position
   gifts   95

5 The art of injury and the ethics of witnessing   98

   viewing (de)position
   'is there anything you wish to ask me?'   117

6 All that remains: image in a place of ruin   121

   Notes   141
   Bibliography   175
   Index   185

Figures

All the figures listed can be found together in a section between pages 97–8

1   Spencer Tunick, *Melbourne 4* (2001)
2   Andres Serrano, *Piss Christ* (1987)
3   Marcus Harvey, *Myra* (1995)
4   Graffiti piece, Adelaide (September 2001)
5   Graffiti throw-up, Adelaide (September 2001)
6   Stencil and tag, Melbourne (April 2003)
7   Stencil, Melbourne (March 2003)
8   Stencil, Melbourne (May 2003)
9   Felix Gonzalez-Torres, *'Untitled' (Loverboy)* (1990)
10   Felix Gonzalez-Torres, *'Untitled' (Placebo)* (1991)
11   Felix Gonzalez-Torres, *'Untitled' (Lover Boy)* (1989)
12   Spencer Tunick, *New Jersey* (1998)
13   Ground Zero, New York (May 2003)
14   Section of a memorial wall at Ground Zero, New York (May 2003)

Acknowledgements

A matrix of support, friendship, thoughtfulness and help both individual and institutional enfolds this book. Its research and writing have been a gift to me, in that I have been able to spend several years thinking about the image and its relation to law. And its completion arises out of a series of gifts to me from others – gifts of time, of ideas and of support.

A great deal of substantive help was provided by interviewees. Numerous graffiti writers talked to me about their involvement in graffiti – thank you for sharing your ideas and histories. Several artists also spent several hours talking with me about their work – thank you for your generosity: Jaguar LaCroix (previously known as Sally McClymont), Andrea Meadows, Andres Serrano and Spencer Tunick.

Research in the early stages of this project was supported by an Australian Research Council Small Grant and a Melbourne University Project Grant. Some of the research underlying Chapter 3 was funded by an Australian Research Council Large Grant. I am grateful for all the financial support provided. Among other things, it enabled me to work with Rebecca Scott Bray, who was a dedicated and creative research assistant. Conversations with her over the years have enriched both this book and my understanding and appreciation of art and law. Derek Dalton saved many interesting press cuttings for me over the years – my thanks to him. And research assistance in the latter stages of the project was very ably provided by Kirsty Duncanson.

Ideas from some of the chapters were presented as conference papers and guest lectures. I am greatly indebted to the audience on each of the following occasions for their discussion of my arguments: the Luce Foundation Lecture, Amherst College; the Australian Law and Literature Association Conference at Beechworth; the Symposium on Law and Cultural Studies at Yale Law School; the Australian Law and Literature Association Conference at Sydney; the departmental seminar in Political Science, University of Massachusetts at Amherst; the Law and Society Association Annual Meeting held in Budapest; the Australian Law and Society Association Conference hosted by Victoria University Law School; the Australian Law and Literature Association Conference at Melbourne University Law School; and the visiting seminar series in the Socio-Legal Centre, Law Faculty, Griffith University.

Earlier versions of two of the chapters in this book have been published elsewhere: Chapter 2 as 'Aesthetic vertigo and the jurisprudence of disgust', *Law and Critique* (2000) 11 (3): 241–65, and Chapter 4 as '"Into the blue": the image written on law', *Yale Journal of Law and the Humanities* (2001) 13: 101–33 and (in shortened form) as 'Compassionate judgments: the cinematic possibility of judgment with passion', in L. Moran (ed.) (2004) *Law's Moving Image*, London: Cavendish.

The space and time to write and think have become incredibly scarce resources for academics, especially in many Australian institutions. Research leave provided the means to begin, develop and then finally to finish this book. I'm very thankful for the generosity of two institutions in hosting me as a visitor during the researching and writing of this book. Amherst College awarded me the Karl Loewenstein Fellowship in Political Science and Jurisprudence, allowing me the chance to spend six months there in 1998 and six months in 2000. During my visits there, I enjoyed conversations with many people – a more thoroughly engaged and engaging group of academics it would be hard to imagine. My time in Amherst was a wonderful intellectual gift. Completion of the project was made possible by sabbatical leave from my department and the opportunity to be a research visitor at the Faculty of Law, Melbourne University, which offered uninterrupted space in which to revise the final manuscript.

Throughout this project, I have benefited from ongoing conversations with a series of supportive friends and academics, who gave up their time and energy to read chapters, suggest ideas or listen to my arguments. My thanks to you all: Mieke Bal, Jennifer Culbert, Tom Dumm, Nasser Hussain, Peter Hutchings, Bill MacNeil, Shaun McVeigh, Nina Philadelphoff-Puren, Austin Sarat, Rebecca Scott Bray, Richard Sherwin. Nasser Hussain, both in Amherst and in the virtual realms of email and telephone, encouraged me at every stage of this project. And Peter Rush lived with this book's intrusions into the everyday, as I agonized about its writing and non-writing. He read and reread each word, and is the most generous of interlocutors. My very greatest admiration and thanks for his intellectual spirit.

This book is dedicated to two people: to Peter, for his art of companionship, and to Sophie, who transformed the text and everything else.

1 The capture of the subject

That illusion, in the final analysis, determines the laws of society cannot and must not be seen.

(Luce Irigaray, *Marine Lover of Friedrich Nietzsche*)

I think an enlightened culture is one that respects the body and doesn't consider it a crime or put a body in jail just because there's an artist working with the nude in public.

(Spencer Tunick)

Becoming image

It's 10 a.m. on a sunny Wednesday morning, and I'm lying naked on a rock at the end of the North Wharf under the Bolte Bridge in Melbourne. I'm in the middle of discovering that, as bell hooks (1995: 136) says, 'writing about art, making art, is not the same as being the subject of art'.

I am naked on this rock because I'm one of more than 200 women who are being photographed by Spencer Tunick, the New York-based artist whose work centres on documenting nude individuals (either solo or as mass groups) in public spaces with photography and video.[1] Tunick is in Melbourne for the Melbourne Fringe Festival, and as part of his *nudeadrift* project, which involves travelling around all seven continents, photographing people naked in public. In the last week, he has already had one installation: he hoped to gather approximately 3,000 people at dawn on the banks of the Yarra River (in fact over 4,000 participants turned up).

Today's event is a closed-to-media, women-only event. I found out about it just this morning, when Tunick called me, in response to my emailed request to carry out an interview with him. He has invited me to interview him afterwards. I turned up at the location – ambitiously called the 'Oriental Gardens' but in reality a concreted stretch of disused wharf past a series of warehouses – intending simply to observe the installation and take notes on what was happening, but now here I am, surrounded by strangers, all of us naked, holding a pose while Tunick shoots the scene.

The participants constitute a formidably diverse group of women. It is supposed to be an event for women aged over 35; most of those present are in the 35–40 age range, a few look younger, and there's a sizeable proportion of older women. The sun is shining fiercely, a strong breeze gusts up from the water. It looks as though there are well over 200 women here.

Upon my arrival, I introduced myself to Tunick. He said, 'Feel free to join in if you like'. I was startled, then transfixed by the idea of sliding from critic into participant. I try to imagine myself taking my clothes off here, in the sun, in this group. I'm apprehensive, but I decided that I would do it. I watched Tunick checking out different sites for him to stand while taking the photographs. Eventually it was decided; he told the group that there will be three locations. We are to take our clothes off and walk to the first; then walk naked to the second; then walk back to our clothes and dress. We will then walk a few hundred metres to the third location, undress again, and pose for a final time.

Everything's ready, his assistant calls out for us to undress. Some women whoop loudly, others are laughing, there's a buzzing noise of excitement as we strip, bundling clothes into bags, stuffing watches and jewellery into pockets. I feel intensely aware of every piece of clothing and every movement necessary to remove it. The T-shirt pulled over my head. The jeans unbuttoned and bundled up. The act of undressing was never so self-conscious for me, so freighted with significance. I look at some of the people undressing around me: there's a tall woman who carries a naked baby with her. A group of three older women remove their clothes to reveal – on their lower backs, hidden in everyday life – tattoos. And *I* feel as though I am both exposing and hiding something: I'm eight weeks pregnant, and standing completely unclothed in public seems like a display of my internally transformed body, although no-one looking at me would yet be able to tell from my body's exterior.

We walk to the first location – rocks by the river's edge, directly under the massive Bolte Bridge ferrying traffic over our heads. Every step I take feels as though I am moving in slow motion. I feel the scratch of gravel under the soft soles of my feet. A film crew, which is documenting Tunick's progress around the world, is filming us.[2] They are standing on the edge of the flowing river of naked women. I walk past one cameraman. I manage not to look at the lens.

We have been told to lie on the rocks, leaning back. Tunick calls instructions: legs to be bent, legs to lean away from the camera, faces to be turned away. He repeats over and over: do not look at the camera. (Tunick's mass photographs are characterized by facelessness, the subjects' heads averted from Tunick's camera.) There are so many of us that we are lying very close to and sometimes touching each other. I'm leaning back on a stranger's lower legs; another stranger's haunches are inches from my face. Women are still laughing and chatting, the buzzing still sounds as we settle into the pose, then silence takes over as Tunick takes the photographs. Tunick takes the photographs and our status as objects of art becomes *subjectified*. We are the objects of the image and we also become subjects by way of the immensity of the act of lying naked on a rock in public in a group of strangers. The experience of becoming image is a movement of subjectification that interrupts the everyday sense of ourselves as individuals separated from the public and its gaze and institutions. Participation in Tunick's installation has enfolded each of us into public space and has infused that space with unexpected intimacy: the shrugging off of clothes, the touch of skin on skin, the immobility of the pose. The silence surrounds us; our bodies could not be less objectified in this moment, the result of a sequence of movements beginning with the removal of clothing, continuing through the walk to the installation location, and held, now, in the sovereign moment of the pose.

It's so quiet while Tunick takes the photographs. I can hear the wind rushing over us, the river paddling at the rocks, the traffic trudging overhead. I can hear my breath. The sun and breeze on my naked skin are shocking. Two hundred naked strangers hold a pose for several minutes. Tunick takes the photographs. It's over; Tunick tells us we can move, there's an outburst of cheering and clapping.

We repeat this twice more. From the rocks, we walk, gingerly over the rough ground, to a disused jetty, and lie down in rows upon the wooden planks. The jetty is covered in gravel; tiny fragments of glass glint in the dirt. I unfold my naked body and lie on my back, head turned away from the camera, feeling the harsh wood, tiny stones and rubble engrave themselves upon my skin. This is not a critical writing *about* art; instead, this is art as the writing of bodies, of my body.

The third location requires a longer walk, through a throng of wharf workers, and so we dress hurriedly in the basics of clothing (jeans but no underwear, T-shirt but no bra) and move to an open space which backs on to the glistening blue harbour, with the prongs of the city's buildings jutting along the horizon. At each location, the same phenomenon: a buzz of excitement, then, as Tunick takes the photographs, the uncanny, beautiful silence, followed by cheers and laughter. People dress and depart, returning to everyday life. Some remain naked, posing for snapshots with Tunick. Many, many women want to hug him and thank him.

Finally, the crowd is gone; Tunick, his assistants, the documentary film crew, myself, and some women who are going to pose in individual installations later in the day remain. We return to Tunick's hotel to do the interview. The film crew wants to film me interviewing Tunick, for possible inclusion of the scene in their documentary. And so I ask him questions and he answers, generously, thoughtfully. I have a brief list of questions to ask, with my usual interview technique being to use them as improvisational tools, so that I can move the interview in particular directions that seem interesting once the conversation has begun. However, the presence of the camera, silently swivelling between myself and Tunick, oscillating with each question and each answer, inhibits my thinking and I can feel myself getting more and more mechanical with the format, mind blanking as the answer comes, unable to generate impromptu questions. Tunick remains completely composed, but when it's over, I'm sweating and pink-faced. As I say my goodbyes, he returns to discussing with a prospective model the locations for his next installation.

I'm left with the enigma of the ground's roughness against my body, of the soft air and the sunlight touching my skin, of the sudden open secret of two hundred naked bodies in a public place. I am writing about art, and I have just made myself the object of art. In the shift from subject to object, what affective dislocation has been achieved? In a performance that reconfigures the anonymous public sphere as intimate, what judgment is involved?

Art as performance: participation/regulation

Subject/object. It is simpler to occupy one side or other of that dividing line than to waver between the two. Attempting to interview Tunick while being filmed doing so was a brief and uncomfortable experience of that oscillation; however, Tunick's great achievement as an artist is that his work is premised upon offering individuals the uncanny experience of being simultaneously the object of the image and the subject of a performance. Tunick remains in control of the event and of the resulting image: it is he who selects locations, who dictates poses, who sets the time of day for the event. It is he who develops the film, crops the image, discards some in favour of others. As photographer, of course, he is the subject of the artistic process; the individuals he photographs, whether alone or in their thousands, are objects of the camera's gaze.[3] And yet: Tunick's photo-sessions are distinguished from those of other photographers by their performative dimension.[4] In electing to photograph people nude in public spaces, Tunick asks of his models a willingness to put themselves on display, in an event existing prior to and independent of the final image. The performance begins as people disrobe and ends as they reclothe themselves. In between those two temporal points (akin to the opening and closing of curtains on a stage), the participants have redefined their bodily relationship to urban space and to other individuals and have enacted a discrete role in a brief drama which problematizes skin, concrete, strangeness and intimacy.

The performative dimension is perhaps the most significant aspect of Tunick's work. The finished images certainly attract attention: when exhibited, they are reviewed in the usual way as completed artworks, without much dwelling on the process of their production.[5] However, in focusing on the product, these responses ignore the effort, risk and effects of how these artworks *came to be*. In accounts given (such as mine above) of posing for Tunick, individuals tend not to speak of the excitement or interest of contributing to an art object that will be displayed in a gallery or book. Rather, it is the experience of performing as nude bodies in public space that is found to be meaningful, remarkable, memorable, transformative. Participants in the Melbourne events described their experience as 'one of the singularly most inspiring things I've ever done';[6] 'it was beautiful';[7] 'we were part of something more beautiful than it was possible to imagine before the event';[8] and 'it made me feel good about being a human being'.[9] One recounted:

There is a feeling of ridiculous, extravagant joie-de-vivre, of fraternal grins and sheepish acknowledgment of complicity. People jump up and down and hug themselves or if they're fortunate, hug a friend, and there is a sweetness, an innocence in this instinctive desire to keep the goose-bumps at bay. Without the accoutrements of class and status, you start thinking about abstract nouns like liberation and democratization.[10]

Participants in Tunick's massed events speak of their performance in terms of beauty, collectivity, personal affirmation and abstraction.[11] Pleasure is found in the displacement of their individuality into the experience of belonging to a larger whole. In contrast, those who have posed for Tunick in his solo portraits describe the experience as a means of expressing something about themselves as individuals, often with a distinctly therapeutic compo-nent. The documentary film *Naked States*, which accompanied Tunick in his (successful) attempt to photograph individuals naked (alone or en masse) in every American state, features many models whose comments exemplify this: a woman in Boston states that posing for Tunick 'was ninety per cent of [her] self-therapy', after having been raped; an older man characterizes his decision to pose as a rejection of the conventions of ageing; and an obese woman, who has suffered constant public humiliation and physical assaults related to her bodily size, described posing naked for Tunick: 'To be naked right before sunrise on the rocks at the Hudson River and the breeze was coming up – it was really wonderful'. Of the resulting photograph, she has stated:

> For me, there is some privacy in the photograph … Not everyone is always poking at me and saying things to me and stopping me and grabbing me. So I think maybe I find a lot of pleasure in the sort of 'public solitude' of the photo.[12]

And these accounts would seem to confirm Tunick's objectives in undertaking this type of art practice; as he says, 'I'm not trying to make spectacles. I'm trying to create art events that are spectacular for the participants'.[13]

For others, such as the police or municipal authorities, the performative dimension is also crucial, although in a far more troubling way than that experienced by the participants. For example, Tunick's attempts to take photographs in New York have repeatedly led to his being arrested.[14] The first such occasion was in 1994, while Tunick was photographing a naked man posing on top of an 8-foot Christmas tree bauble alongside the famous Rockefeller Center Christmas tree. Another arrest came when Tunick was photographing two individuals in a snowstorm. The documentary *Naked States* depicts one of Tunick's mass installations (in Times Square) being interrupted as he is arrested by police officers, and also shows him facing charges of lewd behaviour and public exposure in court (which his lawyer succeeds in having dismissed). In all, Tunick had been arrested five times in

New York, before a ruling was sought in the state courts as to whether Tunick's art practices were exempted from state laws banning public nudity. In 1999, however, police responses to Tunick's events were becoming more aggressive. On 25 April, Tunick was pulled away from his camera and handcuffed before he had even begun to photograph the dozens of people lying naked in Times Square.[15] Charges on this occasion included unlawful assembly, creating a violent act, disorderly conduct, public exposure and reckless endangerment. And on 6 June, when Tunick and the participants arrived to begin the installation, police officers were already waiting for him, displaying handcuffs and an extensive line-up of police wagons, making it clear that if Tunick attempted to take photographs he, and perhaps the participants, would be arrested.

As a result, Tunick's lawyer, Ron Kuby, filed for an injunction preventing the New York Police Department and the City of New York from arresting him as he worked. The injunction was granted by the Federal District Court, and Tunick's next installation was scheduled for 18 July. The City of New York, however, obtained a stay of the injunction at an emergency court hearing on 17 July, and the event was thus prevented from taking place as planned, although Tunick photographed a hundred clothed participants and one naked baby. Police officers stood by in case anyone removed their clothes.[16]

The federal court was then asked to decide whether Tunick's work was exempt from state anti-nudity laws (Tunick's claim being that artistic enterprises were indeed exempt; the City of New York arguing that such exemptions were restricted to indoor performances). The federal court refused to decide the issue, claiming it was a matter for the state, and sent the case to the state courts to decide on three issues: whether Tunick's photo-installations constituted entertainment or a performance in a play, exhibition or show; if they did, whether the exemptions to the state's anti-nudity laws were limited to indoor activities (the current interpretation of the statute); and finally whether an exemption to the law which included Tunick's photo-installations would be valid under the United States Constitution.

On 24 March 2000, the Court of Appeals for the Second Circuit in Manhattan stated that there were inadequate precedents to enable it to decide how to interpret the statute on public nudity, although the judges warned that the City of New York's actions in recent years had generated a 'relentless onslaught' of litigation over the First Amendment right to freedom of speech and expression,[17] and that police officers' decision to stop Tunick taking photographs in the absence of any clear rule against the practice was 'a variation on the classic theme of censorship'.[18] The case was then passed to the New York State Court of Appeals, and on 19 May 2000, a ruling was made in favour of Tunick and stating that the New York Police Department was barred from arresting Tunick as he carried out his art practices. The City of New York then appealed to the United States Supreme Court, asking it to overturn this decision.

Such an action is perfectly consonant with the City's attitude in recent years to both 'controversial' artwork and questions of nudity and sexuality. In the latter years of the 1990s, the then Mayor Rudy Giuliani enacted a series of local laws relating to the advertisement of sexual services and sexual entertainment and restricting the provision of sexual services through the city's brothels. Giuliani also made very public protests against the 'Sensation' exhibition at the Brooklyn Museum in 1999, and attempted to harness the legal process to his criticisms, a move which culminated in Giuliani being found to have violated the Constitution by withholding funds from the museum as a punitive response to its exhibition of such 'controversial' artwork (discussed further in Chapter 2). In relation to Tunick's installations, the Supreme Court refused to allow the City of New York to appeal against the lower court's ruling: Tunick's installation involving 100 nude individuals beneath the Williamsburg Bridge was able to take place on 4 June, and in 2001 the Federal District Court in Manhattan ordered the City of New York to pay Tunick $33,368.75 for his legal fees.[19]

Since 2000, then, in principle Tunick has been able to photograph in New York without interference. However, despite the court victory Tunick and his volunteers are still threatened with arrest and imprisonment by the City of New York, whose Department of Film and Television has continued to refuse to grant a permit for Tunick to work in New York City.[20] Commenting on his struggles with the City of New York, Tunick states: 'I think an enlightened culture is one that respects the body and doesn't consider it a crime, or put a body in jail, just because there's an artist working with the nude in public'.[21]

Tunick's New York images therefore come to exist as part of a struggle between municipal and state agencies, which regard their mode of production as offensive, and the artist and participants who regard these practices as art and the resulting performance as beautiful. The struggle thus takes place around the image's manner of production, or the process of its performance at a moment prior to completion: unlike the artworks discussed in Chapter 2 of this book, there has been no controversy attached to the finished images that Tunick exhibits.

As noted above, participants characterize the event of posing in terms of its beauty or its liberating effects. Tunick himself has described the mass events as 'a way of juxtaposing the human body with a public place so that a living organism of 100 bodies forms a landscape',[22] as 'performance installations',[23] and 'a flood of flesh, like pink water',[24] and the resulting images as arising from an interest in 'the anonymity of public space and the vulnerability of human nakedness'.[25] Michael Hess, lawyer for the City of New York, acknowledged that no complaints had ever been made about Tunick's photographic practices, but asserted that 'people who do not choose to watch it are being exposed to it'.[26] Hess is here invoking the conventional trope about forms of 'offensive' display in public, manifested since *Hicklin*: that pornography or offensive literature or images is particularly problematic when it is available or visible to groups who would ordinarily never seek out such material.[27]

Thus the performance dimension of Tunick's work is elevated, without the emphasis on beauty, stillness, or affirmation that characterizes accounts given by participants. Instead, following the precepts of the modern law of obscenity, the performance is converted into exhibition: thus, naked bodies are being put on display in a public place, a place which should contain only clothed bodies. Performance is made exhibition, and exhibition is quickly translated into exhibitionism with all its attendant lack of propriety and appropriateness.

Thus, we can see in relation to Tunick's aesthetic practice, the resulting images, and responses to them, a series of dichotomies such as public/private, clothed/naked, voluntary/compulsory, art/offence, beauty/obscenity. Underlying all of these is the opposition law/image, which assumes that the realm of the cultural is subject to legal processes and is the object of law's subjective governance. Tunick's work, however, manages to subvert this unidirectional story of law and the image. The naked participants feel empowered rather than objectified by their experiences; the images render the fleshiness of human corporeality abstract and sculptural through their sheer multiplication of bodies; the disorderliness of mass public disrobing results in a silent, meditative stillness; and the apparent obviousness of the transgression (public nudity) becomes an authorized aspect of artistic production.

To a certain extent, it is possible to recount Tunick's engagements with the police and the courts as a story of legal governance: that previously illegal aesthetic practices were recategorized as legitimate thanks to the invocation and intervention of the legal process. However, this story of legal governance leaves out and covers over a number of striking features relating to Tunick's work. Most notably, it erases the performative dimension of the artist's photographic practice, of the subject's role in being photographed, and of the official reception of the artworks. And when it comes to the law, this story of legal governance has no resources to give an account of either the contingency of the law's role in responding to these images or of the indifference towards the legal institution manifested by both the artist, in his courageous persistence, and the participants, in their self-pleasure. A reading of Tunick's photographs provides a site from which it becomes possible to launch a study that questions the place of law in the production of an imaginary domain. Legal discourse represents itself as able to respond to art in a series of modes playing out different aspects of the story of the legal governance of art (as sovereign arbiter of taste, neutral judge of disputes, embodiment of community attitudes). Such a story is too incomplete: so how should we read the tense and tensed relations of law and the image?

Law in/of the realm of art

Law has always had a visual policy and understood the importance of the governance of images for the maintenance of the social bond. Law's force depends partly on the inscription on the soul of a regime of images.

Religion and law have a long history of policing images, coupled with an economy of permitted images or icons, an iconomy, and a criminology of dangerous fallen or graven images, an idolatry.

(Douzinas and Nead 1999a: 9)

Tunick's work is notable for its complication of the dichotomy between object and subject. As an art practice, Tunick's photography is also usually discussed in a profoundly dichotomized manner: commentators tend to focus on either the artistic significance of the artworks or on the ways in which Tunick's practice challenged and was challenged by socio-legal norms about behaviour in public space. The latter type of commentary thus focuses on the various court cases Tunick had faced, varying attitudes to public nudity, and Tunick's place in the panoply of artists whose art practices had led them into conflict with the authorities. There is, then, a marked split between 'law' and 'aesthetics' in the way in which Tunick's work has been discussed.

Such a split is not confined to the reception of Tunick's work; rather, it can be said to characterize much of the discourse on images and law, art and judgment. Acceptance of this dichotomy has a lengthy history and is deeply embedded in both the legal and artistic institutions: Douzinas and Nead note 'the programmatic separation of law and art' and the ways in which

Law pretends that it can close itself off from other discourses and practices, attain a condition of total self-presence and purity, and keep outside its domain the nonlegal, the extraneous, the other – in particular the aesthetic, the beautiful and the image.

(Douzinas and Nead 1999a: 4)

However, such a strenuous separation cannot be maintained. As Goodrich writes:

The memory of law – as custom and tradition, as precedent and antiquity – is held and 'sealed' in images, imprinted through visual depiction or textual figures that bind, work and persist through the power of the image, through a vision, for example, of 'neighborhood', 'reasonableness', 'national security' or simple 'authority'.

(Goodrich 1996: 96)

Legal discourse is irrevocably tied to the insistence and reiteration of the image in law. This may be identified in the metaphorical and analogical techniques of legal discourse and legal reasoning (how do we imagine a family? If we allowed a claim to succeed in that situation, should we also allow it in this, similar, situation?), but also in law's love of images of itself: of the iconography of justice. Courtroom architecture is dedicated to the reproduction and maintenance of a certain appearance: upon entering a courtroom, the architecture and aesthetics of the space do not simply say 'workplace', 'serious business conducted here' or 'state authority resides here' (which could be said of many businesses or public bodies). Rather, they also speak of 'justice' (the statue, the sword, the scales), of a certain kind of 'authority' (which is embodied in the judge, and in the silence or hushed tones used by personnel, and more generally in the affective mood of the buildings), and of 'equity' (a symmetrically organized room with the bench in the middle).[28]

Thus we are at a point of paradox: on the one hand, the legal institution disavows any connection with the aesthetic, or with the imaginary; on the other hand, it relies on a regime of images to found and enforce its authority and to carry on its mode of reasoning and judgment.[29] When an interest in the imaginary or the aesthetic is acknowledged within legal discourse or the legal institution, it tends to be limited to 'specialist' areas, such as copyright law (who owns the image?) or censorship (how far can we go in controlling the production, distribution and replication of images?). Debates on issues such as law's intervention in blasphemy, obscenity and pornography tend to take place without self-reflexiveness: law's ability to control, to intervene, to categorize certain images is taken for granted, obvious. The story of legal governance is reiterated as unproblematic – the image is law's object, and no relation or dialogue between the two can be imagined or admitted.

Both the law/image dichotomy and the paradox that law loves its images while appearing to restrict them function together to render invisible the question of the *implication* of law in the image and the image in law. The relation between law and the image is so much more complicated than the story of legal governance would claim, confining the legal imaginary to a brief roll call of technical topic areas. It is a relation of complexity and complication; indeed, I would suggest that it is one of *co-implication*, in which law and the image are enfolded within each other, their contours and substances passing through and around each other. The task undertaken in this book is to read the conjunction of law and the image, of jurisprudence and aesthetics, while maintaining the relationship between the two as one of co-implication.

Aesthetics and/as jurisprudence

To carry out such a reading interrupts the straightforward story of legal governance and bypasses it in favour of a more uncomfortable one. Immediately, certain penalties might seem to arise – as if speaking thus of the image could be a crime within the laws of a tradition. And if law and legal studies has a tradition, aesthetics might be seen as its betrayal. Legal practice and legal studies involve topics, methods and theory that are generally agreed on and accepted (although accounts of how they should be interpreted or what they might mean would vary). Legal studies constitutes a canon and aesthetics is outside it. So it is with all traditions; for every interiority there must be an externality, for every centre there are many margins. Law has for decades conducted border disputes with psychiatry, history, science, psychology, sociology among others. Is another dispute being staged in the division between legal studies and aesthetics? Does aesthetics betray the legal tradition?

Tradition is always already subject to revision and threat. Tradition, etymologically, suggests 'a handing over or surrender, even betrayal (as in *trahison*); Tacitus uses *traditor* to mean a traitor' (Murphy 1994: 72). The notion of tradition is only ever metaphorical, a relation through which one hands something on or over to another. Since 'tradition' means both passing on (as in necessary or accredited knowledge) and giving up (as in betrayal, defeat, loss), the legal tradition's handing over of its knowledge embodies within itself its own betrayal, its own apparent loss to an outsider.

Just as the relation between law and the image tends to be represented as a series of encounters in which the legal institution governs the practices of art, the relation between legal studies and aesthetics is usually constructed as a hierarchy between two unequal parties, with the legal tradition dominating the marginal domain of aesthetics.[30] In this book, I imagine instead a conversation without such a hierarchy and stage some tropic instances within this imaginary dialogue, asking how are we to imagine the relation between jurisprudence and aesthetics? For some, there is an overlap between the domains. Similarities can be identified, and thus we proceed by means of the relations of resemblance, similarity and substitution – that is, of metaphor. Law might be like art; aesthetics might work in similar ways to jurisprudence.[31]

Legal reasoning, as all law students are taught, proceeds by analogy, by the identification of resemblances between factual situations (so that 'like' cases can be treated alike, according to the same rules and principles) and the identification of difference, so that exclusions can be justified. 'This' can be said to resemble 'that', while 'X' can be disavowed as 'not Y'.[32] When this system of analogical classification is brought to bear upon the domain of aesthetics, many resemblances might appear: as Gearey puts it,

> It may be that aesthetics can cast light on law's rule-based nature . . . Indeed, it might be thought that the artist is like the lawyer, in that both have a working knowledge of rules. Their product, art or legal argument, represents a mature understanding of the ways in which they are constrained and the opportunities to be creative.
>
> (Gearey 2001: 1)

Limits to such a process of comparison might soon become apparent, however. Many artists would baulk at the notion that they were 'like the lawyer', and many lawyers would also resist the comparison. For law students toiling over case reports in the library, the difference between those texts and the delights of the art object are only too obvious. And the defendant being sentenced to a term of imprisonment can immediately explain the difference between an art critic and a judge.

To write *as if law were art* would allow us to speak of the *plaisir du texte* which permeates all legal processes, the pleasures and desires and horrors which structure the trial, the statute, the judgment. To write *as if law were art* would reverse the standard hierarchy whereby law is able to govern and regulate artistic production and is thus much more threatening, provoking the fear that law might be *only* an image. Easier to turn the metaphor around and ask aesthetics to proceed with the analysis of cultural artefacts *as if art were law*, so that cultural forms could be seen to conform to certain rules, to uphold the concept of law because their interpretation would validate it, require it, perpetuate it. Cultural production would be subject to the law of a law; and culture would be subordinated *to* law.

These inclusions and exclusions, however, still operate within a fixed sense of disciplinary and institutional boundaries. The metaphorical systems of contiguity and resemblance that I propose neither force an unsustainable analogy between law and art nor efface the points of distinction between them. Instead, they acknowledge the repressed lines of flight moving between the body of law and the terrain of aesthetics, and they begin to do so at the point where comparison between them becomes *abject*.[33] The co-implication of law and the image, of jurisprudence and aesthetics, engenders discomfort in its juxtaposition of such different terrains, entities and experiences: this is the discomfort of abjection, when one encounters something that has been hidden, evacuated, repressed. The abject locates that which we would rather not see, or reveal, or touch. In the abject discomfort of a co-implicated relation between jurisprudence and aesthetics, we find that which the legal tradition would prefer not to be revealed – uncertainty, affectivity, contingency, difference, the peripatetic and nomadic, the marginal, the image.[34]

And in the repressed recesses of that relation, we find the workings of a legal imaginary. The imaginary quality of law is that which is most repressed within its own discourses and practices, repressed and acknowledged to appear only in its most impoverished and caricatured forms (wigs, insignia, courtroom architecture, uniforms, bowing and ritual). Its chosen form of self-representation is antithetical to an engagement with the imaginary: reason, science, deduction, are all founded, ironically, upon the appearance or image of non-imaginary substances, rules, decrees and regulations. As the most repressed, the image in law exerts a powerful influence: case reports, statutes and so on depend upon and require the written word, the written tradition (the word being, of course, the signifier which imports meaning, the image which contains the decision, the rule, the finding). Similarly, law's reliance on legal personality inspires a system of masks, personae, places from which to speak, which are representations of the authority or standing or (il)legitimacy of the speaker.

Although the legal institution claims to confine its engagement with the image to a purported relation of governance and technical regulation, law founds its authority in a system of the imaginary. As Hachamovitch writes: 'An object of judgement is retained by attaching it to a visual image; it is the visual image which accumulates sense; and alongside sense, the image accrues a series of judgements or perceptions, it is made into a new objectivity' (1994: 42). The image is lost as it acquires 'sense', or meaning, and is then transformed into objectivity, the rule, logic, judgment. Legal discourse takes pleasure in its self-representation as detached, passionless, thorough, impartial, rule based. It has no place for the image, for the imprecise and uncertain creativity of art. Yet such a sense of exclusion is only the expression of a rhetorical wish. The translation of affect into law, into judgment and jurisdiction, takes place precisely through the workings of images, of the imaginary and the imagination.

Ethics and possibilities: looking, performing, judging

Law's relation with art has been continually disavowed within the legal institution and legal discourse, despite law's reliance on a regime of images founding legal authority, language, reasoning and politics. This book offers a reading of the law/art relation that circumvents this central paradox and concentrates instead on the embedded and enfolded relation of law and art. Before introducing the series of readings which follow in subsequent chapters, let me situate them in relation to my accounts of Tunick's performative art, law's aporetic relation to art and my argument for envisioning the law/art relation as one of co-implication.

A number of convictions have animated my reading of these images and law's judgment of them. First: the affective and effective force of the image. Again and again in the following chapters there will arise instances of a spectator moved to violence by an image, or discomfited by an artwork, or overwhelmed by its beauty. Viewing art is a profoundly emotional experience, no matter what level of 'expertise' the viewer has, no matter what one's politics may be. Looking at an image requires an acknowledgement on the part of the viewer that representation exists in the world, that appearance has a place and a force within society. Most viewing experiences do not provoke in the viewer the joy of recognition – 'there I am!' Rather, they arouse the shock and anxiety of an encounter with the Other – 'there I am not'. This unsettling quality in the image, and its effect on the spectator, is sometimes highlighted by commentators on art and social controversy. Dubin, for example, states:

> Serrano's photos taught me a great deal about the force of some images, a latent power which is activated and released by what each person brings to their viewing because of their biography, their present mood, past experiences with art, and a wide variety of additional factors. I left the gallery both confused and enlightened . . . I was some curious amalgam of contradictory feelings and impulses. I was unnerved, but I reveled in that state for some time: I respected a body of work that was able to puncture my sense of smugness to such a degree.
>
> (Dubin 1992: 6)

Here the affective force of the image is foregrounded, although it is trumped by the determinism that is accorded to the spectator's approach to the image, with the experience of viewing the image rendered a product of a number of relative factors (biography, temperament, history). I share with

Dubin an emphasis on the powerful responses that can be engendered in the spectator by looking at an image; however, in this book I have broadened the ambit of response from Dubin's focus on individual reaction and social controversy to include also both the responses offered by law's judgment of various images and also the sense that responses are the product of more than the relativism of individual factors such as mood and experience.[35] Thus, for my argument, response arises within a matrix of intersections between the spectator, the artwork and the context of reception, with perhaps the most important factor in any instance being the possibility that the spectator – including the legal institution as well as the individual – feels *addressed* by the artwork and thus bound up in a relation with it.

It should be stressed that this book does not define 'art' or 'artwork' in the conventional way. Some of the events discussed in subsequent chapters relate to artworks which hang on gallery walls; others do not. 'Art' is defined generously. This is partly because I have endeavoured to examine images in several different cultural realms and resulting from differing cultural practices. Thus, my analysis deals at various points with paintings, photographs, film, installations, performance, buildings and text. But my aim has been not simply to cast a wide net over the cultural realm in order to dredge up a variety of images for analysis. Rather, it is my intention to show the manifest ubiquity of the image and the centrality of the image to contemporary life. The aesthetic has been contested, debated and judged in locations such as city streets, museums, theatres, cinema and the ruined foundations of a destroyed building. Art exists not just in gallery space, but in every corner of quotidian life. To that extent, I would echo bell hooks' rallying call to aesthetics:

> We need to place aesthetics on the agenda. We need to theorize the meaning of beauty in our lives so that we can educate for critical consciousness, talking through the issues: how we acquire and spend money, how we feel about beauty, what the place of beauty is in our lives when we lack material privilege and even basic resources for living, the meaning and significance of luxury and the politics of envy.
>
> (hooks 1995: 124)

Part of that agenda must include a reflexive consideration of the process of interpretation. It will have become obvious that this book does not subscribe to any approach endorsing law's straightforward 'right' to judge the image, or award (members of) society any particular power to censor or control image-making. Rather, my interest is in analysing the means by which any such judgments and controls come into existence as responses to interpretations of the image. That process of interpretation is one of entanglement and implication. The image does not exist in isolation from the spectator (or from law) – looking (and thus interpreting) has a dynamism; responses are, by definition, responsive. The subsequent readings of art and the image deal with the responsive *dance* that ensues between the artwork, the law and the spectator from the moment that the image is created, displayed or sometimes even simply imagined. Bal (1999: 36) calls this 'displac[ing] the object of interpretation from work to process'.

In these displacements and in my argument that law and art exist in a relation of co-implication, we find what could be called the traces of a politics. Writers on law and aesthetics have often asserted a political dimension to their analyses. For example, Gearey uses his thesis on law, aesthetics and poetry to issue an imperative to critical legal thinkers: 'make it new' (2001: 124); while Manderson argues that

> taking aesthetics seriously [has] normative implications . . . [I attempt to] conjoin the ideas of legal pluralism with the changing aesthetic tenor of our times in order to find new approaches to law and new metaphors through which to give them life.
>
> (Manderson 2000: ix)

Underlying this book is a conviction that we must add to the politics of social change and legal transformation the significance of an ethics of visual interpretation, which responds to the project of signification and values the manifold instances of the imaginary in contemporary life. hooks speaks of the need to theorize the meanings of beauty in our lives; let us also give the name beauty to the transformative potential of art, a potential which is continually contested and continually desired:

> Our capacity to signify beauty has no limits. It is born of a loss which can never be adequately named, and whose consequence is, quite simply, the human imperative to engage in a ceaseless signification . . . It is a call to which none of us is adequate by ourselves . . . Only as a collectivity can we be equal to the demand not only to find beauty in all of the world's forms, but to sing forever and in a constantly new way the jubilant song of that beauty.
>
> (Silverman 2000: 146)

Contested beauty: the struggles over Tunick's practice of photographing nudes in public places and the struggles recounted throughout this book represent various attempts to legislate the meaning of beauty in the world. As Bal (1999) indicates, there can be no *one* definition (or judgment) of beauty, and nor should there be. Instead, the continual struggle to make images and the continual contestation of their beauty, legality and propriety constitute us as visual subjects, engaged in an entangling dance of vision, interpretation and judgment.

Affective bodies: image/judgment

In this book, my reading of various cultural or aesthetic events seeks to elaborate upon this dance, thus expanding the sense of the enfolding of judgment and the image and the co-implication of law and art. In doing so, it traverses a series of different terrains and concerns. Each chapter displaces – at times explicitly and at others with indifference – the law-as-governance model of analysis, and provides a more nuanced reading of law's investment in the image and the image's involvement with the structures of law. Chapter 2 begins at the conventional intersection of law and art: a site where an image has been deemed problematic and law has been invoked as the means to regulate that problem and the potential transgression it embodies for the normative order of society. Thus, the chapter studies works by Andres Serrano, Chris Ofili, Robert Mapplethorpe and Marcus Harvey. In most instances, a particular image has come to stand in for the artistic enterprise of the individual artist. For Serrano, it is *Piss Christ*; for Ofili his portrait of the *Holy Virgin Mary*; for Harvey, the attention to his painting of a murderer (*Myra*) has eclipsed any attention given to his other works; while the notoriety of Mapplethorpe's *X Portfolio* outstrips awareness of his portrait photography or his images of flowers.

I situate these artworks in terms of the response and responsibility engendered in relation to contemporary artistic practices. In each instance, the force of law was brought to bear on the image. This force took various forms: a civil lawsuit to prevent a gallery from displaying the artwork, criminal prosecution, vandalism by spectators, the removal of an artwork from display, and so on. Rather than figuring these and related responses in terms of an opposition between 'freedom of expression' and 'community interests' (a construction which reduces the events to cognitive operations structured around the context and content of the artwork and the authorial expression of self through art), this chapter instead explores the artworks and the law's responses to them in terms of their affective or emotional dimension. In particular, it suggests that these aesthetico-legal events are best read as performances of disgust.

Crucial to the regulation of art is the question of exhibition space. Controversial artworks such as those of Serrano and Mapplethorpe become subject to the legal process partly as a result of their display in museum space. Chapter 3 develops the idea of the appropriateness of certain spaces as spaces of display by investigating graffiti as an aesthetic phenomenon within the contemporary city. Graffiti is almost always illegal (unless done with the property owner's permission) and aims to display the writer's identity within a carefully camouflaged aesthetic vocabulary. The writer is on display, yet hidden; while the resulting graffiti manifests a rejection of the codes of propriety and ownership regulating practices of signification in urban space. The chapter examines both public discourse surrounding graffiti and also elaborates writers' experiences of an aesthetic practice deemed illegal by virtue of its being 'out of place'.

Chapter 2 provides a response to the question of what in the artwork – more than the artwork itself – provokes a disgusted response in law. Chapter 3 proceeds from the other direction and considers the legal regulation and cultural understanding of imagistic writing in public space. Whereas these two chapters primarily read the artwork (albeit in the context of a legal response), Chapter 4 turns initially to a reading of the imagistic writing of law. In addition to its interest in literal images (artworks), legal discourse creates its own images, to be put to work in the processes of judgment. And legal discourse manifests a desire for fixity of its created images. Chapter 4 reads several cases in which the images invoked in judgment act as rigid frames around the already marginalized figures who have been brought before the judge. These cases involve law's images of the gay man, and of the HIV positive gay man, and show the power of the image in working to effect repressive judgment. Against these cases, in which the law makes images *appear*, I offer a reading of the aesthetic enterprise of Felix Gonzalez-Torres and the cinematic revisions of Derek Jarman. Both deal in the art of *disappearance*; in the creation of an image which is elsewhere and otherwise than seeing, using the bodily sensations of touch and hearing to invoke a different way of responding to the HIV positive body.

The difficulties and responsibilities of the *visual* in art are further examined in Chapter 5. The artists considered there share the characteristic of exhibiting injury to and for the spectator. Two of the artists, Chris Burden and Ron Athey, either actually injure themselves or invite the audience to injure them, as part of their performances. The third artist, Jenny Holzer, provides a recounting of the experiences of injury from the perspectives of victim, perpetrator and observer. All three explicitly invoke violence as part of their art practices. My main interest is in the demands that are then made upon the spectator. How is one to watch such a performance or approach such an artwork? The chapter interrogates the art of injury and the experience of looking at injury as a forensic event, in which injury becomes testimony and spectatorship becomes witnessing. Chapter 6 follows on from these concerns by considering how the forensic nature of artistic practices can raise questions about how art responds to the violent interruption of the law's smooth surface that is constituted by a mass terrorist attack. The aesthetic enterprise has a lengthy history of providing memorials for violent events or for the victims of violence, injury and death. The final chapter of this book examines the competing tensions of the struggle to create memorial images in the wake of the World Trade Center attacks in New York City, enfolding survivors, architects and citizens in a matrix of trauma, memory and ruins.

Other such implicatory enfoldings can be identified as crucial to the book's argument. The blurring of the boundary between subject and object is crucial for understanding the work of Spencer Tunick (as discussed already in this chapter); and the implication of the art object in the legal subject is an issue that recurs throughout subsequent chapters (see especially Chapters 2, 3 and 4). Thus, witnessing a crime and perpetration of a crime are often taken as markedly separate phenomena: however, a number of artists have refused to uphold this separation, instead sheeting home to the spectator the similarities between looking and doing (see Chapter 5). The persistent separation of public and private spheres finds its own version in relation to art: artworks are generally thought of as for exhibition in gallery space, with a specific name reserved for art which is displayed in public ('public art'). Various chapters demonstrate the confusion and anxiety that can occur when the hurly burly of public life enters the cloistered atmosphere of the gallery (as when protesters smash an image, or prosecute a gallery owner) and when the private activity of art is placed in full public view (as in the case of graffiti, whose illegitimacy derives from its location, unauthorized, in the public sphere). And underlying each of these intersections and each of the chapters is a sense of the co-implication of law and art, of the entwining of judgment and the image. Finally, while each chapter makes explicit how we come to an understanding of these interleavings through the process of looking, the dynamic role of the spectator needs to be highlighted, both in subsequent individual chapters and in the overall structure of the book.

Interleaved between the chapters are short sections entitled *viewing (de)positions*. In each of these, I recount a number of experiences as a spectator. The first deals with various ambivalent exhibitions of the work of Andres Serrano, and the percussive effects of viewing his images. The second begins with an instance of contested public discourse on graffiti and moves into the city space in order to view graffiti as a form of urban writing. Generosity and donation are the subjects of the third piece: focusing particularly on the artist's gift of an image or sensation to the spectator. And in the final section, spectatorship becomes something that is more than 'just looking', when particular representations transform the artwork into testimony and the spectator into forensic interlocutor.

I have named these short pieces viewing (de)positions for a number of reasons. First, I wish to emphasize the *experience* of looking, a prior state which necessarily antedates the critical moment and the distance of analysis. Looking at artworks finds the individual addressed by the image, engaged in a process of projection and interpretation. Such a process can be affected by the gallery space (which provides a frame for the image), the positioning of an artwork next to or near other artworks (perhaps other works in a series, or by juxtaposition with contrasting images), by a lack of legitimizing gallery space (as in public art, or graffiti), or by the expectations raised when the artwork is 'supposed' to bear a certain kind of message (as in 'art about AIDS' or 'memorial art'). All of these issues can be approached indirectly (as in Chapters 2 to 6), through 'third person' critique of the individual work or artist; however, an account of the viewing position itself restores a missing moment in the artwork's aura – that moment when the viewer first sees and is seen by the image, with all the attendant emotions, associations and responses that may flow from there.

Second, viewing is a practice which brings response and responsibilities; the (de)positions foreground the inevitability, pleasures and tensions of looking. In addition to being about viewing and spectatorship, these pieces are de-positions: they recount experiences in which I as a viewing subject was de-posed, unseated, unable to find a secure or comfortable position from which to look. And finally, to that extent, the viewer is always thoroughly implicated in the process of looking. Spectatorship is often perceived to be a comfortably distanced experience: a passive reception of an already existing image without the responsibility of interpretation and projection. One of the aims of this book, however, is to stage a series of readings and viewings derived from the *spectator*'s implication in the processes of judgment of the image.

All viewing positions are, of course, freighted with value and consequence. No moment of first sight can be 'innocent' or independent of cultural structures and devices. To acknowledge this lack of 'innocence', this state of cultural responsibility from which we view images, I wish these short accounts to be regarded as *depositions*: declarations under oath or acts of testimony during a trial. For our viewing experience is a forensic one: it has prosecutorial potential, it can indict and convict. That moment of first sighting the artwork binds the spectator to law and law to the image, inviting condemnation or approval, generating narratives of understanding or dismissal, meting out punishment or reward. These four short pieces, then, should be understood also as snatches of evidence given during the perpetual prosecution of the artwork, and judgment of the image.

In writing this book, I wished to move away from the conventional position of critic and towards a more mobile oscillation between roles. Rather than simply providing my reading of various artworks, legal cases and events surrounding them, it has been my objective to incorporate other positions from which to speak about law, the image, and the cultural frame that enjoins interpretation. Thus some chapters are written as conventional pieces of criticism, while in others I speak as a viewer, from a prior moment of address by the artwork. And, in addition, this opening chapter has attempted to engage with the experience of being the *subjective object* of art, of being in the artwork. Taking part in Tunick's installation for me confounded the pheno-mena both of viewing art and of writing about art and law. At the original time of writing, I had not seen any of the images taken by Tunick that day (it would be two or three months before I saw one of the images from that day, posted on his website, and later would receive a copy of another for inclusion in this book as Figure 1). When writing this chapter, I had no image of how the images would look. I could only recount an experience from inside the frame, a phenomenological story of presenting one's body for re-presentation by the artist. And in posing with two hundred other women, the body of this critic lost its authorial voice and became a single point within the artwork, a mute but evocative single trait participating in a larger whole. There was no image to which I could relate my experience in order to generate a final analysis of the event; there was only the memory of the bright sunshine, the shock of cool breeze on skin, the mind's juddering between the contemporary experience of being naked in public and the traces of texts analysing Tunick's work. And, as Tunick took the photographs, the descending silence which confirms *the capture of the subject*, for aesthetics and law, in the moment of signification.

2 Aesthetic vertigo

Disgust and the illegitimate touchings of art

At the intersection of law, legitimation and aesthetics, certain artworks have come to be the object of social and legal intervention in their production and display. While in Chapter 1 I discussed attempts to prevent an artist from actually making an artwork (for example, the City of New York's endeavours to stop Spencer Tunick photographing nude individuals in public and the New York Police Department's frequent arrests of Tunick as he worked), this chapter examines the vicissitudes of the legal imagination once a discomfiting artwork has come into existence and into circulation in the public sphere. My interest in such images, however, does not arise out of any question of its legitimacy or the legitimacy of intervention against artists, or the rights of artists and audiences *per se*. As pointed out in Chapter 1, much of the preceding discussion of the contested relation between law and aesthetics constructs that relation as one of censorship or *collision*, whereby the tools of the law are brought sharply to bear on the artwork or the artist.

Instead, I investigate the ways in which the relation between law and the image negotiates the *affective jolt* engendered by certain artworks. In particular, this chapter looks at some recent images in contemporary art that have been called 'disgusting', and pursues the consequences of such an appellation. The description of an artwork as disgusting (or as any of its variants: grotesque, horrible, abhorrent, distasteful, repulsive, and so on) allows the legitimacy of the artwork *as artwork* to be brought into doubt and its display by a gallery brought into the realm of judgment.

Since one of the common stories about art relates it to beauty, edification of the human spirit and the sublime, nomination of an artwork as disgusting seeks to exclude it from the very realm of art.[1] 'Disgusting', in many ways, stands in for 'not-art'. An underlying aim, therefore, of the fierce public debates canvassed in this chapter is the policing of the boundary between 'art' and 'not-art', and the ejection of the artworks under discussion out of the domain of art and into those of 'blasphemy', 'outrage', 'abjection', 'transgression' and so on. The possibility of conjunctions between art and abjection, or art and outrage, is not admitted – indeed, it is strenuously avoided.

In my analysis of the various contested works, I do not pose the issues as a matter of censorship or as a case of the infringement of free speech, or as the art establishment's subordination of transgressive artworks. Each of these claims suggests a straightforward duality between the public responses to the artworks and the 'right' response to the artwork. Censorship arguments presuppose the repression of minority points of view in favour of a dominant discourse; free speech arguments are founded on the notion of a right to expression that all can and should utilize, with any variation from that constituting an erosion of universal rights; the notion of the repression of transgressive works constructs a top-down flow of power which can readily identify 'outlaw' artworks. It is my contention that none of these perspectives can accommodate the complexities of the events to be discussed in this chapter.[2] Arguments about censorship tend to posit an instrumentalist structure of power, in which we lose any sense of the shifting and volatile alliances which can form and re-form around transient issues. The free speech perspective valorizes the intentions of the artwork without reading them alongside the varied and hybrid emotional responses of the artwork's spectators. And claims about transgression in art have not yet engaged with the difficulties emphasized in cultural studies, feminist theory and criminology in discussing the outlaw, the transgressive and the borderline. As such, I wish to step to one side in approaching the events under analysis, by focusing upon the key issue of their nomination *as disgusting*, by tracing the consequences of such an appellation, and by locating the force of the epithet in the relations of *touch* within and around the images.

Disgust at an artwork can be embodied in a variety of forms: for example, through individual disapproval, negative media coverage, a lawsuit against a gallery, or an attack on the artwork itself. This chapter concentrates on disgusted responses such as these in relation to two artworks, with a brief detour through the now notorious obscenity trial relating to Robert Mapplethorpe's photographs, and with a postscript examining the metonymic transfers of disgust as they affected a third image, Chris Ofili's *Holy Virgin Mary*. The two works – the objects of similar disapprobation, criticism, assault and intervention at, oddly enough, roughly the same time although on opposite sides of the world – are *Piss Christ*, by Andres Serrano (Figure 2), and the occasion of its short-lived exhibition in Melbourne; and *Myra*, by Marcus Harvey (Figure 3), exhibited in London as part of the 'Sensation' show at the Royal Academy.

Two images, and each deals with a murder. *Piss Christ*, a photograph of the crucified Christ immersed in a vat of the artist's urine, takes place in the context of the foundation of a religion upon the murder of Christ. *Myra*, a painting of a police photograph of a convicted murderer, is an image located in the trauma of the murder of children. And the third image, Ofili's *Holy Virgin Mary*, unites aspects of both Serrano's and Harvey's works. The mother of Christ is represented in portrait form with elephant dung incorporated into the image. The embodiment of evil, Myra, is anagrammatically shuffled into Mary, an icon of the Christian faith brought into proximity with animal faeces, a waste substance even more reviled than urine. As this chapter will show, each artwork calls forth an extraordinary affective charge, resulting from the uncomfortable relationships established within each image.

Uncomfortable aesthetics

In October 1997, as part of the annual Arts Festival in Melbourne, the National Gallery of Victoria hosted a retrospective exhibition entitled 'A History of Andres Serrano'. The exhibition included examples of Serrano's early tableaux; several images from the *Fluids* and *Immersions* series, such as *Piss Christ* and *Black Jesus* (objects photographed immersed in urine or, sometimes, water, and abstract images made from body fluids such as milk and blood); two images from the *Red River* series (menstrual blood dried on a sanitary pad); the *Ejaculate in Trajectory* series (ejaculated semen photographed in a white arcing blur against black); several photographs from the *Nomads* (homeless people) and *Klansmen* (masked members of the Ku Klux Klan) series; a large number from the series *The Morgue (Cause of Death)*, showing fragmented shots of individuals photographed by Serrano after their deaths; and a small number from the *Sex* series (individuals and pairs of people, often naked, usually engaging in various sexual practices).[3] Note that the majority of the *Sex* images were showing at a companion exhibition, 'Andres Serrano: A History of Sex', at a private gallery in Melbourne, the Kirkaldy Davies.

Among the exhibited works was *Piss Christ* (1987), an image which was at the centre of the 'Culture Wars' in the United States.[4] The Culture Wars began in April 1989 when the American Family Association, a Christian fundamentalist organization, targeted *Piss Christ* as a way of protesting against the use of federal funds in contemporary art, since Serrano had received a fellowship from an organization funded by the National Endowment for the Arts (NEA).[5] The protest led to Alphonse D'Amato, a Republican Senator from New York, tearing up a reproduction of *Piss Christ* and throwing the pieces onto the floor of the Senate. Jesse Helms, Republican Senator for North Carolina, joined the farrago, comparing Serrano's work with that of Robert Mapplethorpe (an exhibition, partly funded by the NEA, of Mapplethorpe's work had just been cancelled in Washington) and creating the so-called 'Helms amendment' attached to legislation reauthorizing the funding of the NEA. A compromise version of the Helms amendment was eventually passed, cutting the NEA budget and prohibiting the production of obscene material, with a further requirement on the NEA to take into account 'general standards of decency and respect for the diverse beliefs and values of the American public'.

Piss Christ had also been the object of judicial consideration in the suit against the NEA by four artists whose applications for the federal funding administered by the organization had been turned down.[6] In the Supreme Court's decision in *NEA* v *Finley et al.* (finding in favour of the NEA), *Piss Christ* is mentioned three times. In the main judgment, delivered by Justice

O'Connor, *Piss Christ* is described as a 'provocative work' which, along with the Mapplethorpe exhibit, 'prompted public controversy . . . and led to congressional revaluation of the NEA's funding priorities and efforts to increase oversight of its grant-making procedures'. The court thus awards *Piss Christ* causal significance in the creation of constraints and controls over the NEA.

Justice Scalia described the range of work previously funded by the NEA as 'everything from the playing of Beethoven to a depiction of a crucifix immersed in urine'. Serrano's image is thus firmly located in opposition to what would conventionally be deemed 'art', or 'high art'. Justice Souter, the sole judge to align himself with the artists, states that 'the whole point of the [amendment] was to make sure that works like Serrano's ostensibly blasphemous portrait of Jesus would not be funded . . . while a reverent treatment, conventionally respectful of Christian sensibilities, would not run afoul of the law'. In this minoritarian view *Piss Christ* is a work which challenged categories even before the reorganized NEA procedures were envisaged and which now would not meet the new standards operating at the NEA (due to effects of the Helms amendment).

However, it was more or less assumed that *Piss Christ*'s moment in the legal and political glare had passed. The artwork's reception in Melbourne was thus all the more surprising – appearing to re-enact the struggles of the Culture Wars, albeit in an abbreviated and accelerated fashion. An article in the *Age* newspaper on 29 September 1997 initiated the controversy, describing Serrano's work as 'confronting' and claiming that it had 'sparked a political row with conservative state MPs'.[7] An organization called the Victorian Parliamentary Christian Fellowship was reported as calling the artwork 'blasphemous' and 'deliberately designed to insult Christians'. It cited US Republican Senator Alfonse D'Amato tearing up a copy of the image in 1989. Fellowship members had been urged to protest over the use of taxpayers' money to exhibit the photographs and call for the gallery to withdraw the images.

This article set the terms for the subsequent discussion of Serrano's artworks, with its use of the terms 'poor taste', 'offensive', 'blasphemous' and 'insult', and its concern over taxpayers' money. It also mentions two forms of action, both of which came to be used against the artwork: first, it calls for the gallery to withdraw the image (this became the objective of the lawsuit against the gallery by the Catholic church); second, in adverting to D'Amato's destruction of a *copy* of the image, it set the scene for the subsequent physical attacks on *the image itself*.

At the same time as the National Gallery of Victoria was preparing for the Serrano retrospective, in London the Royal Academy, that epitome of uncontroversial artistic good taste, was mounting an exhibition of British contemporary art. It was cynically commented in the press that the Royal Academy was deliberately seeking controversy in order to generate revenue (the Academy was known to be £4 million in debt). The title of the exhibition did little to dispel the notion that controversy was desired: the show was called 'Sensation: Young British Artists from the Saatchi Collection'. Whether or not the Academy sought scandal, scandal occurred in various forms: extremely negative coverage of the Academy, the show, its curator, and one particular artwork; protests and pickets outside the museum; two attacks upon the artwork in question, which resulted in its being vandalized; and threats to prosecute the museum for its exhibition of the artwork.

The artwork in question is a painting called *Myra*. It is a huge reworking of the (in)famous police photograph taken of Myra Hindley when she and her lover, Ian Brady, were convicted of the murders of two children (she confessed years later to the murders of two other children). The woman in this photograph seemed to embody evil: a woman who killed children, a woman who betrayed not only the law but also her gender. A sexual woman whose peroxide blonde hair and lowered chin and staring eyes seemed to offer confrontation, invitation and murder in one look. One journalist writes:

> It is the belief that it is the terribleness of her 'inner being' that can be plainly seen etched on the 30-year-old police mugshot of Hindley – the cavernous, upturned eyes, the heavy bones, the holed hedge of bleached-blonde fringe, the fondant of deep shadow, like a choke-collar, under Hindley's chin – that gives it its power as a symbol of evil.[8]

It is important to emphasize at the outset how significant Hindley is in the British imagination. Her name is remembered while that of her lover and accomplice is fading from the collective memory. The Moors murders – so called after Hindley and Brady's choice of Saddleworth Moor in Yorkshire as the location for the killings and the burial of the bodies – were notorious for their cruelty: Hindley and Brady had tape-recorded their victims' screams.

Hindley admitted in the 1980s that she and Brady had indeed killed two other children (it was long suspected but never proved that they had) and directed the police to the location of one child's body (the other's has never been found). Hindley's cooperation with the police was considered by many to be motivated by self-interest, part of her fight to be released from prison. Indeed, Hindley's name retained currency partly as a result of her struggles to achieve parole (Hindley received an indefinite life sentence in 1966 and remained in prison until her death in 2002).[9] In 1997, some months before the 'Sensation' exhibition was to open, Hindley had been featured prominently in the news, thanks to a High Court judgment in May allowing her to challenge a recent decision by the Home Secretary that her life sentence did indeed mean life. And on the same day that a tabloid newspaper would publish the first story about the artwork *Myra*, another newspaper carried a report on the House of Lords confirmation of Hindley's right to challenge her life sentence.[10]

During many of Hindley's campaigns to be released, the media used the 1966 police photograph to illustrate their stories about her. This continued well into the 1980s; Hindley eventually succeeded in having another photograph of herself (taken in prison) used to accompany such stories: this later photograph showed a middle-aged woman with dark brown hair. (Hindley was no doubt correct to assume that the police photograph perpetuated a public image of her as a hypersexual, sullen, aggressive woman.) By the 1990s, it had become a truism, both in public and in academic discourse, that Hindley's police photograph was taken to embody 'feminine evil'. One journalist describes the police photograph and its status in public consciousness as follows:

> an image that has been in the public domain so long, and has so seared itself into the collective retina, as to become a modern icon. Had Andy Warhol been English, he would no doubt have seized upon it 30 years ago, as he did with Chairman Mao.[11]

It was this police photograph that Marcus Harvey selected for his artwork. The image *Myra* is enormous: its dimensions are 396 × 320 cm, or 11 × 9 feet. It is not, however, the photograph blown up to great size. It is a painting of the photograph. And the 'dots', which are revealed when a photograph is enlarged, are constituted in this painting by imprints made from a cast of a child's hand.

Responses both to *Myra* and to *Piss Christ* were marked by intense anxiety. In this respect, the first point to note is that in both instances the form of the artwork confuses genres. *Myra* is a painting that looks like a photograph, using pointillism that looks like pixelization. *Piss Christ* is a photograph that looks like a devotional icon. The second point to remark is that the anxiety repeatedly returns to the manner of the production of the artwork, and persistently misrecognizes the processes involved (in the notions of Serrano urinating on the crucifix and Harvey compelling children to make handprints that would become Hindley's face). It is as if it was impossible to tell the difference between product and production. In the subsequent judgment of the artworks, the implications and effects of their exhibition in major national galleries came to dominate legal and media discourse. Yet the discourse of judgment remained replete with an anxiety that withdrew the very possibility of judging (discriminating, differentiating, determining) at the very moment that it called forth the moment of judgment.

Newspapers in particular, as I will show, condemned the galleries for contemplating the display of such offensive works, while, in the lawsuit over *Piss Christ*, the court struggled with the paradox that an artwork might be beautiful and (yet) obscene. Without explicitly stating that no artwork such as these should exist, nevertheless that sentiment structures the responses to the artworks' public display: disgust at the very existence of these images (a disgust deriving from anxiety about the artworks' confusion of genres and about the supposed manner of their production) allows for calls to prevent the images *being seen*. In the case of *Piss Christ*, this jurisprudence of disgust can be seen in fiercely negative media writings; a lawsuit by the Catholic Church against the gallery; and two attacks on the artwork. With *Myra*, we find a vituperative public discourse against the artwork and two attacks on the artwork.

The 'obscenity' of *Piss Christ*, by way of Mapplethorpe

On 8 October 1997, the Most Reverend George Pell, the then Archbishop of Melbourne and head of the Catholic Archdiocese, sued in the Supreme Court of Victoria for an injunction against the National Gallery, on the grounds that:

> The public display of the work would constitute: (a) the exhibiting or display of an indecent or obscene figure or representation . . . and (b) the common law misdemeanour of publishing a blasphemous libel by reason of the fact that the photograph is so offensive, scurrilous and insulting to the Christian religion that it is beyond the decent limits of legitimate difference of opinion and is calculated to outrage the feelings of sympathisers or believers in the Christian religion.[12]

Pell claimed that since the gallery had refused requests to withdraw the image, there was 'no option other than launching legal proceedings against the gallery' in order to prevent 'Christians be[ing] insulted at government expense in our most prestigious art gallery'.[13] In the following analysis of the lawsuit, I will focus on the question of obscenity, with reference also to the allegations of obscenity previously made against the images of Robert Mapplethorpe (an artist whose work has long been entwined with Serrano's in the Culture Wars). While Pell's lawsuit was underway, the Victoria Police vice squad inspected both the retrospective at the National Gallery of Victoria and the companion exhibition at the Kirkaldy Davies Gallery, and referred the exhibition's catalogue and reproductions of some of the images to the Office of Film and Literature Classification, further versions of the investigation into the artwork's possible obscenity.[14]

Pell's lawsuit against the National Gallery of Victoria replays uncannily in civil law a previous challenge to the legitimacy of artworks made in the criminal law of obscenity. A travelling exhibition of photographs by Robert Mapplethorpe, 'The Perfect Moment', had been installed at the Contemporary Art Center (CAC) in Cincinnati, Ohio, in 1990. Dennis Barrie, the gallery's director, and the gallery were each charged with the criminal offences of pandering obscenity (*Hustler* publisher Larry Flynt received a prison sentence in 1977 in Cincinnati for the same charge of pandering obscenity) and illegally depicting minors in a state of nudity (see Barrie 1991; Cembalest 1990: 140–1; Higonnet 1998; Merkel 1990; Steiner 1995). Their prosecution seemed to question the Supreme Court ruling in *Miller* v *California*,[15] that art and obscenity were mutually exclusive categories (if, taken as a whole, the work has 'artistic merit', it cannot be obscene), although the *Miller* ruling had been somewhat diluted by subsequent cases relating to representations of children. *New York* v *Ferber* ruled that child pornography could have no artistic significance,[16] and *Massachusetts* v *Oakes* extended this to include images of mere nudity, if the image showed 'lascivious intent'.[17]

The Mapplethorpe exhibition had been an originary part of the Culture Wars in 1989, when the Corcoran Gallery in Washington DC, ostensibly to avoid further controversy in the wake of the Serrano furore, cancelled its scheduled Mapplethorpe show (for which it had received NEA funding).[18] Stripped of NEA funding, the Mapplethorpe exhibition travelled to a number of other venues, such as the Cincinnati CAC. Barrie had even returned a grant of US$30,000 to a local government authority so that the gallery could not be said to be using taxpayer funds in displaying the works (Beal 1990: 320). Unable to attack the gallery on the civil grounds of misuse of funds, the city's strict anti-obscenity laws were used instead. Seven of the works were selected as evidencing the charges: five of Mapplethorpe's homoerotic photographs, and two of his images of children. The homoerotic pictures, part of the *X Portfolio*, showed one man urinating into the mouth of another man; a self-portrait of Mapplethorpe with a bullwhip inserted in his anus; a man fisting another man; a man inserting his finger into his penis; and a man inserting an object into his rectum. The two photographs of children were *Jesse McBride*, a naked boy sitting on a chair, and *Honey* (also known as *Rosie*), a girl whose dress is raised, showing her genitalia.

The potential significance of the case was acknowledged in the prosecutor's opening statement, when he said to the eight jurors:

> You people have a unique circumstance. There has never been a museum or art gallery charged with obscenity before, and you have the chance to decide – where do you draw the line? Are these the kind of pictures that should be permitted in a gallery?
>
> (quoted in Carr 1993: 274)

The line to be drawn – in a perhaps unconscious artistic metaphor – is the boundary between obscenity and art. The prosecution won its motions to have the CAC considered as a 'gallery' rather than as a 'museum' (and thus entitled to less protection from criminal prosecution) and to have the seven works considered in isolation (rather than as parts of different series of works, as parts of an exhibition as a whole, or as parts of Mapplethorpe's work as a whole), and their trial strategy seemed to assume that a jury would look at the images and immediately 'see' their offensiveness. The defence had hoped to contextualize the photographs, and thus dilute their potential offensiveness, but – deprived of this option – were forced instead to offer readings of the images which emphasized their status *as legitimate artworks*.

To do so, the defence sought to educate the jury on the nature of art. This involved taking the jury to a museum to view paintings (only three of the jurors had ever attended an art exhibition) and calling a number of expert witnesses, such as Janet Kardon, who had curated 'The Perfect Moment' when it originated in Philadelphia. Kardon described the sadomasochistic images in the language of art criticism, in order to authorize the photographs as works of art rather than as obscene shots. On Mapplethorpe's *Self-Portrait* with the bullwhip, she said:

> The human figure is centered. The horizon line is two-thirds of the way up, almost the classical two-thirds to one-third proportions. The way the light is cast so there's light all around the figure. It's very symmetrical.
>
> (quoted in Merkel 1990: 47)

Although the experts emphasized the artistic nature of the works, they also sought to endorse the view that a work could be disgusting and still be art (perhaps to avoid the jurors feeling that their emotional reactions to the photographs were being disparaged). Thus a local art critic testifying for the defence stated: 'I said I felt they were repulsive . . . they're disgusting, but it's still art' (quoted in Cembalest 1990: 139). The strategy clearly succeeded: not only did the jury return a verdict of acquittal, but also they repeated versions of the experts' testimony in giving their views on the case to the media, with comments such as 'if I had put my morals in I would have said guilty', 'as far as we were concerned they were gross and lewd' being trumped by findings that 'even though we may not have liked the pictures, we learned that art doesn't have to be pretty' (quoted in Cembalest 1990: 136–7).

Such comments, of course, depend on the notion that categories such as 'prettiness' and 'art' are decidable and unambiguous. Mapplethorpe's work clearly shows that this is not so: although the jurors in Cincinnati found the images to be art, but 'not pretty', Mapplethorpe's work is also associated with the beauty of an extreme aestheticism. The images have a profound purity of line, the black and white tones honed to sharp resolution, the bodies portrayed evoke baroque representations of figure and composition.[19] Yet the images seem as capable of being described as 'disgusting yet art' as they could be called 'beautiful and art'. As Nead writes, 'obscenity's beginning is art's end; art starts where obscenity terminates' (1999: 205). Perhaps, however, in some works the two categories are irrevocably insinuated within each other, as the images of Serrano, Mapplethorpe, Ofili and Harvey demonstrate, their confusion of genres and dissolution of borderlines causing anxiety in the spectator and difficulties for the discriminations of judgement.

In the aftermath of the case, the artistic community celebrated its victory, as if the question of obscenity in artworks had been settled. Yet despite the Cincinnati verdict, several years later when a retrospective of Mapplethorpe's work was put on at the Hayward Gallery in London, *Honey* (*Rosie*) was withheld from exhibition on the advice of police and children's charity groups.[20] That the problem of 'obscene' artworks has not been settled (and indeed could be said to be by definition *unsettling* and therefore continually requiring judgment) is further demonstrated by the Catholic Church's suit against the National Gallery of Victoria for its planned display of *Piss Christ*. Although the demand for an injunction against the gallery would be dismissed, the undecidability of the obscene artwork can be read in the hesitancy of the judgment.

Of *Piss Christ*, Harper J said:

> It shows the crucified Christ as if enveloped in a mist which is infused with the colours of a red and gold sunset. Of itself, it is not only inoffensive, but might be thought to be a reverent treatment of a sacred symbol of the Christian Church, membership of which is claimed by the artist himself. (p. 1)

As to why such a delicately beautiful image might cause 'much controversy', Harper J goes on to speculate:

> This is entirely understandable. The title 'Piss Christ' provides one reason why. The account of its creation provides another. The crucifix was, according to the artist, immersed in urine when the photograph was taken. In other words, the person who for Christians is the son of God and the founder of their church, is shown immersed in excrement. (p. 1)

'Excrement' usually connotes faeces. The judge uses the metonymic relation between urine and faeces to generate the offensiveness of the artwork. Although both are waste products, in the contemporary hierarchy of abjection faeces are regarded as more disgusting than urine. The judge's selection of the word 'excrement' intensifies the 'understandability' of the work's offensiveness. Harper J then cited Serrano explaining why he had chosen urine:

> Mr Serrano is quoted . . . as saying 'It dawned on me that piss would give a nice yellow'. He is also quoted . . . as saying 'Urine symbolizes waste, but is also a necessary bodily function; and perhaps the urine humanized Christ'. (p. 1)

Serrano's interest in urine should therefore be understood partly in relation to its capacities as a fluid to bring about certain formal effects on an immersed object (air bubbles clinging to a statuette, a golden or red hue when lit in various ways). Serrano was also interested in a wide range of bodily fluids: he had photographed urine, blood, semen and milk for an earlier series of works (*Fluids*). Some of these works (such as *Milk*, *Blood* and *Blood Cross*) evoked and commented on the famous abstracts of Mondrian. Others were created as submissions to a show at the New Museum of Contemporary Art in New York in 1987. The show was called 'Fake'; Serrano was interested in using bodily fluids such as urine and blood as if they were paint.[21] Other works, such as *Piss and Blood*, *Bloodstream*, *Blood and Semen* and the *Ejaculate in Trajectory* series, depict various aspects of bodily fluids: he photographed these fluids external to and independent of the body although they were normally hidden within the body's boundaries; he made images out of them in a way similar to how paint had been used for centuries although they were considered waste or taboo substances.[22]

It should not be forgotten that there is also something of a tradition concerning urination in art.[23] Jackson Pollock's infamous act of urinating in the fireplace seemed to mimic the drips he used to construct his massive artworks; Andy Warhol subsequently collapsed the two events into one (by urinating, along with several assistants, on canvasses painted in copper metallic paint) in his oxidation paintings. Gilbert and George, in addition to their *Shit Pictures*, provide images of men urinating together. Marcel Duchamp's *Fountain* presented the sculptural beauty in an item normally deemed antithetical to aestheticism in general and display in a museum in particular.

While much 'urination art' seems heavily masculine, works by two women artists address the gendered nature of attitudes towards urination. Helen Chadwick's *Piss Flowers* names a series of bronze sculptural forms cast from the cavities left in the snow by the urinating artist and a male collaborator. The sculptures made by the more concentrated female urine are far more phallic in shape than those cast from the man's puddled urine.[24] Sophy Rickett's series (*Pissing Women*) of computer-generated photographs shows women urinating, standing up, out of doors, alone in various urban locations that would normally be experienced by women as threatening.[25]

In *Pell* v *NGV*, *Piss Christ*'s juxtaposition of urine and crucifix, regardless of any longstanding artistic interest in urine as a medium, is certainly seen as problematic by the judge. And this is said to be compounded by Serrano's choice of title. On the fact that much controversy had surrounded the artwork, Harper J stated: 'This is entirely understandable. The title "Piss Christ" provides one reason why' (p. 1). The judgment identifies (and is uncomfortable with) the fact that the artwork's title might depend upon the suggested omission of a preposition. *The Age* newspaper wrote of the image that it was a preposition away from a statement of utter disdain (the preposition, presumably, being 'on': therefore, 'piss on Christ' – although 'off' might work almost as well).[26]

It is worth interrogating Serrano's use of the term 'piss', rather than, say, the more clinical 'urine'. Although some of the works described above (such as Gilbert and George's *Shit Pictures* and Rickett's *Pissing Women*) use appellations that come close to the vernacular without receiving comparable critical disapprobation, Serrano's selection of 'piss' seems at the least ambiguous. In some interviews, Serrano has indicated that he used 'piss' in the title in order to achieve a greater ambiguity in the artwork.[27] 'Piss' is, of course, an important component of the lexicon of swearing. Hughes (1998) explains its being borrowed into English from Old French (the earliest recorded instance of its use is circa 1290) and notes its varying uses as a noun and as a verb. It is supposed to have originated as a euphemism, although exactly for what has now been forgotten (Hughes 1998: 25–7, 31).

The word 'piss' is regarded as echoic or onomatopoeic, so that even saying the word evokes the activity. Some of the provocative potential of *Piss Christ* thus derives from the artwork's determined transformation of the spectator's position: anyone who says its title moves from a distanced viewer into some-one orally imitating the activity of urination. At least part of the artwork's provocation derives, of course, from the positioning in the title of 'piss' next to 'Christ'; perhaps also hinting at the latter word's use as a profane oath in its own right (an uncomfortable association which mirrors the discomfiting juxtaposition of urine and the crucifix).[28] The title thus mimetically reminds the viewer of the acts which led to *Piss Christ*'s existence as artwork. *Piss Christ* therefore does not exist in a present tense, rather the image continually speaks of a state of coming-to-being, in which the artist placed a crucifix in a vat and urinated on it.

For the court, and for the Catholic Church and the work's detractors, the offensiveness of *Piss Christ* relates to its prepositional nature: that there is an anterior state to the photograph. Its present condition and the artist's imputed intentions or motivations are thus read through its prior making. The artist's seemingly naive statements thus both exacerbate the offensiveness of the artwork (in claiming that urine was necessary only to broaden his colour palette) and also assert that *Piss Christ* does not in itself take a position except in so far as it ambivalently points out the paradox underlying the foundational nature of such a symbol (that a murder might be commemorated as religion).

In coming to judgment, Harper J refused to see the role of the court as having anything to do with the determination of what is or is not art (unlike the decision required of the jury in Cincinnati). He stated:

> [There has been no] assumption by me of the role of art critic. It would not merely be presumptuous, but quite wrong, of me to attempt any such thing. It is not relevant to my task and it would take the court into places in which it has no business to be. There is much wisdom . . . in the words of Landau J., the Israeli judge who presided over the trial of Adolf Eichmann. The courts, he said, speak with an authority whose very weight depends upon its limitations. No-one has made us judges of matters outside the realm of law. (p. 3)

The evocation of Eichmann in Jerusalem at first seems strange. However, this associative leap underscores the offensiveness of *Piss Christ*: the indefensi-bility of the crime against humanity perpetrated through religious hate lends a judgmental sensibility to the offence of an artwork which brings a man's penis and its emission of urine next to a religious symbol – again, a metonymic association. Not, however, that the judgment rests easily on the notion that the artwork is straightforwardly offensive, or at least not in any readily juridical manner. Rather, it is taken for granted that the image is *both* art *and* offensive. Harper J argues that the gallery did not manage to cast serious doubt on the proposition that the photograph is offensive, scurrilous and insulting at least to a very large number of Christians, including a very large number of Catholics, and has outraged their feelings. It has been argued that this outrage can be accommodated by refusing to attend the exhibition; but this is at best a partial answer. The outrage is generated as much by the knowledge that this work is being exhibited, in public, within the Archdiocese, and in a Gallery of which this State is very proud, as it is by viewing the picture itself. (p. 2)

He goes on to say: 'There can be no doubt that Mr Serrano's work is deeply offensive to many Christians, as well as to many non-Christians, who are offended at the offence given to others' (p. 4).

With the ambit of offensiveness thus drawn extremely widely (being offended at knowing the artwork exists, or being offended at the offence taken by others – a kind of circulating sensibility of offence), the judge then considered whether *Piss Christ* amounted in law either to a blasphemous libel, indecency or obscenity. Indecency and obscenity, according to the judge, exist on a continuum of failure to meet recognized standards of propriety, with indecency at one end and obscenity at the other. The judge consulted a number of legal dictionaries in order to discover that indecency connoted an affront to modesty, or something offensive to common propriety; and obscenity connoted, variously, filth, lewdness, disgustingness, incitement to sexual depravity, something abominable, disgusting, repulsive and offensive to modesty or decency.

It is interesting that Harper J took the view that *Piss Christ* was indecent or obscene in some *factual* manner: 'The fact that [this photograph's] indecent or obscene quality comes not from the image as such, but from its title and the viewer's knowledge of its background, does not make the task [of judgment] easier' (p. 8). The problem for the judge is that the image can easily be described in aesthetically pleasing terms (the sunset hues), but it is the ordinary person's imputed understanding of the title and knowledge of the manner of the image's making that might evidence the offensiveness and the possible obscenity. The judge might wish to locate legal obscenity or indecency in the artwork, but is ultimately unable to do so, due to the conflict he finds between the aesthetics of the image (the 'beauty' of its appearance) and the prepositional condition of the artwork (the 'disgusting' nature of its creation confessed by the title). And it seems to be this surface 'beauty' of the image that saves it from obscenity.[29] In Cincinnati, the jury found that Mapplethorpe's images were 'not pretty' but still 'art' (allowing the 'disgusting' content of the images to degrade the formal beauty of the works without removing them from the realm of aesthetics). In Melbourne, the court sees the image as formally beautiful, but precariously so, subject to a degradation wrought by its title and by the manner of its making. With this juridical oscillation between surface beauty and disgusting production, it becomes impossible to tell the difference between art and obscenity, to judge the difference that obscenity makes.

And so *Piss Christ* went on display. The exhibition had been open for only a few hours (with a crowd outside of two hundred demonstrators representing various religious groups) when a man, John Haywood, tried to take the artwork down from the wall. He was arrested and charged with criminal damage and burglary. The image was slightly scuffed as a result and was removed for the rest of the day for cleaning and restoration. In court after the event, the magistrate sentenced Haywood to a suspended term of imprisonment, taking into account his guilty plea as evidence of remorse. Haywood did not demonstrate much remorse after his court hearing, when he told reporters that he would not hesitate to attack the artwork again. He said, in a perhaps unconscious witticism: 'You can go so far in taking the piss, you understand. It riles me, it really gets me very upset.'[30]

On the second day of the exhibition, *Piss Christ* was rehung. Two teenagers entered the exhibition: one created a diversion by kicking from the wall one of the *Klansmen* portraits, distracting security guards, while the other boy used a hammer to smash *Piss Christ* nine times. The boys were arrested and the exhibition was closed. The next day, the gallery director announced that the show was to be abandoned.[31]

The older of the two second attackers, 18-year-old Timur Grin, pleaded guilty to two counts of damaging property.[32] Grin's accomplice, 'X' (he could not be named by the media because he was only 16 years old), was charged with only one count of criminal damage, but his act was the more serious of the two, since he had effectively destroyed the artwork and caused damage estimated at AU\$25,000. In explaining his actions, X stated that he had decided to smash *Piss Christ* after watching his mother weep upon hearing the news that the Catholic Church had failed in its attempt to prevent *Piss Christ*'s exhibition. X's explanation for his actions could not have fitted more neatly into the frame of the event. With its references to both religious iconography (the emblem of the woman's tears as cleansing sin) and art history (where the 'weeping woman' returns repeatedly as paradigmatic trope), the story of X's mother's tears linked the hammer attack upon the artwork to the Catholic Church's failed lawsuit and the wound of the artwork's alleged obscenity and blasphemy.

This, then, is the jurisprudence of disgust as it operated around *Piss Christ*: a lawsuit, tentatively and ambivalently dismissed; and two violent physical attacks upon the artwork. The chapter will next elaborate the judgment of a second artwork, *Myra*. Although no specific legal action takes place in relation to the artwork, responses to the image are animated by the effects of the same jurisprudence of disgust: a disgusting artwork should not exist, and if it must exist, it should not be displayed. Responses to *Myra* are also impelled by the memory of a criminal trial for murder, more than thirty years before, and by the phantasmatic presence read into the artwork of a victim whose body has never been found – the absent trace of the crime.

Myra: this face, these hands . . .

Myra (Figure 3) was exhibited in London in 1997 as part of the 'Sensation' exhibition of young British artists at the Royal Academy.[33] Judgment of *Myra* began almost two months before the 'Sensation' exhibition was due even to open. As with *Piss Christ* in Melbourne, a newspaper announced the existence of *Myra* to the general public: 'An anti-child abuse charity has urged the public to boycott the Royal Academy over plans to exhibit a portrait of Myra Hindley'.[34] Over the following days and weeks, *Myra* was repeatedly put on trial, as if Hindley was being retried for murder. The broadsheet newspapers' views were mixed: some ran a 'freedom of expression' argument; some claimed that Harvey's work was of a great artistic merit that was being lost in the brouhaha; others denounced the work as meretricious. The tabloid verdict unanimously denounced the artwork. The *Mirror* wrote: **'The portrait of Myra Hindley using a four-year-old's hand prints is worse than sick.** It is not art – it is a disgrace . . . It is disgusting' (emphasis in original).[35] An editorial in the *Sun* called the artwork 'nauseating' and wrote: 'Why not simply hang a bucket of sewer water in the gallery? **. . . It would smell a whole lot sweeter than this monstrosity**' (double emphasis in original).[36]

The *Sun* also invited readers to phone in their views in a telephone poll called 'YOU THE JURY'. The issue to be judged: 'Is the Royal Academy right to exhibit the portrait of Hindley?' The results were published two days later: 'Furious *Sun* readers yesterday condemned by a massive 42 to one a plan to display a portrait of child-killer Myra Hindley, made using a tot's hand-prints'. A total of 4,621 callers wanted the artwork withdrawn; only 111 favoured its retention in the show.[37] Hindley herself, no doubt suspecting that any outcry over an image of her might damage her already limited chances of gaining parole, wrote to the *Guardian* newspaper, asking for the Royal Academy to withdraw the artwork. She wrote:

> I find the forthcoming Sensation Exhibition due to open at the Royal Academy totally abhorrent . . . The . . . Royal Academy [shows] . . . disregard not only for the emotional pain and trauma that would inevitably be experienced by the families of the Moors victims but also the families of any child victim.[38]

Shortly after this, the Royal Academy issued a public statement saying that it was not attempting to glorify violence and that it would take the views of victims' families into account in voting on whether to retain *Myra* in the show: the vote in favour of its retention was close (26 votes to 19). At this point four Academicians resigned in protest over the artwork's inclusion in the exhibition.

For the exhibition's opening on 18 September, Winnie Johnson (mother of Keith Bennett, one of Hindley's victims) had travelled to London (her expenses paid by the *Daily Express*) in order to mount a protest in the forecourt of the

Royal Academy as the exhibition opened (along with representatives of a group called Mothers Against Murder and Aggression, or MAMA). The Royal Academy had invited Johnson and other family members to view *Myra* privately in the hope that she would cease her protest outside the museum. Reaction to the invitation was reported to be 'fury' and 'instead of taking up the academy's offer to view the work, they urged the public to boycott the show'.[39] The group of protesters, with placards and sandwich boards, used megaphones to exhort those queuing for tickets to boycott the exhibition. As was the case with Serrano's exhibition in Melbourne, among the first to visit the show were representatives of the police, Scotland Yard's Clubs and Vice Unit, investigating the exhibition for possible obscenity. A police spokesperson stated afterwards that there was insufficient evidence for a prosecution under the Obscene Publications Act.[40] Johnson's family also discussed with the Office of Public Prosecutions the possibility of prosecuting the Academy over the work's exhibition (no action was taken).

During the afternoon of the exhibition's first day, two separate physical attacks were made on *Myra*. First, a man called Peter Fisher threw red and blue Indian ink at the artwork (the ink had been smuggled into the museum in two film cartridges, despite the Royal Academy's searching visitors' bags for items which could be used to damage the artwork). A visitor to the museum saw: 'this guy flailing his arms about and smearing the paint with his hands into Myra's eyes. He seemed like a man possessed. He was kicking at the painting and managed to knock it off the wall.'[41] Another visitor to the museum who witnessed Fisher's vandalism of the artwork was inspired to commit his own act of assault upon the image: he left the museum and went across Piccadilly to the expensive food hall of Fortnum and Mason where he bought half a dozen free range eggs. He returned to the exhibit (presumably queuing once more for admission and paying again the entrance fee of seven pounds),[42] whereupon he threw three or four eggs at the artwork before being stopped by security guards.

The artwork stayed on display (after restoration work), viewed behind security glass with additional security guards stationed next to it. The protesters eventually went home, the exhibition ended up being one of the most successful (in terms of numbers attending – and therefore revenue gained) held at the Royal Academy.

And Myra Hindley was proved an astute judge of the media in her desire for the artwork *Myra* not to be exhibited. Her application to be considered for parole failed in November 1998. As she had no doubt predicted, newspapers used the story about Harvey's artwork in order to remind the public about Hindley's status as monster, as an indirect conjunct to the much more significant question of her release (for one deals only with an image, the other with the actual woman). Hindley's renewed campaign for release and the success of her claim (to be considered some day for parole) in the House of Lords meant that the artwork could not be viewed except as an extension of the woman herself. The existence of *Myra* was taken as a reminder of the existence of

Myra Hindley; it was as if the woman herself were standing in the Royal Academy, as young and vital and *present* as she was in 1966.[43]

This may serve to explain much of the pleasure taken in the imagination of Hindley's annihilation. A pun on the notion of 'hanging' frequently appeared in newspapers. The most explicit use of the pun came in an editorial in the *Sun*, which stated: '**Myra Hindley is to be hung in the Royal Academy**. Sadly it is only a painting of her' (double emphasis in original).[44] The pleasure taken in such innuendo reveals the desire for Hindley's annihilation in place of the display of her image.[45] But sadistic desire for Hindley's death is also matched by the violent abjection of the artwork. The nature of Hindley's crimes and her status as an almost mythic figure of evil mean that any artwork representing her and the murders would meet at least an unreceptive mainstream audience. However, particular features of *Myra* contributed to its being labeled disgusting. Many emphasized the sheer size of the image: 11 feet by 9 feet. One critic stated: 'A portrait measuring 11 feet by nine feet was bound to be interpreted as an affront to common decency'.[46] Marcus Harvey, the artist, said: 'The only way you can talk about the power that image has is by allowing it to operate on people. And that meant making it big. You're in a sea of Myra, lashing over you.'[47] The image is a size which invites the adjective 'monumental'. A monument, of course, commemorates an event or person: Hindley's status as monster could not allow the existence of an image that was at least capable of being read as a monument *to her* or *to her crimes*.[48] Comments by the artist and by the artist's dealer, to the effect that the image's size related to its status as an icon of evil could not countervail against the suspicion that size does matter, that enormity equals approbation.[49]

In addition to its size, a second feature of *Myra* constituted its provocation. This concerns its nature as a painting of a photograph. In its massive size, the painting enlarges the original photograph. Despite our belief or hope that enlargement will reveal more and more of the 'truths' hidden within a photograph, a point is reached at which all that is shown is the constitution of the image itself, its grain, its myriad indistinct dots (see Mitchell 1992: 2). Enlargement of any photograph inevitably reaches such a vanishing point. Harvey's painting, however, enlarges the photograph to and beyond the point where form and shape and meaning should dissolve into the morass of significatory dots. And those meaningless dots he replaces with marks in paint impressed by the cast of a child's hand. Harvey stated his intention thus:

> I just thought that the hand-print was one of the most dignified images that I could find. The most simple image of innocence in all that pain. And that kicks the thing into reality. There's an absolute realism. It's a real event. I realised you had to break the surface of this image, so it's not just a glamorous posturing. That wouldn't have been enough. It wouldn't have struck the nerve you needed to strike if you were going to get people to realise that what they loved to hate – what gave it the heat – was the idea

that a woman and innocent children were in there, and the children were dying.[50]

The child's handprint is a profoundly ambiguous mark. Children make prints of their hands at play, in day care, in games played with parents and with non-toxic paints. The very word 'handprint', however, echoes 'fingerprint' with its forensic drive and function. And the marks made by a bloodied hand have been used by other artists to denote the occasion of a crime, the traces of violence, just as forensic science seeks out the handprint or the fingerprint at the scene of a crime.[51] The ambiguity of the handprint gives *Myra* much of its voltage as an image. And yet, it makes no difference whether the handprint is understood as a mark of play or as a mark of victimization. If it denotes a child at play, its conjunction with the face of a child-killer horribly jars the spectator. If it is the mark of victimization, it draws attention, coolly, to the acts Hindley committed in the early 1960s, as if the hand was a sign that points to a crime too terrible to be itself the subject of representation.

It has been interpreted, inevitably, as a mark of violence. At first, most tabloid newspapers reported, erroneously, that Harvey had actually made children press their hands into the paint and then onto the canvas.[52] Such an assumption springs from the same place as the fascination with the notion that Serrano's actual urine had been used in the making of *Piss Christ*.[53] Discovering that Harvey had made casts of two toddlers' hands (which he had used himself to press paint onto the canvas) did not dilute the force of the idea that children's bodies and labour were involved in creating *Myra*. It did not help that when searching Saddleworth Moor for the dead children in the 1960s, police discovered the remains of one victim when they spotted a hand they described as 'beckoning' from a shallow grave.[54] In *Myra*, it is as if all four dead children are beckoning from the canvas. One of the Academicians who did not support the inclusion of *Myra* in 'Sensation' had said: 'I am not talking about censorship. It is about common decency. When there is a child buried on Saddleworth Moor, we should put decency before art'.[55] The child still buried on Saddleworth Moor is Keith Bennett, son of Winnie Johnson, who protested outside the Royal Academy. He is the lost child, his phantasmatic body the absent trace of murder.

And, finally, it is the *repetition* of the handprint, hundreds of times over, which finally ensures that the image has such a dreadful charge. The mass of handprints combine to make *Myra*, the image of Hindley. It is as though the children dissolve into her being. The means of making the image repeats as metaphor the fact of the crimes: in the coming-to-existence of the image *Myra*, each individual mark of signification (the handprint) is lost in the massive, overwhelming image that develops around it and as a result of it. The child – and all that 'the child' means – is reduced to an item of massification, condensed into a dot. In *Myra*'s reference to technological reproducibility (the photograph and its repetition in the media), the child is frozen forever at the point of vanishing into the image of the murderer.

Another sensation (again)

Revenue, crowds, protesters and lawsuits. The elements which characterized the public reception of both *Piss Christ* and *Myra* can be found, once more, in the response to an exhibition at the Brooklyn Museum. Once again, it was the Saatchi artworks of 'Sensation', which had travelled to New York City in September 1999, meeting with controversy and disapprobation. On this occasion, however, it was not *Myra* at the centre of the fierce dispute; instead it was Chris Ofili's *Holy Virgin Mary*. Ofili is one of the so-called YBAs, the young British artists championed by Saatchi, and came to prominence in 1998 when he won the Turner Prize for contemporary art. His paintings and drawings traverse and combine references from Black culture, hip hop, Catholicism, pornography, and traditional African aesthetic and cultural practices.

Holy Virgin Mary had been exhibited in London without criticism; in New York, its inclusion in the 'Sensation' exhibition prompted the same kind of outcry that had attached itself in London to *Myra*, in Melbourne to *Piss Christ* and in Cincinnati to Mapplethorpe's *X Portfolio*. The then Mayor of New York, Rudy Giuliani, called the painting 'sick stuff'; the President of the Catholic League for Religious and Civil Rights stated that it found the image 'offensive' and demanded that people picket the museum; and John Cardinal O'Connor called *Holy Virgin Mary* (and the exhibition) 'an attack on religion itself'.[56]

What provocation did this artwork offer? The image, 8 feet high and 6 feet wide, features a black woman as the Virgin, robed in traditional blue and posed against a gold background which evokes Renaissance religious iconography. The painting glows; 'Ofili uses lots of glitter and splashes of resin to give his surfaces a shimmer, like mosaic'.[57] Two decorative facets undermine the superficial shine of the artwork. The first involves tiny cutout images from pornographic magazines: these are dotted around the figure of the Virgin. Tiny vaginas and buttocks flutter around the canvas like butterflies or cherubs. The second decorative feature is the incorporation of elephant dung. The artwork stands, as do most of Ofili's paintings, upon two balls of elephant dung which raise it up off the floor. Another ball of dung is fastened to the body of the Virgin, in proximity to her right breast.

Both of these decorative devices (especially the elephant dung) are used throughout Ofili's works.[58] Pornographic cutouts appear in paintings such as *She*, *Blossom* and *Foxy Roxy*. The balls of elephant dung are often studded with beads forming words (sometimes the name of a depicted figure, as in *Holy Virgin Mary* where one ball states 'Virgin' and the other 'Mary', and sometimes the names of the elephants at London Zoo, who donate the dung). Ofili has also developed artworks around cultural attitudes to faeces: his painting *The Adoration of Captain Shit and the Legend of the Black Stars* marries an homage to Picabia with both the blaxploitation film genre and cultural distaste for faecal waste.[59] Ofili's work stirred no protests in London (it was also exhibited without any problems in Hamburg in 1998), but its enmixing of revered and reviled tokens sparked not only a media furore and large-scale protests at the Brooklyn Museum but also a lengthy legal struggle between the Museum and the City of New York.

Just as the media coverage of *Piss Christ* and *Myra* tended to sensationalize the nature of the artworks and to invest the artists with an intention to shock, so the New York news media overwhelmingly characterized *Holy Virgin Mary* as a profoundly distasteful image, dwelling on the connections made by the image between a religious icon and waste materials. And just as *Piss Christ* and *Myra* were represented as distasteful in large part due to the manner of their making, so *Holy Virgin Mary* was depicted as offensive due to the ways in which it was made. News reports repeatedly used expressions such as 'smeared' or 'thrown at' to describe the way the dung was applied to the figure of the Virgin, creating an imaginary moment in which Ofili aimed and launched clods of faeces at an icon or image of the mother of God and rubbed them into it.[60]

Protesters crowded the forecourt of the Brooklyn Museum for the exhibition's opening (just as they did in Melbourne and London). Close to one thousand Catholics prayed on their knees, waving rosary beads and placards at visitors. Some Catholic groups handed out vomit bags to those queuing for tickets. Anti-Giuliani protesters held placards declaiming 'Jerk' and 'Arrest Giuliani'. The museum had taken various precautionary steps in planning the exhibition, such as a possible age limit (over-18s) for visitors or prohibiting entry for under-18 year olds unless accompanied by an adult, and, once the antagonism to *Holy Virgin Mary* became apparent, exhibiting that painting behind bulletproof Plexiglass, situating museum security guards next to it, and installing metal detectors at the museum doorway. In the end, a record-breaking number of visitors attended the exhibition.[61]

Protest against the exhibition was not limited to pickets and mayoral ire in the news media. The City of New York, spearheaded by Giuliani, undertook a series of legal actions against the Brooklyn Museum in order to compel it to shut the exhibition down. At first, the City simply blustered and threatened, claiming that the museum was violating the terms of its lease in various ways (for example, by planning to restrict entry to 'Sensation' to the over-18s) and that the museum was 'shilling' for Charles Saatchi (exhibiting the works shortly before a sale of some of Saatchi's art collection was to be held at Christie's in London with the aim of increasing the value of the artworks, although none of the works in 'Sensation' was included in the upcoming sale). However, the City then began a federal suit against the museum, seeking to withhold its funding. At the same time, it instituted a suit in state court to evict the museum from its premises, on the grounds that it was in violation of the terms of its lease in planning to charge an entry fee of US$9.75.

At this point, the museum began a series of counter-suits, first of all for dismissal of the City claims and for violation of its First Amendment rights. The museum also entered a suit against Giuliani personally for making a frivolous claim and seeking damages from him. It also claimed that Giuliani had violated the Constitutional guarantee to the museum of equal protection under the law, and that he had violated the State Constitution and the City Charter in withholding from the museum funds that had already been allocated to them. A string of other New York museums, including the Metropolitan Museum of Art, filed amicus briefs in support of the Brooklyn Museum, which was now suing for an injunction against the City to prevent it from withholding funds. The City's actions to evict the museum and to cut its funding were refused by Judge Nina Gershon; this failure was then followed up by an unsuccessful appeal to the Second Circuit Court, claiming that Judge Gershon had abused her discretion in making her ruling.[62]

Although the threats to the museum were eventually defused, Ofili's artwork did not escape untouched. Shortly before the exhibition was due to end, several months after going on display in the museum, *Holy Virgin Mary* was the object of an attack by an elderly man. Dennis Heiner, aged 72, feigned illness to distract the security guards, before slipping behind the painting's Plexiglass shield and applying white paint to the image. According to some accounts, he shouted 'Blasphemy!' while he threw the paint at the artwork; according to others, he answered quietly, 'It's blasphemous', when asked why he attacked the painting.[63] Heiner was charged with three misdemeanour counts: criminal mischief, making graffiti and possessing instruments of graffiti.[64]

Like one of *Myra*'s attackers in London (who smuggled ink into the Royal Academy concealed inside film cartridges), Heiner secreted white latex paint inside an empty tube of hand cream. And like *Piss Christ*'s attackers in Melbourne, it is a religious imperative that dictates his actions. His wife, who is blind, explained his motivations: 'This painting is your mother, the painting of the Blessed Mother, the mother of Christ. So he said, "I will go there today and try to clean it"'.[65] The painting is therefore 'dirty'; the iconic figure's contact with waste materials renders it offensive and in need of cleaning. Just as *Piss Christ* was attacked by a boy who wanted to assuage his mother's tears (tears which fell when she heard about, rather than saw, the painting), so Heiner was acting in an emotional state shared by him and his wife, described as 'being upset for a very long time' and being 'angry Roman Catholics'.[66]

The artwork was rapidly restored by the museum and put back on display, not only behind its Plexiglass shield, but with the addition of a velvet rope and a police officer. The exhibition ended, the artworks were returned to the Saatchi Gallery, the protesters dispersed until the next small culture war.[67] And in reiterating the features of these three examples of contested display, I have sought to show how public protests and legal disputes over the exhibition of art tend to share common characteristics and interchangeable features (such as a prominent public personage heading a campaign against the artwork or gallery, and a coalition of interest groups whose focus is public morality or the defence of religious doctrine).

Interchangeability almost seems written into the letter of these examples, whereby Myra anagrammatically transforms into Mary. Indeed, some of the New York press coverage of 'Sensation', in their reporting of the previous aesthetic struggle, could not even manage to reproduce the correct spelling of

Hindley's and Harvey's names, calling them 'Myra Handle' and 'Marcus Heavey'.[68] Although these nominal lapses can to a certain extent be put down to the vagaries of the spell-checker or sub-editor, in other respects such slips reveal the way in which the substance of a previous contest matters little each time a new one rolls around. Thus it was of little consolation for Serrano, when *Piss Christ* was attacked in Melbourne, that the artwork had been exhibited without fuss for years: all that mattered was that there had been controversy in the past and that it could be invoked and stirred up again. And, indeed, all such struggles since and all those which are no doubt unfortunately yet to come take place simply in the shadow of the Culture Wars, which lend historical credence to *the fact of contestation* and allow disputes to be repeatedly rehearsed.[69] In the remainder of this chapter, I will reconsider and further explore the organizing dynamic of these contested artworks, and suggest that their provocation derives from two relationships: first, a relation interior to the artwork and centred on the illegitimate touching of things which are supposed, culturally, to be kept separate; second, a relation of address between the artwork and the spectator, through which the artwork extends its touch towards the spectator, in a spiral of aesthetic vertigo.

Touching: aesthetic vertigo

In *Piss Christ*, urine has flowed over and around a crucifix. In *Myra*, a child's hand touches the face of a child murderer. In *Holy Virgin Mary*, balls of dung press on a canvas depicting the mother of the Christian God. Each of these artworks, therefore, insists on the physical commingling of elements which are not only usually separate(d) but also normally held utterly distant from each other. Each artwork is composed of endless illegitimate touchings, the sight of which creates shock, distress or queasiness in the viewer.[70] However, the spectator's sense of disgust at the artwork does not derive solely from the disturbing conjunctions represented within it. What is crucial here is the effect of the 'disgusting' artwork's *address to the spectator*, its intimation of connection with her and its erosion of any sense of separate space from which it can be viewed – its unbearable *proximity* to the spectator. Out of this proximity comes the shuddering sensation that can be called 'aesthetic vertigo'.

In what way does disgust prompt vertigo? Actual touching of a disgusting thing – a mouldering piece of food, for example – produces the shudder characteristic of disgust.[71] Korsmeyer describes the physical movements that display disgust:

> The disgust response is . . . a physical recoil, often with a notable gesture of repulsion as the body folds inward and turns away. The verbal response . . . is an expulsion of air, a 'yyeech!' sound, expelling the presence of the disgusting object as though it were a bodily contaminant.
>
> (Korsmeyer 1998: 4)

However, near touching or simple sighting of a disgusting thing usually produces the same sensation (although it may be less intense). This adverts to the
power of the imaginary: the shudder arises out of the imagined sensation of a
touch which has not taken place.

Such is the affect of representation. Add to this a further dimension: the
spectator in a gallery understands that she is looking at an image of something
which may be disgusting rather than at a disgusting thing in itself. There is an
important difference between a photograph of a crucifix in a vat of urine and a
physically present vat of urine with immersed crucifix: such a hypothetical
artwork as the latter might well be deemed 'disgusting', but its relation to the
spectator would lack the specific character of metaphorical disgustingness
that interests me here. The picture on the gallery wall does not literally touch
the spectator; however, the visceral response to artworks such as *Piss Christ*
and *Myra* can be interpreted as the shudder arising from an image which
transcends the cushioning effect of the fact of representation and threatens
metaphorically to touch the spectator.

Claims have been made that disgusting or 'abject' art such as *Piss Christ* and
Myra (among many other examples, including the work of Kiki Smith, Mike
Kelley, Hannah Wilke, Carolee Schneeman, some works by Cindy Sherman
and so on) constitutes a radical and critical rewriting of the laws of aesthetics.
However, there are clear limits to its radical potential, as Molesworth adverts:
'it is as if the exhibition, the religious right, and Kristeva could all agree that
[a] sculpture really is a pile of shit' (in Bois et al. 1994: 7). Thus, the depiction
of excrement (for example) as a strategy in abject art collapses into the
artwork being called excrement: denunciation of the artwork as not-art ('it's
shit') or as bad art ('this is a shitty artwork') or as too easy and therefore
lacking the laboriousness that defines artworks ('it's a piece of piss').

Abjection – in its requirement that the disgusting object be expelled,
outlawed and repressed – *demands* a regulatory responsiveness in the subject.
As Foster states:

> the danger, of course, is that . . . an abject artist (like Andres Serrano) may
> call out for an evangelical senator (like Jesse Helms), who then completes
> the work, as it were, negatively. Moreover, as left and right may agree on
> the social representatives of the abject, they may shore each other up in a
> public exchange of disgust.
>
> (Foster 1996: 116)

Disgust is certainly a condition of responsiveness to an object's address. But
Foster, however, would insist that artists such as Serrano seek more than the
simple shudder of revulsion, desiring instead the full weight of censure from
the paternal Law. He states:

> Often [the Surrealists] did act like juvenile victims who provoked the
> paternal law *as if to ensure that it was still there* – at best in a neurotic plea
> for punishment, at worst in a paranoid demand for order. And this Icarian

pose is again assumed by contemporary artists who are almost too eager to talk dirty in the museum, almost too ready to be . . . spanked by Jesse Helms . . . Is this, then, the option that abject art offers us – Oedipal naughtiness with the secret wish to be spanked, or to wallow in shit with the secret faith that the most defiled might reverse into the most sacred, the most perverse into the most potent?

(Foster 1996: 118, emphasis in original)

Thus the artwork addresses the spectator through the image and requires disgust as a reaction and as a platform for its own censure. If we follow Foster's logic, *Piss Christ* is not 'complete' until Helms, D'Amato, Pell and the hammer-wielding boy proffer their responses of disgust. This, however, reads *Piss Christ* through a retrospective narrative frame which imputes a desire for discipline to Serrano and reduces the artwork to the product of his intentions, a mere device to stimulate the Law of the Father. The same retrospective frame is deployed by McAuliffe, when he writes that artists such as Serrano 'recommissioned effrontery not by discovering new ways to shock the bourgeoisie but by offering themselves up as sacrificial victims in the so-called "Culture Wars" of the Reagan–Bush era'.[72]

Instead of simply reading an artwork such as *Myra* or *Piss Christ* retrospectively – through its controversy – I wish to read it *as an artwork*, situated on the gallery wall, in its address to the spectator. As noted earlier, artworks such as *Holy Virgin Mary*, *Piss Christ* and *Myra* seem disgusting due to their threat of metaphorical contact with the spectator. Two types of defensive response are then occasioned. For the first, it is less the fact of the artwork's existence than its *exposure* which is problematic. Giuliani's actions against the Brooklyn Museum, the lawsuit by Archbishop Pell against the National Gallery of Victoria, and the exhortations of British newspapers for individuals to boycott the 'Sensation' exhibition fall into this category by preventing or inhibiting the exhibition or display of a disgusting artwork. The second category is represented by the individuals who threw paint and eggs at *Myra* and who kicked and hammered at *Piss Christ*.[73] The sheer physicality of these vandalizing assaults responds directly to the threat of the artwork: that the image might touch and contaminate the spectator, and that the image depicts illegitimate touchings within its frame. Such is the threat of a disgusting artwork that the vandal overcomes the considerable museal prohibitions on touching the artworks: not only does the disfigurer touch the artwork, she attempts to destroy it.

I do not wish to suggest that the viewer who sees an artwork as disgusting is somehow 'duped' by the image into believing that there is a literal threat of contamination. Rather, the *sense* of threat arises in two places at once. First, the affective charge of the artwork's illegitimate touch (crucifix and urine, faeces and religious figure, or child's hand and child-killer) reduces the interim space between the viewer and the artwork (the space in which the viewer knows that 'it is only an image'). Such a lack of an interim space might in itself be challenging to viewers. In addition, however, the spectator must confront the duplicity of representation, or the 'emptiness of the image'.[74] At the same time as the image looms ever closer with its threat of contamination, the viewer knows that what she sees is only a reproduction. As Weber notes:

> Where . . . what is 'brought closer' is itself a reproduction – and as such, separated from itself – the closer it comes, the more distant it is. This tendency is rooted not only in works that are, from the very start, as it were, constituted as reproductions. It results no less from the nature of those to whom such works are addressed.
>
> (Weber 1996: 88)

This is the dynamic of 'aesthetic vertigo'. Rather than provoking a simple 'disgusted' response, artworks such as *Holy Virgin Mary*, *Piss Christ* and *Myra* make the spectator dizzy, teetering on the verge of a representational abyss. The illegitimate touchings within the image; the threat of metaphorical contamination by the image; the lack of an interim space in which the image can be viewed as an image; the defensiveness generated by disgust; and the spiralling emptiness within the image (for it is, after all, 'only' an image): all combine to effect a vertiginous collapse, or falling away, within the spectator. For some, this will manifest as a sense of admiration at the transgressive beauty of the image. For others, it will require the corporeal motions of disgust as the spectator passes on to the next image on the gallery wall. For others, it will invite a physical reaction that mirrors the vertiginous collapse within, and the spectator will strike, or kick, at the image. For others, perhaps even without seeing the image, the jurisprudence of disgust will demand normative judgment and the prohibition of its appearance.

The illegitimacy of the image, its touchings and juxtapositions, is thus imagined as desiring a repressive response. In contrast to those who would see the abject artwork as requiring this repression to confirm its critical status or those who would focus on the censorious or repressive response as part of the artwork's controversial status, it is my contention that *the spectator desires the abjection of the artwork* as a response to its uncomfortable address (an address in which the spectator is implicated). Artworks such as *Holy Virgin Mary*, *Myra* and *Piss Christ* suggest an other order to the familiar economy of images, an order in which waste materials can look beautiful, or in which a victim might stroke the murderer's face. These artworks therefore merge the two orders of the imaginary which law has struggled to keep separate: as Douzinas and Nead (1999a: 9) put it, the 'iconomy', or gallery of permitted images, and the 'idolatry', or criminology of dangerous images. The desire to judge these artworks not only as disgusting but also as indecent, or obscene or blasphemous, is a desire for the reinstatement of the law (of community, of religion, of representation) and for a continued segregation of images into the sanctioned and the unwarranted. The satisfied fascination manifested in public discourse when an exhibition is closed down and when images are vandalized confirms that the law of representation governs display through veiling, and the smooth surface of the community is founded upon disorder and defacement.

viewing (de)position
hidings

It's April 1995 and I'm in New York City, coming to the end of a four-month sabbatical. I've started thinking about a book on crime, law and the legitimacy of images, so when I hear about a retrospective exhibition of the work of Andres Serrano at the New Museum of Contemporary Art, I am keen to go – to see for the first time, in gallery space instead of as reproductions, the artworks which became famously contested in the late 1980s and early 1990s.

The exhibition occupies the ground floor of the museum. It's an attractive space, and the images, which are huge, are given room to project without overwhelming each other. The exhibition ranges from Serrano's earliest works, like *Heaven and Hell* (a bishop turning away from a bloodied girl strung from a hook) to his later portraits of hooded Ku Klux Klan members. In between are included the almost abstract shapes produced by close-up photographs of guns, the steady gazes of New York's homeless, and the blocks of colour produced by bodily fluids such as milk and blood. *Piss Christ*, probably the most notorious of Serrano's images, comes early in the museum, in one of its outer rooms, as befits its chronological position early in Serrano's body of work. It is flanked by others in the *Immersions* series: *Piss Discus* and *Black Jesus*, for example. It is good to see it like this – a work in a series of works, a work to be understood not just in its own right (which is partly how it became so misread and misrecognized in conservative responses to it), but also in relation to other, similar, artworks. All the *Immersions* images play with fluid, exploiting the effects produced by submerging a solid object in water or urine. Each of the drowned plaster statues is fringed with delicate bubbles which cling to the statue's outline like lacy decorations. Varied lighting effects lead to either the roseate glow found in *Piss Christ* or to the chiaroscuro of *Black Supper III* or *Black Jesus*. Looking at *Piss Christ* here, it's hard to see how it could have inspired such fury, such hatred and determination, which still reverberates in the chilling to a trickle the financing of contemporary art with federal funds.

After wandering through several rooms, I'm about to turn and leave, when a museum custodian steps forward and calls to me. 'Don't miss the last room,' he says, gesturing to a small door at the top of a short flight of stairs. 'You won't want to miss that one'. I go up the stairs. They lead to a tiny enclosed room on a sort of interim, mezzanine level. The ceiling is low, the walls and floor white. There are about eight enormous images hanging on the walls around me. And they really feel as though they are around me – it is not as if I am viewing the images any more, like downstairs, rather I feel enveloped in them, wrapped in them. They press on me.

My gaze grazes over them – a close-up of a head, a close-up of a tiny foot, a side-on shot of a woman's torso with arms rigidly lifted across her chest. Walking closer to the wall, I consult the title card for one: it reads *The Morgue (Infectious Pneumonia)*. The next: *The Morgue (Rat Poison Suicide)*. Of course, these are the *Morgue* pictures, I realize, some of Serrano's more recent work.

The next image that I notice is an abstracted, flattened, landscaped and luminous red with black(ened) blotches on it. I'm admiring the hues, and thinking back to Serrano's early works like *Milk/Blood*, where he used the juxtaposition of fluids to present abstract shapes and colours, when I see the title card: *The Morgue (Burnt to Death III)*. Suddenly I recognize the image as a close-up of burnt skin, burnt skin on a body, the burnt skin of a person who has died from those burns, those reds and blacks, whose body is now a glowing landscape of colour and luminosity. At the same moment, my memory is flooded with a story told by a colleague and friend, years before, recounting the experience of suffering extensive burns to her legs after the skirt she was wearing ignited while she stood next to an open fireplace.

In a swirling, sweating rush, I connect the image, the dead person behind the abstraction, and my friend – all coalesce in a visceral, vertiginous rush (in my head I feel a kind of whoosh) that homes in on my legs (exactly where my friend was burned). I actually feel dizzy: 'going weak at the knees' is no longer a cliché but describes exactly what is happening in my body. I grope into a seat with my head down. I'm breathing hard. After a few minutes, I make an effort to look at other images on the walls (keeping my eyes averted from *Burnt to Death*). But it's no good – I've been jolted out of spectatorship by that one image and into an intimate relationship with it: I saw it as if it documented the burned flesh of my friend.

I get up and walk out, leaving behind a shuttering room, the images leaning down from the walls, fragments of dead bodies made artefacts after pain, mementos of the negation of subjectivity. Past the peaceful, glowing *Piss Christ* and onto Broadway, a hurtling rush of legs, eyes, voices, bodies, cars, buildings. The image of my friend's injury I leave behind in that small room – but it is also travelling with me, an electric charge of reminder whenever I contemplate Serrano's artworks and their admirable and appalling address of and to the flesh.

*   *   *

Six years later, walking – lost – down a street in Prague, I'm brought to a standstill by a poster proclaiming 'Andres Serrano Pobody Zla'. It's advertising an exhibition of Serrano's work at a local gallery (I couldn't tell if it was a solo show or Serrano in conjunction with another artist called 'Pobody Zla'; later I discover that 'pobody zla' means 'placing time and evil'). I track my way through the cobbled, curved streets to the Prague City Gallery (Galerie hlavniho mesta Prahy). The exhibition is installed in the museum's basement, the artworks crowded onto arching, cellar-like walls. On the upper floors there is an exhibition of twentieth-century Czech art. Serrano's artworks – the fluids, the corpses, the naked lovers, the churches, the bodybuilders, the guns – are crammed into this nether space, hidden away like troublesome reminders of corporeal imperfection.

* * *

The containment of Serrano's exorbitancy in tiny underground rooms reminds me of the brief and ambivalent attempt to exhibit his work in Melbourne in October 1997. The retrospective was heralded with much publicity; the National Gallery of Victoria advertised the show (called 'A History of Andres Serrano') on banners cascading down its outer walls.

However, when I entered the gallery, on the exhibition's second day, it was impossible to tell that there was any Serrano exhibition taking place. A massive Rembrandt exhibition was also occurring, and all signs in the gallery foyer directed visitors towards that. No signs advertised the Serrano retrospective. I asked at the information desk whereabouts 'A History of Andres Serrano' was located: the gallery employee produced a floor plan and started explaining in a low voice where I could find it (located in a far corner of the gallery, with a small entry way situated in the back of a room showing another exhibition – of Japanese flower-arranging). I asked her why it was in such a remote corner of the gallery and why there were no signs directing visitors towards it. She replied, 'Well, they don't want people to just stumble upon it, you know'.

Visitors thus had to pick their way through a warren of rooms to reach the exhibition; ticketing was also organized separately from the main ticket desks in the foyer (perhaps to avoid tempting the Rembrandt-goers with the ambiguous pleasures of Serrano's work). Unlike most galleries, which would usually try to encourage visitors to attend as many exhibitions as possible (sometimes offering packages of tickets to two or more exhibitions at discounted rates), the National Gallery of Victoria seemed to be denying the existence of the Serrano exhibition, hiding it away so that only the determined spectator could find it, purchase a ticket, and view the images. A further barrier was provided at the entrance to 'A History of Andres Serrano', in the form of a notice posted next to the ticket booth stating that the exhibition was restricted to those over 18 years old and that proof of age could be demanded.

Entering the exhibition space, I wandered around the beautifully installed artworks for a while, and then stopped, puzzled. Where was *Piss Christ* (the display of which here had inspired a lawsuit by the Catholic Archdiocese against the National Gallery only a few days previously)? After circling the space again, I came upon a gap between two images. A small title card was still in place, quietly positioned beneath a blank space. *Piss Christ*, however, was gone, with only the card as a trace of its display. 'What's happened?', I asked the museum guard. 'Where's *Piss Christ*?' 'Smashed,' he said. 'Two kids with a sledgehammer smashed it this morning.'

I could not reconcile my memory of that silent, radiating image I had seen in New York with the idea of an artwork which had been attacked with a hammer. But there it was – the empty space framed by two other images, the mute remnant of *Piss Christ*'s brief exhibition. Spectators continued to swirl through the gallery, their viewing went on uninterrupted, but at the heart of the exhibition there was now a wound, a hole.

Meanwhile, outside the National Gallery of Victoria, on its forecourt, protesters continue to lament the exhibition's very existence. When I had entered the gallery, I had had to walk through a crowd of approximately forty people – many on their knees reciting the Lord's Prayer, a Greek Orthodox priest in full regalia, people sitting by the entrance doors holding placards which read 'I'm Fanatical About the Arts – Also Christian – Also Deeply Offended' and 'Andres Serrano Take Your Blasphemy and Pornography Out Of Our City', young men walking up and down with banners and placards which state 'Christ's Cross Is Our Salvation'. A sandwich board had been placed on the forecourt. It reads:

Christians Against Blasphemy

As Christians we are opposed to Andres Serrano's blasphemous exhibition at the gallery.

IF URINE, a bodily waste, was used to immerse Mohammed or Princess Diana or John Versace [sic], the justified outrage would be enormous.

WE SEE THIS AS A DOUBLE STANDARD AND DISCRIMINATION AGAINST ALL CHRISTIANS AND THEIR SACRED SYMBOLS.

The outside space of the museum, with its posters for Rembrandt and Serrano and the Melbourne Arts Festival, had been appropriated by the protest: it jostled and shifted and heaved with discontent. Two teenaged boys had carried the protest inside – finding their way to the hidden exhibition, buying their tickets despite being under 18 years old, swinging a hammer at *Piss Christ* where it hung, looking at them, on the wall, smashing the artwork in nine places. This mobile, penetrating, chanting protest had become an anti-portrait of *Piss Christ*, an image which represented only a frozen moment, a plaster statue of the crucified Christ immersed in liquid, an invitation to interpretation suspended before the spectator.

Withdrawn into the rear of the gallery, with only muffled voices acknowledging its existence and only circuitous, unguided paths leading to its location, 'A History of Andres Serrano' was exhibited as little as any gallery could exhibit artwork without actively removing it from the walls. That this is what the gallery did the next day, in shutting the retrospective down, perfectly demonstrates its reluctant exhibition of Serrano's work. While the protest sat in comfortable full view of the city and its inhabitants and visitors, Serrano's images had to be on display as covertly as possible.

In showing to us the repressed relations and remainders of corporeality (blood, semen, urine, sado-masochism, the homeless, guns, nuns, sanitary pads, religious artefacts, corpses), Serrano's work is repeatedly secreted away, like a bodily secretion itself. Its manifestation of the fragility of the layers we invoke to hide our corporeal selves is met with vituperative dissent and given a hiding with a sledgehammer by two boys. Its uncovering of hidden spaces and things requires its hiding away in the interim, remote and nether reaches of gallery space.

3 Written on the skin of the city

This chapter begins at an unremarkable place, on a New York street. In early October 2000, the Deitch Projects Gallery in SoHo was about to open an exhibition showing artwork inspired by graffiti, and aiming to challenge the separateness of the aesthetics of exterior and interior spaces. The three exhibiting artists were graffiti writers. On 2 October, one of the artists, Todd James, was arrested as he left the gallery where he had been helping to install the works. Two days later, Josh Laczano, who had been at the gallery to help with preparations for the opening, was also arrested. The men were arrested by a New York Police Department Vandals Unit, which had stationed itself outside the gallery, to await the artists as they exited the building. Todd James was charged with three graffiti-related misdemeanours, in connection with allegedly painting his tag, Reas, on walls at a school in the Bronx in November 1999. Josh Laczano was charged with the felony of criminal mischief in the second degree, relating to his allegedly tagging 'Amaze' on a building in 1997.[1]

As the two men each left the gallery, they were accosted by police officers. The path of the artist crossed with that of the police officer arresting a vandal. This chapter takes as its beginning that point of intersection on Wooster Street, New York City. The artists' display of their work *as art* led to their being identified and targeted *as criminals*. Display of an artwork in the legitimized space of the gallery permitted the prosecution of illegitimized writing on other buildings. And the encounter between artist and police officer took place on a New York street, in public space, where, for over thirty years, writers and agents of the law have struggled over the status of graffiti. In this encounter, the bodies of artists are transformed into the bodies of criminals.

This chapter traces the intersection between two irreconcilable discourses, the oscillation between claiming graffiti as art and condemning it as crime. It also addresses the undecidable question of *the sense of graffiti* in the contemporary city. To question the sense of graffiti requires imagining it as sensation and as challenge to conventional sensibility. Graffiti as sensation provokes investigation of the experiences of writing and reading graffiti; graffiti's challenge to sensibility proceeds from its apparently nonsensical nature and its construction as illegal, inept, wasteful, transgressive and aggressive. The sense of graffiti will be investigated in two sections: one examining the experiences, claims and objectives of graffiti writers; the other interrogating the determination of legal and criminal justice agencies to condemn graffiti as an illegitimate signifying practice in public space. As Chapter 1 concluded, 'the law of representation governs display through veiling, and the smooth surface of the community is founded upon disorder and defacement'. That foundation will be investigated in this chapter through an interrogation of the techniques of (de)legitimation of signifying strategies in the city. To that extent, my reading of graffiti and the public discourse on graffiti continues the investigation begun in Chapter 2, asking what it might be in a particular artwork or artistic practice which seems to invite a set of responses from the spectator. I also seek to ask what it could be that the spectator desires, in constructing the artwork or artistic practice as if it were seeking such a response. My intention is therefore to view graffiti as existing within an imaginary matrix of desires, whereby a range of signifying practices which put words and images upon walls can be understood as 'graffiti' through a relational economy drawing on notions of propriety, property, the bounded self, the city and the other.

Graffiti as cultural practice

Graffiti should not be considered as if it were a unitary, homogeneous category. It is not, as will become clear. It should be noted at the outset that this chapter's focus is on graffiti as a contemporary cultural practice and thus does not deal in any depth with historical graffiti. It also does not engage with the type of graffiti that has come to be known as 'latrinalia' (that is, writing on public lavatory walls) because it is not a target for socio-legal intervention in the way that political slogans, tagging or murals on train-line walls have been. Latrinalia has a specific communicative tone (often involving a conversational format) and is 'public' only to the extent that members of the public see it when they use toilet facilities and that it occurs on someone's else's property. (Graffiti on school or university desks is very similar: often conversational, public in a limited way, and involving commonly used tools such as ordinary biro pens.)

The graffiti that is the focus of this chapter takes place firmly in the public sphere: on street walls, on billboards, on train lines, on trains. It is often viewed as affecting a whole community, not just the owner of the property or the limited numbers who happen to see it. A commonly held view splits public graffiti into 'art' on the one hand, and 'vandalism' on the other. 'Graffiti art' might include the elaborate murals painted by artists such as Futura 2000 and Keith Haring, the graffiti-like images incorporated by recognized artists into their canvasses (such as Cy Twombly or Jean-Michel Basquiat), and the carefully designed, cartoon-like imagery which goes into the graffiti mural known as a 'piece' (short for 'masterpiece') (for example, see Figure 4). On the other hand, for many 'graffiti vandalism' would be exemplified by the most common form of graffiti, tagging, which probably originated in the United States in the late 1960s, and in which an adopted name is written in complicated calligraphy on any available surface (for example, see Figures 5 and 6).[2] Hip hop writers speak of graffiti as being about 'getting up' (successfully writing one's tag or piecing on selected surfaces), with the main objective of having the work seen by other writers.

The struggle over whether graffiti might be 'art' or 'crime' has persisted unresolved since at least the 1970s. The dichotomy is useful for adverting to the fact that graffiti takes more than one form; however, it also perpetuates the commonly held view that graffiti is *either* 'art' or 'crime'. As Lachmann comments, however:

> [M]uch of the previous scholarly and popular work on graffiti has tended to ignore the differences among graffiti writers and their creations and either has championed all graffiti from scrawled obscenities to elaborate murals as art . . . or has viewed graffiti as [uncontrollable crime].
>
> (Lachmann 1988: 231)

Graffiti culture and practice is more complicated than this dichotomy would indicate, in that both the aesthetic of graffiti and its toleration, criminalization or appreciation in the community depend upon issues such as placement, content, style and mode of address. It is clear that a simplistic polarization of graffiti into either art or crime cannot be sustained when two factors are taken into consideration. First, the art/crime divide is challenged by the existence of two further types of graffiti: the slogan and the stencil.

Slogans range from the personal ('Sally loves Ted', or 'J. Kaminski is a slut'), through the gamut of political issues (environmental concerns, feminism, state politics, international relations and so on), but all share the common feature of being declaratory or exhortative in nature, expressing a view to an audience (much like a letter to a newspaper, or a phone call to a talkback radio show). Stencils have become an extremely popular form of graffiti in recent years, particularly in cities such as Paris, London and Melbourne. The work of stencillers such as Banksy and Nylon (based in Britain) and Blek, Némo and Jérôme Mesnager, and Miss-Tic (based in Paris) has been exhibited and collected in books and on websites.[3] To make a stencil, an image is created (often using a computer program such as Adobe Photoshop) and translated into a cardboard template which can be placed flat against a wall or other surface and sprayed, to leave behind the stencilled image (for example, see Figures 6, 7 and 8). Stencils range from the highly political through the allusive to the whimsical. They are highly reproducible, by their very nature: when a stencil is painted out, the stenciller need only return later with the template to replace the erased image. To that extent, the stencil straddles some of the divide between the piece and the tag in hip hop graffiti culture.

Neither slogans nor stencils can be readily categorized by means of the art/crime dichotomy. And, as the encounter between the two writers and the police officers waiting outside the Deitch Projects Gallery in New York demonstrates, the art/crime dichotomy is volatile, straddling shifting lines which can capture and recapture bodies, names and images.

'Often violent and uncontrolled in its visual image'[4]

The public discourse that is manifested through newspaper coverage of graffiti writing focuses on the public's sense of being addressed by the graffiti: the emotional force behind the discourse, as will become apparent, depends upon an identification of the graffiti as directed towards the individual in a particular way.[5] Media discourse about graffiti tends to construct graffiti in a metonymical relation to a reviled object or phenomenon distinctive for its own subjugated and distasteful relation to the individual. The urban spectator's relationship to graffiti therefore becomes an always already determined matter. Such a metonymical relation means that graffiti is rarely considered *as itself* (whatever that would mean), but rather always by reference to and through some other – usually quite distinct – phenomenon. Facets of this phenomenon are selected and resemblance asserted by invoking them in the specific context of graffiti. Public discourse therefore concentrates on these asserted resemblances, to the exclusion of other possible similarities, comparisons or qualities. Thus, as will be elaborated, public discourse also tends to invoke a metonymical relation with phenomena such as waste matter or criminal behaviour, rather than with art or culture, when discussing graffiti and its practitioners.

The waste of graffiti

The linking of graffiti with waste draws connections between the written image and a series of highly pejorative, distancing associations. The waste that is evoked is usually bodily waste, although references are also made to dirt in general. Thus graffiti produces 'squalor in our cities' and is 'sticky, tenacious muck'.[6] It is also linked to the dirt or infection of disease: it is an 'epidemic', a 'plague of biblical proportions' and it leaves scars: the paint 'etches like acid into stone walls', with 'poisonous pigments' and 'caustic calligraphy'.[7] On the New York City subway, 'many [cars] have not a single unscarred window'.[8] In a gesture towards the abjection of human bodily detritus, graffiti along the train-line fences in Melbourne 'only reaches a certain level on the track-side fences and walls, like the tide mark on a bath'.[9]

By far the most common device to configure graffiti with dirt is that which links it to bodily waste fluids, especially urine. The comparison of the writer with a urinating animal is repeatedly made. A tag is described as 'one of those scribbled signatures teenagers spray around their beat like a urinating dog'.[10] The employee of a graffiti removal company compares the graffiti writer to 'a dog marking [its] territory'.[11] Graffiti is 'a bit like wild animals peeing to stake out their territory' and writers 'treat the finest buildings humans have ever created as if they were the insides of public dunnies [toilets]'.[12] Council-run workshops designed to improve graffiti techniques are derided as only comparable 'in civic terms, to courses in how to drop litter or training dogs to foul pavements'.[13]

As is well known, thanks to the work of Douglas (1966), Miller (1998), Stallybrass and White (1986) and others, dirt and waste (which Douglas famously defined as 'matter out of place') are culturally and psychically troubling: a great deal of social and individual effort goes into limiting the moments of contact with or proximity to waste products. Entire industries are built around 'waste management'. Children are trained from infancy to regulate the production of and the location of waste; advertisements show 'dirty' households cleansed with powerful disinfectants.

The discourse of (the need to control) waste and dirt is also evoked when particular events cause individual or social anxiety. For example, in the controversies surrounding the exhibition of Andre Serrano's *Piss Christ* or Chris Ofili's *Holy Virgin Mary* (as discussed in Chapter Two), anxiety regarding the artworks (and their presentation to the viewer of waste matter which was thought to be very much 'out of place') inspired a strongly regulatory discourse which demanded strict limitations on the display of the artworks. Political protesters, such as the feminist anti-nuclear protest at Greenham Common (A. Young 1990) or the protests at Stonehenge (Cresswell 1996), have also been described as 'dirty' and the discourse of waste operationalized in order to justify harsh responses to their activism and to the substance of their political demands.

That graffiti gets represented in public discourse in ways which draw heavily on cultural distaste for waste should in some ways be unsurprising, given the versatility of our dislike for dirt and our ability to direct it flexibly at political protest, artwork, and even, as Miller (1998) shows in great detail, moral states such as cowardice. In other respects, however, the graffiti–waste association should be revealingly unexpected: study of the historical ubiquity of graffiti has led many commentators to suggest that graffiti in ancient and premodern societies was a commonplace phenomenon (Pritchard 1967), to the extent, for example, that individuals in the Shakespearean era even wrote graffiti on the walls of their own homes (Fleming 1997). The notion that graffiti somehow constitutes a blot or stain on the social landscape is a relatively recent one, and it should be all the more surprising given that throughout the modern age that social landscape has become increasingly cluttered with other signs and markings, such as billboards, street signs and road signage.

Despite the contemporary saturation of the urban visual field with corporate or official signage to an extent that far exceeds anything graffiti writers could hope to accomplish, graffiti is still commonly represented as a polluting flood of dirty signifiers. As is to be expected with the discourse of dirt and waste, these media representations animate a common cultural imperative to remove the polluting substance or fluid. When skin is scarred, we long for its healing; when a surface is dirtied, we work to clean it. Urine is flushed away in the sewage system; dog faeces on the streets are frowned at and (increasingly) compulsorily removed. Such is the implicit imperative underlying the representation of graffiti as waste: it establishes the need for its removal as an unquestioned precondition of its existence. A graffiti piece or tag is experienced, then, as if it were a rotting piece of garbage, or the stinking evidence that someone urinated in public. The public response to graffiti is represented as always already one of disgust, awaiting the cleansing and purifying actions of criminal justice and municipal regulation.

Thus the impetus behind municipal strategies of removal is plain: the graffiti is seen as something out of place, which must be erased in order to return the social space to its proper condition. Removal is thus a way of *reappropriating* the space, both taking back the space from the graffiti writer, and returning the space to a condition of propriety. In the Australian states of Victoria and South Australia, almost every council municipality is committed to the removal of graffiti from public property. Council strategies may provide for removal to be done by council employees, by a contractor (such as the Australian company 'Graffiti Eaters'), by volunteers or by the local resident or trader whose property has been affected. It matters little who is the agent of the graffiti's removal. The significant aspect is the socio-legal desire to make clean that which is seen as dirty.[14] Removal strategies are founded upon the assumptions that graffiti is a blot on the visual field and that its erasure returns the urban landscape to a pristine condition.

Writing ineptitude

An often-cited critical reaction to contemporary art involves the claim that 'a child could do it'. Whether 'it' be the drips of Pollock, Basquiat's crowns or the paint slurs of de Kooning, a popular sense of art demands that it manifest skill, in accordance with conventional definitions of what 'real' artists do and what 'proper' art looks like. Artworks that vary from these conventions may meet derision for appearing too simple, too *un*skilled. The second metonymical association to be found in public discourse on graffiti draws on this dislike of artworks that are perceived to be 'unskilled'. It is as if graffiti looks too easy, as if anyone could do it, should the impulse arise. To that extent, graffiti is defined contiguously with vandalism, of which it *can* be said that anyone – should they wish to – could do it, since it takes no skill to slash a train seat with a knife, or to throw a stone through a window. The graffiti–vandalism elision will be discussed in more detail shortly; here, I am more concerned with the specific contours of graffiti's supposed 'unskilledness'. Public discourse on graffiti deploys terms which perpetuate the notion that graffiti is illegible because its writers lack ability, that graffiti is evidence of a writing *ineptitude*.

Two terms recur: that graffiti is 'daubed' and that it is 'scrawl' (or variations thereon). Subway graffiti on the New York subway has been called 'gibberish' and 'indecipherable scrawl';[15] walls are 'besmirched with asinine squiggles'; tags are 'hieroglyphs'.[16] The interior walls of a Melbourne train carriage are 'scrawled with codes'.[17] A magistrate sentencing three writers for the painting of a train refers to 'the spectre of trains daubed with paint, luridly done'.[18] The installation of alarm buttons on some trains and video cameras on trams in Melbourne is claimed to be a response to 'thug[s] daubing graffiti on the seats',[19] and 'gang[s] of teenagers daubing graffiti on . . . tram seats'.[20] In a gesture uniting 'commonsense' scepticism at certain modern art with the condemnation of graffiti writing as artless, writers are said to have 'Jackson Pollock'd every cityscape and many of the beautiful nooks and crannies of the natural world'.[21]

'Scrawl' – together with its synonyms, 'squiggles', 'scribble' and 'hiero-glyphs' – is a deliberately critical representation of graffiti writing. If it is 'scrawl', it is not 'calligraphy', it is not 'script'. Words that are scrawled or scribbled are written awkwardly, hastily or carelessly; the completed writing looks inept or negligently done. Writers may carry out their graffiti in haste (they are often forced to, in fear of apprehension); not every writer is highly skilled (and many leave apologetic messages when they feel that they have not succeeded in constructing a well-turned set of letters). And so much graffiti is produced by people learning its demands in situations which are not conducive to good handwriting. Characterization of all graffiti as 'scrawl', however, cements the notion that graffiti's illegibility is the product of all writers' ineptitude and disregards the writer's skilled achievement of a camouflaged display.

In the register of art criticism, 'daub' has strongly pejorative meanings. Calling a painting a 'daub' would indicate dislike for the work, criticism of the artist's abilities and condemnation of the effort applied to the work. 'Daub' derives from Middle French and connotes the act of coating with soft adhesive matter such as plaster, coating a surface with a dirty substance, and applying or smearing colours crudely. The notion of daubing as coating a surface with something adhesive or dirty quickly returns us to the association of graffiti with waste, where it was described as 'sticky, tenacious muck', or as a 'tide-mark on a bath'. 'Smearing' material onto a surface often denotes an unappealing substance (often, in fact, something with the abject qualities of waste fluids), probably deriving from its original meanings in Old High German (grease) and in Middle Irish (marrow). To 'smear' also means to sully, stain or besmirch, a vilification through sneakily spreading unpleasant charges or rumours. The 'asinine squiggles' that 'besmirch' the cities, as mentioned above, thus render graffiti writing a vilification of the city, with writers the rumour-mongers, and graffiti the stains which stick to the surfaces of the streets.

The crimes of writing

Graffiti is often bundled into the same category as vandalism and yet the act of throwing a stone through a window is very different from the act of painting an image or a word upon a surface. However, the elision of graffiti and vandalism, or graffiti and other types of criminal behaviour, is a common device through which official representations of graffiti display their sense of its illegitimacy. A strongly held official view is that the very act of graffiti frequently or always involves damage to public and private property (due to its effects on the surface it is written on, its effects on the visual field, or adjunct effects which might include damaging locks, gates and doors to gain access to favoured sites such as train stations, factories, schools, sports facilities and so forth).[22] It is important to emphasize that the act of graffiti is fundamentally different from an act such as seat-slashing. Where vandalism leaves behind torn fabric or broken glass, graffiti leaves a type of image or message (no matter what one's opinion may be of its aesthetic merits). Thus graffiti's ambiguous status as art *and* damage should require it to be treated separately from simple acts of vandalism.[23]

According to law, graffiti is a crime.[24] What concerns me here is not the details of the 'art versus crime' debate, but rather the ways in which the specifics of the crime of graffiti (painting or writing on property belonging to another without permission) are either subsumed by other aspects of the category of damage to property (so that graffiti and vandalism can then be discussed as if they are the same thing) or are made comparable to other types of criminal behaviour, such as drug dealing and use, or assault (with aspects of those offences adhering to the public sense of graffiti writing). As such, graffiti becomes part of an intensified nexus of criminality.

It is common in official discourse to find the compound term 'graffiti vandalism', a convenient catch-all term which encourages the forgetting of any differences between window-breaking and word-writing. News articles may also deploy this term, calling writers 'graffiti vandals'.[25] The equation of graffiti with vandalism may also be explicitly asserted: one letter writer stated: '[Graffiti] is not art at all, it is pure vandalism';[26] another said: 'Those involved are neither writers nor artists. They are vandals involved in a criminal act. They should be vilified, not glorified'.[27] At other times, 'vandalism' is an epithet used to condemn the activity of writing, without distinguishing between writing and the traditional acts of vandalism such as seat-slashing: thus painted trains can be represented as 'vandalized trains' which need to be 'repaired',[28] and a writer can be called a 'mindless vandal'.[29]

The word 'vandal' derives from the appellation of a Germanic 'Barbarian' people (which also included the Batavi, Goths and Marcomanni, among others) who lived in the area south of the Baltic sea between the Vistula and the Oder rivers. The Barbarian peoples are commonly remembered for inflicting a crushing defeat on the Roman legions at the battle of Adranople in AD 378, and for following this up, in AD 410, with an invasion of central Italy. During this invasion, they laid siege to Rome and sacked it, taking the city.[30] The Vandals, at the head of a Barbarian army, also overran Gaul, then pushed their raiding and looting into Spain. For over four years the Roman army was unable to control the Vandals' activities (they eventually did so by setting an army of Visigoths upon them). Pushed southwards out of Spain, the Vandals crossed the sea into Northern Africa, where they continued to loot, ultimately forcing the Romans to recognize them as federates.

A word denoting a member of a particular Germanic people has migrated through history and culture to name one who destroys or damages or alters another's property. Even the generic name for the group of peoples in Germania at the time, the Barbarians, has become an adjective which describes inhabitants of an alien land, culture or people who are usually believed to be inferior to another land, culture, or people, or who lack refinement, learning, or artistic or literary culture. The barbarians are sometimes said to be 'at the gates', threatening the sacking of a citadel, bringing with them chaos, destruction, slaughter.[31] A city such as Rome stands for civilization, learning, refinement; countries such as Gaul and Spain are also imagined to have noble traditions of intellect and culture which would have been threatened by the Vandal invasion. To name graffiti writers as 'vandals' therefore aligns them with the barbarian horde who bring chaos and destruction to the gates of the city (with our cities being imagined as 'Rome', centres of learning and tradition). The immediate response required to the vandalistic threat is defence: exclusion and eradication. Just as the Romans set a Visigoth army on the Vandals to end their looting of Gaul, so local government and criminal justice set police officers, Neighbourhood Watch schemes, and security guards on the 'vandals' who threaten the modern city.

An extended effect of the contiguity with vandalism can also be traced through the appearance in news discourse of terms focusing on the *effects* of vandalism. Thus writers have been described as 'train wreckers',[32] and graffiti has been called 'defacement', 'mutilation'[33] and 'desecration'.[34] Graffiti is sometimes cited alongside vandalism in discussions of criminal behaviour, so that it becomes hard to separate the two. For, example, train operators were said to 'blame graffiti for a significant increase in delayed trains' with '27% of . . . services delayed between January and May because of vandalism alone', and the head of Melbourne's Transit Police was quoted as follows:

> It [vandalism] is actually on the decline overall, particularly graffiti. It's still alive and well and that criminal offence is a daily occurrence, but not as bad as it used to be . . . The perception is that it's an unsafe environment and that is why we target graffiti especially. It's a criminal activity and it has to be stamped out and it will be stamped out.[35]

Graffiti and vandalism thus appear within the same sentence, and the same overall frame, as if they were identical or interchangeable, and the opening qualification – that vandalism is on the decline – is muted by the insistence on the everyday nature of graffiti and its impact.

The graffiti–crime nexus can also be intensified by representing graffiti as one stage in a progression to or from other offences. Press coverage of a government report on young people in Victoria described the survey's attempt to measure involvement in 'anti-social behavior': 'according to the survey, the most common aspects over the past 12 months were shoplifting (29.7%), daubing graffiti (22.9%), taking part in a fight or a riot (18.3%), carrying a weapon (17.9%) or handling something stolen (17.6%)'.[36] The effect is to suggest that the person who engages in graffiti may move on to the other activities listed, as if on a slippery slope downwards into criminality. We see this again in a story about two teenaged boys arrested for arson (and identified as suspects in the arson because they allegedly left their tags at the scene) and described as 'teenagers who had 'graduated' from skateboarding to graffiti and vandalism'.[37] Graffiti is also claimed to be an impetus towards drug use. A newspaper article on heroin use in Melbourne described one user: 'Ten years ago, he and all his friends wrote graffiti on trains. Eighty per cent of the graffiti writers he knows went on to heroin. 'Heroin is in the next street to the graffiti street, you know', he says'.[38]

Graffiti is also represented as predisposing writers to interpersonal violence, perhaps drawing on longstanding and popular associations. The Barbarian sack of Rome was associated with slaughter of its citizenry, although, as Todd states:

> In truth, few of the inhabitants seem to have been slaughtered and it was mainly the houses of the aristocracy that were looted and destroyed. The ancient buildings of Rome did not greatly suffer and the fact that [the Barbarian leader] was a Christian preserved the churches.
>
> (Todd 1972: 20)

Despite such restraint, the 'sack of Rome' connotes menace and violence; a matrix that persists today around the graffiti writers being named as vandals. When alarm buttons were installed on some Melbourne trains, passengers were advised to use the alarms when they saw 'a thug daubing graffiti on the seats, being abusive or engaging in any other threatening behaviour'.[39] Writers are thus 'thugs', a term more usually applied to those who use physical intimidation or commit acts of physical violence, and graffiti is elided with abusive behaviour (again, an aspect of interpersonal violence) and one component of a larger category of 'threatening behaviour'.

It is often assumed that graffiti is evidence of gang activity in an area. One writer says: 'As the street gangs prowl they leave their hieroglyphs all over the place'.[40] The assumptions that all graffiti means the presence of gangs or that all graffiti writers are gang members may derive from a confusion of a 'crew' with a gang. A graffiti 'crew' may seem to outsiders to be similar to a gang; however, they are very different. A crew is a group of writers who share a tag and who write, or 'get up', as a group. Members of the crew are also likely to have individual tags and to get up on a solo basis.[41]

However, as hip hop music increasingly embraces 'gangsta' ideology and imagery, graffiti's association with this musical form contributes to the popular linking of graffiti with gang culture and activity. While it is true that in the United States, some graffiti is produced as a means of gang communication, it should not be assumed that the presence of graffiti automatically means gangs are found in the area (gang graffiti has a distinctive calligraphy and looks very different from hip hop graffiti).[42] In Australia, gang-related graffiti constitutes a small proportion of contemporary graffiti culture, and graffiti appears to be a minor activity for those involved in street gangs (activities such as drug use, drug dealing, car theft, property crime and interpersonal violence all seem to be more important within gang culture than graffiti). Writers sometimes get into disputes ('beefs') with each other which may escalate into violence, but actual assaults tend to be rare and internal to the culture.

Still, the association of graffiti with violence persists. It is now a commonplace of public discourse that graffiti makes people feel unsafe. The British Home Secretary, Jack Straw, described graffiti as a 'much neglected crime', 'often violent and uncontrolled in its visual image [which] correctly gives an impression of a lack of order on the streets'.[43] Straw is responding to the graffiti aesthetic, which can involve an aggressive style, with its three-dimensional lettering, its cartoonish characters (closer to the cartoons of Japanese animation than the cuddlesome figures of Disney). However, a leap of bad faith is still necessary to impute the aggression of the aesthetic to the mentality of the writer, and another leap again to extend that aggression from the production of the image towards the passerby. The bad faith involved in such a metonymy has rarely been interrogated; most municipalities and cities have experienced no difficulty in defining graffiti as having a key role in the production of (further) crime and social disorder.[44]

The notion that graffiti evidences aggression towards the passer-by and thus makes people feel unsafe has been expressed in public discourse since the late 1970s. In 2000, a British police officer spoke of 'the demoralizing effect of graffiti and its inevitable consequences on our living and working space', with 'crime and fear . . . at stake for the community',[45] while in 1979 Glazer wrote:

> [the subway rider] is assaulted continuously, not only by the evidence that every subway car has been vandalized, but by the inescapable knowledge that the environment he must endure for an hour or more a day is uncontrolled and uncontrollable, and that anyone can invade it and do whatever damage and mischief the mind suggests.
>
> (Glazer 1979: 4)

According to Glazer, then, the presence of graffiti in a train leads the passenger to think that the person who wrote the graffiti may also commit *any other crime*. Glazer expands on this point as follows:

> while I do not find myself consciously making the connection between the graffiti-makers and the criminals who occasionally rob, rape, assault and murder passengers, the sense that all are part of one world of uncontrollable predators seems inescapable.
>
> (Glazer 1979: 4)

From writing on train car walls to murder: the metonymical progression is complete. Graffiti *is* damage to property *is* damage to the passenger's environment *is* injury to the passenger *is* murder.

What is going on in this representation of graffiti as emanating aggression towards the spectator? What does this tell us about the spectator's desire for and from the images he or she sees upon the city walls? It may be that the illegibility of the writing makes outsiders feel excluded from the image. Such a sense of exclusion is intensified into a projection that they have been threatened by the image, its illegibility communicating menace instead of any specific content. In addition to this sense of exclusion, the hip hop style compounds the attribution of aggressive motive to the writer: the letters, divorced from any cultural context relating to their production or purpose, seem to speak aggression. Just as in online conversations the use of capital letters is understood to mean 'shouting' or anger, so the capitalized letters of most graffiti might seem to shout angrily across the urban landscape. Attribution of volume to graffiti writing was made by one writer, who stated, of the New York City subway writers:

> But the kids weren't content with the outsides of the trains. Soon every internal surface was painted as well, producing a visual cacophony that deafened the eyes of travellers. It became an epidemic of aggression and intimidation, another form of communal abuse, like the sounds of ghetto-blasters.[46]

In response to the sense of such 'communal abuse', some have advocated that violence is justified towards writers, fantasizing that they or someone else might encounter and injure a writer (oblivious to the irony that if a writer produced *graffiti* inciting violence, they would face even harsher penalties). One stated:

> How pleasing it would be to stumble upon a group of these 'artists' defacing public property. One could then exercise one's own artistic inclinations by covering these sneaky so-and-so's from head-to-toe with some of their own paint. Or perhaps a few bursts of capsicum spray or mace.[47]

Another expresses the hope that 'maybe some of these vandals will break their arms and be knocked out of commission. And if you think that sounds mean-spirited, you . . . have not ridden the subways lately'.[48]

What is remarkable about this vituperative theme of public discourse is not the fact that graffiti claimed to be a crime. Rather, it is the willingness with which the criminality of graffiti is both *multiplied* and *amplified*. Its criminality is multiplied in that any mention of graffiti can occasion the citation of a proliferating number of other crimes: graffiti can lead to drug use or arson; graffiti can be counted alongside incidents of vandalism such as window-smashing. Graffiti is thus rarely considered on its own terms and as a discrete phenomenon. It is represented instead as one component in a nexus of interconnected criminal behaviours. Once an individual starts writing, they may be progressing from some other criminal activity (thus graffiti may be a symptom to trace past criminality), or they may be inspired by graffiti to move on to other types of criminal behaviour, such as assault, robbery, and arson. Graffiti's criminality is amplified in that it is often represented in terms associated with serious crime (its victims are whole neighbourhoods, it is said to inspire great fear, it is imagined as being written by the same individuals who smash windows, commit assaults and burn buildings). It becomes impossible for graffiti to be considered in public discourse without metonymical reference to other forms of criminal behaviour (and metonymical reference also to waste and lack of skill, as discussed above). How graffiti might be made sense of in its singularity and specificity is lost in the chains of metonymy, leaving only the sensibility that graffiti is wasteful, inept, and criminal.

'Some of the feeling I get when I look at graffiti'[49]

Who writes graffiti? Most people have never seen a writer spraying a tag or a slogan on a wall; the writing is simply there, existing in a space that was previously blank, or covering a previous piece of graffiti. The words or images simply appear, usually overnight, impersonal, often hard to read, sometimes incomplete. And *the writer* is unseen, long gone. As I have shown, public discourse generates a relational matrix around graffiti. In this representational matrix we can find an imaginary 'graffiti writer'. This section investigates the unseen graffiti writer and elaborates on aspects of the writer's experience of putting words and images on walls.[50]

Invisible writers

Common stereotypes in the literature on graffiti portray the graffiti writer as bored (with graffiti resulting from a lack of useful economic or social activity: as if 'idle hands' write graffiti) or rebellious (graffiti resulting from a desire to reject the dominant social order or an older generation). One writer commented on such stereotypes:

> I'm just saying that when the common person thinks of a 'graffiti artist' an image pops up in their head of a 14 year old baggy pants, Nike-wearing boy who scratches windows and might roll you with a knife if it's dark'.[51]

The stereotypes of boredom and rebellion might be better applied to vandalism than graffiti; and graffiti writers often state that they abhor acts such as seat-slashing and window-smashing. According to one writer, those who smash windows are just your average yobbos ... they can be drunken dickheads on a trip. Proper writers don't do stuff like that because if you completely smash a train, then the train's going to immediately get fixed and any artwork that you have done is going to get erased.[52]

Writers do not view their graffiti practice as the product of a bored, vandalistic anomie; rather, graffiti functions as a project, a pastime or form of work which consumes their available time and which is approached with dedication and commitment. Many writers are in school, college or employment; they are not unemployed or truants, or school drop-outs, as another stereotype would have it.[53] G stated that he tried to piece once a week:

> Depending on the school, on what else is happening, but yeah, you did it every week ... sometimes you save up, save up, you get a lot of paint and then you do something real nice ... That's what you want.

Piecing regularly is a common theme: many writers speak of going out to write 'every week'. P said that he did a piece every week, for over two years. Planning is also an important component of the activity: G would 'really plan it all out instead of just going there and doing it'. According to A (a member of a feminist crew which painted a series of messages relating to images of women at sites around Melbourne), locations were picked and monitored a few weeks in advance, and the crew would aim to paint a site every week: 'It's very, you know, upper middle-class, we go and have dinner at someone's house and then we go and do a wee bit of crime [laughs]. So, it's done every week'. Graffiti is therefore part of *a schedule*; it is timetabled, in the same way work, entertainment and hobbies are.

Some graffiti does get written on the spur of the moment. G recognized moments when 'sometimes, you know, you've just got that urge to paint and you've just gotta go, you know'. D described tagging on impulse on the night of his birthday, and also how his awareness of the risks of being caught can be overcome:

> If I get caught, I'm fucked. I'll go to court and my life's going to be a complete mess again. But as usual when I have a couple of drinks I just forget about all that and I'm a teenager again and I don't consider the consequences.

However, graffiti is more frequently the result of planning and preparation – such as practising pieces in sketchbooks, research on the Internet, consultation with other crew members – than the stereotype allows. To this extent, Feiner and Klein remark:

> The quest for excellence and originality is an underacknowledged aspect of adolescence. Much practice goes into the writing of graffiti, as evidenced

by the sketchbooks that many writers keep and in which they practice stylistic innovations. In this regard it is like other adolescent activities in which constant individual practice to attain an acceptable level of competence allows close involvement with others. Participating in sports and playing a musical instruments are other examples. But, in under-funded urban areas, such facilities are not always available . . . For many writers, the day gets organized around plans to write – where, when, with what, with whom.

(Feiner and Klein 1982: 52)

The emphasis on careless scrawl that characterizes public discourse on graffiti cannot accommodate the considerable efforts, planning and labour usually involved for most writers. The conventional representation of writing as casual, impulsive and thoughtless makes it easier to construe graffiti as illegitimate.

Writers' involvement with graffiti also does not usually come about through the anomic drift that is often imagined to explain a person becoming a writer. For many, the impetus to write came through hip hop subculture in the early 1980s: P and D attested to the popularity of breakdancing at school and the impact of movies such as *Beat Street*.[54] Graffiti was seen as an integral part of early hip hop subculture, along with breakdancing and hip hop music. Liking one part of the culture oriented fans to its other components. This subcultural effect was not confined to the early 1980s: in the late 1990s, G was given a copy of *Style Wars* (a film from 1984 about the breakdancing, graffiti and music that contributed to hip hop subculture): 'So I put *Style Wars* inside the video player and I was just like amazed, and I thought seeing that I already had an arts background, [graffiti] would be a really good thing to do'. Other writers were inducted into graffiti culture by friends: W 'met this girl at school who taught me a little bit about it all and I started to draw'; while X 'was at graphic art school and a friend got me into it'.

For all these writers, proximity to cultural knowledge initiated their activity, whether that knowledge was communicated interpersonally or through cinema or music. For the feminist crew grr, as A recounted, their motivation was to change the way people thought about particular issues: 'it was kind of being sick of sitting around talking about stuff and wanting to do something practical'. Of their work in writing on advertising billboards, she explained:

> Billboards are put there to be seen, and, um, because they're trying to be seen, they're quite, they bring things down to basics and often we have a problem with the basics that they're basing themselves on.

Thus, grr were attempting to effect cultural change, through alterations in how people might interpret cultural images of women. All of these accounts emphasize a determined participation in a cultural practice, rather than any kind of alienation or apathetic drift into the activity.

Far from being an undifferentiated mass of scrawl, graffiti writing is a highly nuanced, subtle form of communication with clearly developed styles and a sense of its own history. This is most apparent in hip hop graffiti culture, where writers make use of a complex and opaque vocabulary and participate in massive information-sharing exercises such as the posting of photographs on the Internet, the publication and consumption of graffiti 'zines', and the painting of murals at legal graffiti sites. Writers describe themselves as 'old school' or 'new school', to denote belonging to particular periods in graffiti history, and speak of their writing as having certain recognizable stylistic characteristics ('wildstyle', 'semi-wild', bubble letters, types of arrows and so on).[55] The variety and technical difficulty of graffiti was made plain by P:

> There's a lot of different styles. Aesthetically, it's pretty aggressive, I'd say. It depends, there are people that are very graphic, they take a really solid, flat-colour approach, really clean and crisp. That's where technique comes into it as well. Like there's some people that use a lot of stencils, which is something different as well, or straight edges and things like that. Then . . . a traditional, funky piece that gets a lot of credibility is a really aggressive, really mean and stylized looking piece, you know? I mean, a bit more of a darker side than the actual graphic side? Because that holds character . . . and it's about almost making each one of your letters into, have a personality of its own. So when you do a piece, I mean, you're writing your name, and you're writing it in such a style that is giving basically a personality to the way the letter forms are transformed onto the wall. But I mean there's sort of more arty approaches where people get right into the intricacies, fades, and I mean, like splattering paint and things like that. And colour as well, I mean like that's another pretty important thing, the selection of colour.[56]

To write your (own chosen) name, and 'writing it in such a style that is giving basically a personality to the way the letter forms are transformed onto the wall', bespeaks the process of identification that connects the writer to the image. In hip hop graffiti, the image is almost always the writer's tag, often painted in 'wildstyle'; that is, in an imagistic way so that at times the letters of the name are impossible to read within the swirling shapes of the image. The writer experiences the thrill of privacy, while being at the same time utterly exposing and exposed, writing the tag in a public place. As P commented:

> It's like camouflage. That comes with having a different identity as well. I mean you've got an identity which no-one understands, like a name, and you've got a style like a camouflage of being able to even take it a step further and camouflage your name.

The paradox of being camouflaged while being on display raises the question of the writer's intended audience (as opposed to the general audience that may arise in a busy city): to whom is the writer writing?

Few hip hop writers claim to have a generalized audience in mind, although E writes 'for society' and H for 'the whole city, then worldwide and I go from there'. Usually the audience is imagined as 'other writers', but some writers split their target of address: C also writes for 'other writers' but will 'do characters for the public', thus recognizing a division between what a specialist and non-specialist audience might appreciate or understand. G writes 'pretty much for other writers, especially when it's illegal . . . but yeah, sometimes for the general public, or sometimes even the Transit Police, you always get people doing "F. . . the DSG"'.[57] L also directs his graffiti at 'authority figures', as well as other writers. X recognized that he was unusual in addressing his work less to other writers than to the general public, and said:

> I see most writers as being not the types of people I could care less about impressing, it is always good to have some member of the public come up to you while you are doing a wall (some have been as old as 70) and say 'I really like this'. So for me as a person it is a good feeling that I am maybe giving some of the feeling I get when I look at graffiti to the public. But most of all the most important person to impress is me, I want to have the feeling you get when at the end of a piece (sometimes a piece will take a few days) you stand back and look at it and it gives you this feeling, and you can't get the smile off your face.

However, P was explicit about the closed-off nature of hip hop graffiti, saying:

> So it's like, OK, you're using an identity that you've come up with yourself, literally, and then you've got a style that just takes it a step further and hides it even more, because then people can't read it. It's not meant to be read if you can't read it, you know.

Hence the paradox of hip hop graffiti: it *displays illegibility*, it offers up for reading that which cannot be read (except by the initiated few). No doubt part of the animus directed at graffiti in public discourse derives from the manifest tension between its apparent legibility and its actual semantic opacity.

Writers of political slogans have very different audiences to those of hip hop graffiti. A slogan writer is generally expressing an opinion in the same way as another individual might by writing a letter to a newspaper or phoning a talkback radio show. At times, a slogan seems simultaneously to name and criticize its object, as in the phrase 'corporate whore', which was painted on a wall in Melbourne.[58] Some slogans exhort readers to political action or activism, as in the statement 'silence is yellow not golden'. Other slogans simply declare opinions, such as 'Save Goolengook' (a forest under threat from logging). The feminist crew grr, according to A, saw themselves as '[doing] something that was fairly accessible in terms of just spreading opinions'. They focused on television images of women, and wrote various slogans based on this central idea: 'more bisexual women on tv', 'more hairy women on tv', 'more Koorie women on tv', 'more dykes on telly', 'more migrant women on tv', 'more political women' and many more. The crew also wrote commentary on billboards. A described one example: 'There's a pantyhose ad, the "don't let one prick ruin your day, try such-and-such pantyhose" ad, and we wrote "forget the pantyhose, try lesbian sex".' On grr's intended audience, A stated:

> I kind of imagine, when I'm doing something, I want women to be empowered by it and to think about it, and I want men to think about it. I guess primarily I'm thinking of women when I do it, mainly because having that focus means you can have a positive message rather than a negative one . . . I'd love for everyone to be supportive of it, but obviously I do imagine that there will be some guys who go past and go, urrgh. But, you know, it's putting it out there that's important – that somebody's willing to do that and somebody gutsy enough to do it.

Stencillers combine some of the communicative desires of slogan writers with elements of the sense of a discrete and autonomous culture that characterizes hip hop graffiti. Summarizing the choices made by stencillers in their selection of locations and in their motivations (and perhaps being slightly unfair to many hip hop graffiti writers who spend a great deal of time selecting locations, examining their surfaces and choosing paint), Manco writes:

> Stencils are more self-conscious than the spontaneous tagged graffiti messages or the coded confidence of hip hop style. A stencillist will have a location in mind for both aesthetic reasons and for an audience. Generally the artists have an affinity with the place they choose, they know its aspect and have considered its qualities of colour, shape and surface. Some choose a humble spot, perhaps an old, disused door with aged and peeling paint. The audience in this case will be small but, when stumbled upon, the piece will feel like a hidden treasure. Other stencillists pick locations for their associations . . . Fashionable districts are also popular sites for art-based stencils since they will be seen by young people, the media, and perhaps galleries. Stencillist activists tend to want to communicate to wide audiences so they target shopping districts or government buildings.
>
> (Manco 2002: 11)

Melbourne stenciller Ha Ha stated: 'If you put your viewpoint across in a visual way, like with a stencil, it's a good way to pass on a political message'.[59] J said of his stencilling that he intended it to act as a counterpoint to advertising in public space and to change the way people think.[60] This view is echoed by another stencil artist, Tom Civil, who links stencil art to the culture-jamming movement, which adapted 'images from the mainstream, and [gave] them a political bent'. Another stenciller, Dominic Allen, sees stencils as 'promoting activist thought and actively encouraging people to do something about changing the current political situation'.[61] JS was more modest, claiming that he simply wanted to make people smile, or to 'have a laugh' when they look at his stencils (which depict scenes from well-known Hollywood films).[62] Famed British stenciller Banksy acknowledged both the political and the amusing elements of stencils, stating:

> All graffiti is low-level dissent, but stencils have an extra history . . . They look political just through the style. Even a picture of a rabbit playing a piano looks hard as a stencil. It's like the charge of the light entertainment brigade.
>
> (quoted in Manco 2002: 76, 78)

As Banksy puts it, 'all graffiti is low-level dissent'. Simply making a mark, whether with a pen, a spraycan or a stencil on any urban surface such as a wall, a door or a pavement, means that the writer has made a decision to reject the norms of signification and authority within city spaces. Signifying practices are considered to be legal only when authorized – thus street signs, advertisements, billboards and public information notices are never considered graffiti. Although there may be variations in the specificity of intent that motivates stencillers, slogan writers and hip hop graffitists, what is probably more important is their shared willingness to enter this sphere of signification as authors rather than as passive consumers, to write in public space and to emphasize the porous textuality of the city streets.

The letters and the name

In rendering the city a mutable, permeable space, what is the significance of the graffiti writer's text? What is written by the graffiti writer? In this section, I will focus on the writing of the hip hop graffitist, for whom the business of lettering and the selection of a tag name is the constitutive element of graffiti, denoting the writer's identity and belonging within hip hop graffiti culture. This form of graffiti deals in the repetition of a name, in the forms of tagging (a handwriting that is usually done by texter pen), throw-ups (a fairly basic bubble-style version of a tag, often in silver spray paint) and pieces (complex, multi-coloured, usually large and often incorporating cartoon-like figures). Public responses to hip hop graffiti often depends on whether tagging or pieces are being discussed. K complained about the uninformed view predominant among the general public that murals or pieces are acceptable while tags are just 'scribble':

> What people have got to know is that *they are the same people 'scribbling' on the trains and doing the 'murals'* . . . Do people realize just how hard it is to tag? I know myself, it took me about three years to learn how to perfect it, and if they think it's so damn easy give them a 20mm marker and tell them to go try it. [his emphasis][63]

Antipathy to tagging as 'scrawl' is certainly a prominent theme in public discourse on graffiti, as discussed above. Even some writers express a dislike for it. B will do 'anything except tagging', and S (who specializes in legal graffiti) commented that tags look to him 'like cold spaghetti'. However, tagging – as senseless and random as it may seem to outside observers – is a socially learned skill with a coherent internal hierarchy of symbols, practices and techniques.[64] Some writers apologize when they perceive themselves to have written a poorly executed tag (or piece): 'too late, too tired', 'sorry about the drips' or 'hands were cold' are comments left beside graffiti.[65] Most writers of illegal graffiti admire a well-written tag. G explained:

> What people don't understand is – well, this is how I see it – that's sort of our artwork . . . A tag is like calligraphy to me, and if you really look at it and appreciate it you just see style, you know? I mean, I collect photos of pieces, but sometimes I've been walking and I'll see like an old school tag and I'll just get a photo of it because it's calligraphy, you know? It's just . . . it does look ugly if you see it from far away, but if you really sit there and look at it and just see how much control the writer has over the can, you just appreciate it, you know? . . . I do, like if I do like a real nice piece then I do put a nice tag next to it, you know? Something really nice that makes it . . . that finishes it off. It's your signature. Say like Michael Jordan on a basketball or whatever, that's just how it is.

Tags are practised in order to progress upwards in the hierarchy of graffiti culture towards piecing. It is also an ineradicable part of hip hop graffiti culture. As P commented: 'tagging and piecing are pretty much hand in hand. It's all about getting up'. Tagging is generally how writers begin their graffiti practice and is seen as either a necessary stage to pass through (progressing up the hierarchy towards being able to piece with style) or a necessary adjunct activity (to be able to sign a stylish piece with a good tag). And, of course, tagging is primarily about the transmission of the writer's tag, or name.

As Handler Spitz (1991: 40) notes, 'the name, unlike our ever-changing face, figure and physique, denotes and survives us and is, finally, engraved as our memorial'.[66] In graffiti writing, the name is a camouflaged exposure: camouflaged not just through the selection of an alias but also through the illegibility of the calligraphy, a manifest anonymity of the name.[67] Writers have selected a tag for themselves, allowing anonymity (given the illegality of the activity, the alias makes it harder to trace the writer) and also rejecting the individual's given name. The explicit rationale given by writers is usually to do with their liking for particular letters, but the content of the tag sometimes has meaning for the individual. Thus, in contemporary New York City, Ader derived his from the British comedy show, *Blackadder*; while Mosco chose his because it means 'mosquito' in Spanish, an insect of which he says 'it's an irritating bug coming in at night and they sting but it's hard to get rid of them', and which he compared to graffiti writers 'hitting' the city at night.[68] Most writers choose their tag by selecting a combination of letters that they can write with the most style. As Y noted, 'it's all about the letters'. Stewart (1988: 167) relates the example of Parish, whose tag was originally 'Paris', but who felt, once he began writing it, that the word looked unfinished and required the 'H' for visual closure. To demonstrate the importance of the letter as governing force in writing practice, writers often have more than one tag, to enable them to practice different styles, as appropriate to the varying of letters from one tag to the next.[69] (This practice also helps elude detection by the police.)

Although writers assert the primacy of the letter form as determining their tag, it should also be noted that other formal and semantic considerations apply. First, tags are usually short, to enable fast spraying or writing (especially important for a writer who does more tags or throw-ups than pieces). Second, tags are often unconventional (or 'street') spellings of familiar words (such as 'Phake', 'Sens', 'Phiber', 'Puzle', 'Mpire', 'Chek', 'Kage' and so on). Some are witty or whimsical ('Pnut', 'Diem', 'Yeha'). Ambiguity and wordplay is also common (seen in tags such as 'Futura', 'Shear', 'Spek', 'Seen' and 'Reach').[70] When tags are legible to members of the public, it may contribute to their sense that graffiti is threatening to them in the tags' potential to be read as implying violence: tags such as 'Krush', 'Shear', 'Mash', 'Shok' and 'Bear' might seem to outsiders to denote anger or menace. Such interpretations mistake the object of any such anger: just as writers speak of 'bombing' a train, or 'destroy[ing] everything in your path' (as D described graffiti practice), the implied violence is not directed against the passerby later viewing the graffiti. Such a discourse is rather the product of a culture that acknowledges its outlaw foundations and which valorizes speedy writing and extensive coverage of the city. It also perhaps derives from a certain 'masculinity' within graffiti culture, which is less to do with the fact that most (though not all) writers are male and more to do with the culture's elevation and repetition of versions of 'macho' discourse.[71]

Writers assert a commonality between the centrality of the tag name in hip hop graffiti culture and the circulation of product names or brands in advertising:

> Okay: Mr. Mobil; Mr. Amoco; Mr. Exxon. They're rich. They can put their name on any sign, any place. Build a gas station and there's their *name* . . . Okay, now you're on a poor economic level and what do you have? Years ago, and even today, a boxer makes a name for himself in the boxing ring. So when this art form starts developing, why would it be any different? It's all in the name. When you're poor, that's all you've got.[72]

In contradistinction to the assumptions of public and official discourse on graffiti, that it results from a desire to leave evidence that the writer was present at a particular site (see especially the comparison made to animals marking territory by urination), the centrality of the name in graffiti practice points towards another sense of graffiti. Although some writers say that they do tag in order to mark their presence (for example, L said that he tags 'to show I've been here, to express how I feel or to prove something to mates'), a deeper and less remarked aspect of writing relates to the sensations experienced by the writer when he or she looks at the name they have written. Writers describe feelings of satisfaction and pleasure that outstrip any gratification deriving simply from completing a piece of work or marking their presence in the streetscape. G stated, 'it's something that you put all this effort into and then you get a good result when you get your photos back, you're like, damn I did this'. The corporeal sensations are intense: when G saw his piece on a train that was standing at a platform in Melbourne's main station, he said, 'I just ran up and, like, my heart was pounding and I was just proud and people would walk past and look at it'.

The writer obtains this powerful, bodily pleasure from looking at an image of the self, at a representation of his or her identity, manifested through the stylized name on the wall or train or fence. The pleasure that writers experience derives much less from leaving proof for others of their presence than from a confirmation of self and subjectivity. It is like looking into a mirror, a mirror that reflects a self-constructed image rather than a 'natural' or given one. To that extent, the graffiti name, painted or written onto the chosen surface, looks back at the writer, a projection that affirms his or her identity in the image. Control strategies fixated on criminalization and the immediate removal of all graffiti therefore take no account of the deleterious consequences that accrue to writers when tags – their projected selves – are erased from the public sphere. As P notes, 'I was never really proud of being a graffiti writer . . . the general public perception was always pretty negative surrounding my, you know, *my existence*' (emphasis added). The endless dance of writing and removal replicates the policing practice of 'moving on' apparently 'risky' people from public spaces and in the assumed dangerousness of their presence in the city landscape.[73] A signifying practice that is, for its practitioners, profoundly about identity and existence is viewed as something to be erased, something to be displaced, something *illegible and illegitimate*. The spectator's imputation of aggression to graffiti writing erases the writer's identity, subjectivity and self; and the labour, pleasure and love that wrote the graffiti is replaced with blank space.

Authority and signification in the city

Not all urban signifying practices are rendered illegitimate. For the contemporary city is awash in signs: the city swims in signage at a depth far beyond any that graffiti writers could achieve. This signage is of course composed of the 'official graffiti of the everyday', 'corporate tagging' and the 'sign wars' of advertising.[74] On the constant writing and rewriting of New York City, Austin writes:

In this forest of signs, public space itself is a medium of communication, but there is no DJ, no production manager, no editor organizing all the messages being broadcast through the glance of everyday life. Instead, the messages are organized through the denizens' attention, sometimes focused and intent, sometimes wandering. We might notice, preoccupied: litter, the *Daily News* and the *New York Times*, street addresses, new advertising advertising old advertising, dilapidated buildings, people in rags and suits, billboards and neon, ART SALE!, the sidewalk detours around the de/construction of another skyscraper, groups of people, a change in the price of roses and crack, intention and confusion and conflict, peddlers selling books new and used, traffic on empty streets, food and eating and no food, flyers being handed to you now in the garbage cans now blowing down the street, a dozen languages on the subways and that's not enough. The city's public space ... is encoded, overcoded and coded over: a palimpsest order of change and monu-mentality, constantly rewritten, never blank, in dialogue with people and space.

(Austin 1996: 271)

In this glorious evocation of the city's perpetual significatory motion, Austin directs us towards a crucial issue for the sense of graffiti: the cityscape as text and the implication of the passer-by within that text. It is not possible for the citizen to look at the city without also being in the city: there is no separation of viewer and object as there might be with a painting in a gallery. Media discourse on graffiti excoriates writers for creating stains on a visual field implied to be unblemished; criminal justice interventions penalize writers for the supposed impact of such a stain in an unsullied public sphere. Yet any cursory glance at the urban public sphere confirms that it is a roiling sea of signification, a competing jumble of signs and statements, much of which is produced by public authorities and agencies, or by 'authorized' writers such as corporations. How then does graffiti come to be singled out as a unique form of visual pollution?

As a preliminary matter, it should be noted that public discourse on graffiti not only overlooks the visual clutter of the urban public sphere but also forgets the occasional struggle over limits and legitimacy in modes of authorized signification. The legitimacy of signs in the city is a mutable phenomenon, subject to seismic shifts in planning regulations or fractional adjustments in notions of taste.[75] Thus, for example, the longstanding convention of placing sandwich boards on the pavement outside a shop or café has been subject to dispute in South Australia.[76] Large billboards became the object of criticism in Geelong, a Victorian city, where the National Trust claimed that streets were 'a laboratory of bad signs', many of which were illegal under the city's planning regulations.[77] In Melbourne, amendments to state planning regulations permitted companies to build giant billboards called 'sky signs', despite protests from local residents about the excessively bright lighting required for the signs at night.[78] And, on sunny days, skywriting by small planes colonizes the blue dome of the sky as if it were one large overhead billboard.

The ubiquity of authorized signage in the cityscape is rooted in the assumption that its presence *per se* is not problematic, although there might be contestation over its quantity, location or type. Its eradication is never discussed. A considerable amount of authorized signage is therefore taken for granted as the normal condition of the city; in fact, its presence in the city is rendered so normal that it is unremarkable or even invisible in comparison with the mark of graffiti. The graffiti tag or stencil or slogan, with its supposedly blighting and staining effect, is imagined as sprayed on a smooth, empty wall in a visual field composed of other smooth, empty walls. The wall's textural qualities, products of paint and stone or wood, are not even imagined to exist; the wall is in fact a *notional* or *conceptual* wall. Such a visual field would conform to 'the clear text of the planned, readable city' and 'the geometric space of city-planners and architects', written of by de Certeau (1985: 126, 136). A streetscape like this did not exist even in the premodern period to which the imagination no doubt harks back – as noted earlier, Victorians, Elizabethans and ancient Greeks and Romans painted, carved and etched images and words on walls. In the fantasy of the *tabula rasa* on which graffiti inscribes itself, we can read a tell-tale *signophobia*, a fear of signification with very particular targets.

The target of fear is always the product of judgment, of discrimination and choice. Here, graffiti is targeted while the 'official graffiti of the everyday' and advertising's corporate tagging are continually *overlooked*. We have succeeded in hiding it in plain sight. Its very visibility renders it invisible. The manifest legibility of its messages (official graffiti strives for plain meaning; advertising requires decodability in order to sell products) sinks into a visual blur which is no longer perceived. The illegibility of graffiti, however, becomes hypervisibility, a flaunting of nonsense in an exclusive conversation between invisible writers. Graffiti, in its choice of the cityscape as canvas, has infringed upon the determination of the citizen to relegate the sign to a comforting blur. In an encounter with a swirl of wildstyle letters and characters, the citizen translates the sign into an exclusionary device which dares to traffic meaning in the urban sphere without using the simple visual vernacular of the everyday sign.

The artist Claes Oldenburg commented, 'The city is like a newspaper anyway, so it's natural to see writing all over the place' (quoted in Austin 1996: 271). Oldenburg was attempting to situate New York's graffiti-covered trains within the network of signs and textuality which constructs the contemporary city. As I have shown, however, not all writing is authorized; some texts are unwritten, *de-legitimized*. Graffiti is an urban text which is unauthorized, which does not belong to anyone. As P asserted:

> The beauty of it is, it's so pure, there isn't *one* financial element to it. There's no profit, there's no corporate infrastructure or anything like

that, it'll never get involved, especially while it's illegal. So no-one owns it, like, no-one can re-sell it, because it is temporary and disposable.

The very quality which writers identify as its merit is confirmation of its illegitimacy. A mural or stencil is an image without an artist, a tag or slogan is script without a writer. They are unauthorized; they lack authorship. They are anonymous letters to the city sent by secret correspondents; they are unsolicited spam emails which clog the inboxes of the streets. It could be said that the graffiti writer personifies 'a form of culture in which [textuality] would not be limited by the figure of the author' (adapted slightly from Foucault 1998: 222). The graffiti writer has already achieved the disappearance Foucault imagined (although such invisibility is always subject to the efforts of public discourse to drag the writer into the public sphere of inspection). Foucault writes:

> All discourses, whatever their status, form, value, and whatever the treat-ment to which they will be subjected, would then develop in the anonymity of a murmur. We would no longer hear the questions that have been rehashed for so long: Who really spoke? Is it really he and not someone else? . . . and behind all these questions, we would hear hardly anything but the stirring of an indifference: What difference does it make who is speaking?
>
> (Foucault 1998: 222)

I am not arguing that we should cultivate a devotion to the graffiti aesthetic, that we should become its fans, acolytes or practitioners. Rather, as Foucault would put it, we should listen for 'the stirring of an indifference' to graffiti and to its writers. In this indifference, writers would be able to inscribe their texts upon the city surfaces, not as objects of fear, or anxiety-inducing invisible vandals, but *as writers*. Graffiti could be regarded, not as the spoiled destruc-tion of the cityscape, but as urban texts which simply appear, as if through permeable city walls. Stencils might be regarded as temporary, site-related art. Slogans could be read as though participating without attachment in a dialogue with the city itself. And when the question is raised, 'who wrote this graffiti?' we should answer, 'no-one; the city is writing itself'.

viewing (de)position
'where do you live?'

This afternoon I have to speak at a public meeting on graffiti. It's been organized by a local council in Melbourne, to allow residents and traders to voice their opinions on graffiti, after listening to a number of brief talks from a member of the local police force, from a council worker, from an anti-graffiti activist and from me. I'm there to speak as an academic researcher about who does graffiti, why they do it and the consequences of various attempts to regulate it.

While we're setting up before the meeting starts, a man approaches me. He introduces himself as the anti-graffiti activist, a spokesperson for a group which wants all graffiti prohibited and prosecuted. I recognize his name: both he and I have been quoted (giving rather different opinions) on graffiti in recent newspaper articles.

He immediately makes reference to these media reports, saying that he keeps getting phonecalls from angry and bemused homeowners and traders, wanting to know who *I* am. He says: 'They say to me, where does she live? I bet she's never had graffiti on her property'. He pauses, then asks me directly: 'So – where *do* you live?'

I'm wondering if he seriously expects me to tell him, to recite my address as some proof of credibility or in some naive failure to recognize the possible threat in what he's asking. Instead, I simply say, 'I live in an area that has lots of graffiti'.

The meeting starts. The activist and I are seated next to each other. At one point he leans over and whispers to me, 'I've a feeling you and I are going to be seeing a lot more of each other'. I ask him, 'What, at meetings like this?', and he shakes his head, smiling, 'No, at bigger and better things, I hope'. While I'm examining the sleazy combination of flirtation and menace bound up in his comments, he adds, 'You know, if we got together we could make the perfect graffiti policy. Ninety-five per cent my ideas, and I've got room for about five per cent of yours'.

I'm feeling threatened, objectified, sexualized, unsure what to say or do, when the person on my other side tugs at my arm. This is the token graffiti writer invited to speak at the meeting, a 16-year-old boy who used to do only illegal graffiti and who now, thanks to a council graffiti workshop, seeks out commissions for legal murals. He passes me an A4 sheet of paper, saying, 'I got bored with all this talking, and I did this for you'.

On the paper he has written, in the fat, bubble letters used in some graffiti, 'HIP HOP DON'T STOP'. Below it is my name, 'ALISON', which he has rendered as a graffiti tag. Lettered beside my name is a message: 'good luck with your work'. I smile at him, at his gift, and at his ability to keep on doing what he wants to (a graffiti sketch) in the midst of a heated debate in which residents and traders are calling him and his fellow writers 'mongrels' and 'scumbags'. It makes me feel that no matter what graffiti policy gets adopted in this – or any other – council area, writers will keep on writing, doing graffiti in the face of insult and condemnation. It helps me turn my shoulder so I am facing away from the anti-graffiti activist – I don't speak to him or let him speak to me for the rest of the meeting.

*   *   *

The meeting's over. I leave the building and go walking to clear my head. I'm on a main street – shops, houses, offices in jumbled succession, and on each corner a range of graffiti tags, each announcing a name and confirming an identity as writer. I walk down the street – the names look out from the walls at me: Phact, Deks, Fokul, Sick, Vend, Phiber, Scion, Acre, Flex, Reach, Kut. Some names appear once or twice; others come up again and again, written by 'bombers' on expeditions to cover the area with their tag: Hoon, Logo, Inn, Zork, BBQ. The ubiquity of their signatures: I see them on lampposts, walls, post boxes, bus stops, crash barriers, posters, street signs.

I turn a corner and suddenly there's a small 'piece', a mural I haven't seen here before. It's been done in the last few days, I guess. It's as though it has simply appeared on the wall: one day there would have been a blank space, the next day this 4 feet by 5 feet signature, executed in blues and greens, is there, saying VGO. I know this is short for Vergo, a prolific writer who has produced pieces in a huge range of locations around the city. One piece is a 'stay-up', so called because Vergo must have gone to considerable risk to write it, high up on a building several storeys up on the wall of an office building in the city centre. Since it can be removed only at some risk to the cleaning crew, it'll 'stay up' there for some time, gaining Vergo a great deal of respect within the writing community.

I get out my camera and photograph Vergo's abbreviated piece. I've also remembered seeing a slogan further down this street that I haven't photographed yet. I walk on, past some faded slogans which record the debates and concerns of the last several years: 'No Gulf War'; 'more dykes on telly'; 'Fight Homophobia'; 'Cars = Carnage'. The slogan I want to photograph appeared just last week. It says 'Refugees Ain't Got Fleas' and I want to document it.

But it's gone, painted over by the property owner or some enthusiastic council cleaning crew. I photograph the fresh paint instead.

De Certeau (1985) called graffiti 'transit images'. He was writing specifically about graffiti on the New York subway trains, but it's a good way to describe graffiti generally. Graffiti leaves transient, transitory images. Whether they remain for a decade or get painted over in a week seems a matter of chance, of an accident of location, of sea changes in public policies. Even writing that isn't painted over fades through the years, gets weathered by the sun, gets written over by other writers, has posters stuck over it, becomes part of the palimpsest legible as the walls of the city.

As well as graffiti being utterly transient, I've always thought graffiti was meant to be experienced while *in transit* around the city. Looking out from a train window and catching sight of a mural running the length of a factory wall. Noticing a cluster of tags as I drive down a certain street. Once, while on the subway in New York, the lights came on in a tunnel, as the train trundled through it. Normally, on the subway, outside the window is simply a depth of darkness, but *this time* – this time I realized that the subway walls are covered in graffiti from top to bottom, forming a huge canvas wrapped around the train. It was a momentary glimpse (the lights went off again after about sixty seconds) which proved to me that the story told by officials (that the subway is graffiti-free) is a lie, that the network of subway tunnels under New York City is a testament to the commitment of writers, and that even when graffiti is rendered invisible by blacking out the tunnels, it is still there.

4 Disappearing images and the laws of appearance

I am disappearing. I am disappearing, but not fast enough.

(David Wojnarowicz 1992)

If we trace the space between an idea and its referent, between the move to judge and the act of judgment, a shadow falls within it. Between the opening mouth, the scratching pen or the blank stare of the judge and the materialization of decision, a shadow is indelibly if illegibly inscribed. This shadow names and marks the always fading subject. This chapter is broken in two parts. In the first part, my concern is with the written texts of law; in the second, it is with the visual texts of culture. The theme of both parts is nevertheless with the interpretation of HIV and its relation to the process of judgment, its force as a limit or liminal case in revealing the imaginary order of judgment.

Chapters 1, 2 and 3 were each concerned with the problem of appearance in art and artworks; for example, the construction of an artwork's appearance as threatening, illegal or disgusting. Nudity in public or writing on walls can be called illegal and said to threaten the public, the property owner or the passer-by. The conjoining of iconic figures with abject substances such as urine or faeces can provoke a disgusted response in the spectator. All of these events demonstrate the powerful consequences of the *appearance* of art. In this chapter, I will investigate the similarly powerful consequences of appearance *in law*, by reading a number of cases concerning the judgment of the gay man – and, more specifically, the HIV positive gay man – before the law. I will then turn to the work of two artists who – through installation art and cinema – have sketched a possible terrain for an other judgment, a judgment beyond the appearance of the image. The intent of this chapter is not to advocate withdrawal from the legal sphere, any opting-out of legal discourse. Rather, my intent is to find hopefulness in paradox: it is only in *the disappearance of images* that the compassionate envisioning of the other can take place.[1] And it is in the disappearing images of art and cinema that reflections of an ethics of judgment in law might be glimpsed.

To this end, I begin by emphasizing a largely unremarked feature of modern judgment – namely, the legal *recognition* of phantasy as a distinct order of reality. The specific phantasy in question involves a narrative of abuse variously thematized in terms of homosexual sex and HIV infection. This phantasy is set in motion in an attempt to gain exemption from the ordinary responsibilities of legal subjecthood. I explore the judicial response to this move – namely, a narrative of the betrayal of trust between men. My argument in the first half of the chapter will be that the modern textuality of law has been occupied by a visual order of representation: to the extent that judgment has not been reduced to the anaesthetic product of administration, judgment becomes *an aesthetics of appearance* which returns law to the horizon of 'our' values.

The second part of the chapter turns this understanding of judgment on its head. The resources for this task are the artworks of Felix Gonzalez-Torres and the cinema of Derek Jarman. These texts comprehend the judgment of HIV/AIDS as *an aesthetics of disappearance*. Paradoxically, the visual texts are iconoclastic. As Jarman put it, our prayer or plea must be to be delivered from image. My gloss on the visual texts of culture draws this iconoclastic process into relation with an ethics of alterity and the materials for reconstructing judgment.

HIV and the legal aesthetics of appearance

Legal phantasies

In *Green* v *R*,[2] the accused, Malcolm Green, had been convicted of murdering his friend Don Gillies, the local real estate agent. It was well known, by Green and in the small town in which they lived, that Gillies was gay. One night, Green and Gillies ate dinner and watched television together. They drank a lot of alcohol, and at least one of them used amyl nitrate. Green stayed the night. At some point, Green beat Gillies, and killed him by stabbing him with scissors and bashing his head against the bedroom wall. Green tried to clean up the blood, failed, and called the police.

At the trial, the prosecution case was that Green had planned to kill Gillies, had then done so, and then had invented a story in his defence. The defence claim was that Gillies had made persistent homosexual advances to Green, which had prompted in Green an image of his father beating his mother and sexually assaulting his sisters, causing him to lose self-control and kill Gillies. He was convicted of murder; unsuccessfully appealed against the conviction to the Court of Criminal Appeal of New South Wales, and then successfully appealed to the High Court of Australia. His case was sent back for retrial; at the second trial, Green was acquitted of murder and convicted of manslaughter on the grounds of provocation, receiving a sentence of ten years' imprisonment.

The case, then, is one of a number of so-called 'homosexual advance' cases: in a series of Australian and North American cases, heterosexually identified male defendants have argued that an alleged homosexual advance provides a basis for the defences of provocation (and sometimes self-defence).[3] It has become increasingly common in homicide trials.[4] Although straightforward claims that the accused killed in direct response to a homosexual advance have been successful, defence lawyers soon realized that an argument based on homosexual advance would be more persuasive if it could be tethered to some additional feature. Use of the homosexual advance defense had become increasingly opportunistic: for example, the defendant in *Parsons* v *Galetka* attempted to claim that the victim had made a homosexual advance to him,[5] despite evidence from others that the victim was heterosexual and that no advance had been made. In *Jones* v *Johnson* (in the context of a killing motivated by theft),[6] the defendant still tried to claim that a homosexual advance had provoked a homicidal response.

In order to raise the chances of succeeding with a claim that a homosexual advance had been made, defence lawyers would link the alleged discomfort of such an advance with the memory of abuse at an earlier age. Thus, in *Bibbee* v *Scott*,[7] the defence led psychiatric evidence that after an unwanted homosexual experience as a teenager, any subsequent advance by a gay man would trigger a violent response from Bibbee. In his attempt to raise the homosexual advance defence, one of Matthew Shepard's killers, Aaron McKinney, cited a retrospective trail of traumatic homosexual encounters: forced oral sex with a neighborhood bully at the age of 7, 'more trauma' caused by sex at 15 with his male cousin, and, at 20, breaking down in tears after accidentally entering a 'gay church' and seeing men kissing.[8] The conventional tactic thus asserts that the interconnection of a contemporary homosexual advance and a previous abusive experience causes a homicidal reaction.

However, the case of *Green* is distinctive for its linking of homosexual advance to a *phantasy* of abuse (as opposed to any actual experience of abuse). During police questioning, Green said two crucial things. The first arose soon after he arrived at the police station: 'He told the police: "Yeah, I killed him, but he did worse to me." When asked why he had done it, the appellant said: "Because he tried to root me"' (p. 700).[9] Green thus constructed himself in the now-classic manner as the object of a homosexual advance, wherein the possibility of homosexual anal intercourse is viewed as worse than death. However, later in the interrogation, Green also added the following: 'In relation to what had happened this night I tried to take it as a funny joke but in relation to what my father had done to four of my sisters it forced me to open more than I could bear' (p. 667). Green was asked at trial to explain what he meant by this:

> Well, it's just that when I tried to push Don away and that and I started hitting him it's just – I saw the image of my father over two of my sisters ... and they were crying and I just lost it ... Because of those thoughts of me father just going through me mind ... About [him] sexually assaulting me sisters' (p. 700).

In short, the defence that was persuasive for the High Court and for the jury at the retrial comprised two elements: one, a homosexual advance by a male friend; and two, an image of heterosexual and incestuous abuse. As McHugh stated: 'The sexual, rather than homosexual, nature of the assault filtered through the memory of what the accused believed his father had done to his sisters, was the trigger that provoked the accused's violent response' (p. 683).[10] In the arguments of the defence, accepted by the majority of the High Court, these two elements are fused so that Gillies' actions become characterized as sexual abuse by a father figure. Only on the basis of the displacement of homosexuality and its replacement with abuse by a father figure does the judiciary bind the objectivity of what has now become 'sexual abuse' with a subjective phantasy.

In respect of the image of the abuse that the accused said he experienced, the prosecution argued that it was concocted, or irrelevant. But the reality of this image of abuse was endorsed in the High Court, and endorsed in a distinctive way. All the judges noted that the accused did not witness directly the sexual abuse of his sisters; all noted that whether or not such abuse occurred is immaterial. What was important is that the accused was told of the abuse and told by his mother and sisters. What the accused heard from the lips of others became a visual scene that he played in his head. The accused became, as described by his lawyer and the High Court judges, a person carrying around 'mental baggage',[11] with the image of abuse a burdensome prosthesis. Gillies' sexual overtures – a touching of Green on the hip as they lay in bed together – animated this prosthesis so that, the defence argued, in killing Gillies, Green was killing the image (of his father). As McHugh J (dissenting in the Court of Criminal Appeal) confirms: 'He sees the advance through the spectacles of what his father had done to his sisters'.[12] The validity of Green's substitution mechanism is affirmed by the High Court's determination to reconstruct the victim as a 'father figure': as Brennan CJ comments:

> The real sting of the provocation could have been found not in the force used by the deceased but in his attempt to violate the sexual integrity of a man who had trusted him as a friend and father figure . . . and in the evoking of the appellant's recollection of the abuse of trust on the part of his father. (p. 665)[13]

The victim, then, in his sexual touching of Green, betrayed the trust between friends, between men.

The case of *Green* marks the recognition by law of the visual force of phantasy. More than this, however, it recognizes a visual phantasy that exists through a conversion of *oral* familial stories into the realm of the *visual*.[14] The force of such phantasy cannot be evaluated by reference to an empirical reduction: there is no derivation of the image from the father's behaviour as seen by Green (in fact, Green had not seen his father for approximately twelve years). And it cannot be reduced to the symbolic order of law: this is not homophobia *per se* (although the majority in the High Court and the minority in the Court of Criminal Appeal cannot restrain themselves from commenting on the moral reprehensibility and horror of an amorous homosexual encounter).[15] In short, phantasy emerges here as a space of the imaginary: it is the specular phantasy of law. As Lacan emphasizes, phantasy has a protective quality for the subject: Lacan compares the scene of phantasy to a frozen image on a cinema screen, as if the film had been stopped in order to avoid showing a traumatic scene (Lacan 1994: 119–20).[16] Phantasy fixes and immobilizes a threat or trauma, which can then be excluded from representation. The tales told in law become specularized as a visual phantasy which can screen out or guard against the threat embodied by the object of law – here, portrayed as the gay man.

Killing the image

The following recent cases show how the law's recognition of the visual phantasy of the gay man as a betrayer of the trust between men can be given additional force through its reconfiguration with HIV. The two cases also show the judiciary actively participating in the defendant's phantasy of the gay man. In *Andrew and Kane*, also involving the murder of a gay man, the phantasy again involves the narrative of abuse and betrayal by the gay man but it is conjoined with the imagined embodiment of the gay man as a repository of HIV infection. In this case, two 16-year-old boys killed a man called Wayne Tonks.[17] They were prosecuted for murder: the jury found Peter Kane guilty of murder and Benjamin Andrew guilty of manslaughter.

At the trial, Andrew argued that, several weeks earlier, he had been forced to have sex with Tonks, and that he became increasingly aggrieved over this. Andrew had come into contact with Tonks by finding his name and phone number in a public toilet. Andrew was being teased at school for possibly being gay; he said at trial that he wanted to ask Tonks, whom he did not know, for advice. It turned out that Tonks was a schoolteacher, albeit at a different school and with his identity as a gay man unknown to family and colleagues. Andrew went to Tonks' apartment in the early hours of one morning; they drank alcohol, they watched a porn video; Andrew alleged that he was then forced to have anal sex with Tonks. Some time later, he became convinced that he was infected with HIV and obtained an HIV test (pp. 11, 15). Tonks was not HIV positive and the accused did not test positive. In a state of anxiety about the encounter he had had, Andrew, with his friend Kane, returned to Tonks' apartment equipped with baseball bat, duct tape and a plastic bag: they had agreed beforehand that Andrew would verbally abuse Tonks and if necessary hit him (p. 11).

The sentencing judge, Sully J, commented that it was plain that Andrew's aim was 'to avenge himself on the victim by inflicting . . . bodily injury serious enough to expunge what . . . was his firm conviction that he had been subjected to vile and degrading conduct wholly unprovoked by, and wholly unwelcome to, him' (pp. 18–19). Together, Andrew and Kane beat Tonks with the baseball bat, bound, gagged and blindfolded him and left him with the plastic bag fastened over his head, so that he later suffocated. While Kane was convicted of murder, Andrew was convicted of manslaughter by reason of provocation.

His defence had succeeded in ways similar to those played out in *Green*. In both cases, gay sex is identified with sexual abuse. In both cases, sexual abuse is then hitched to a phantasy – of familial abuse in *Green*, and of HIV infection in *Andrew and Kane*. In both cases, the salience of the phantasies is that they are elements in a legal narrative of the betrayal of trust between men (in *Andrew and Kane*, Tonks is judicially constructed as the teacher, the older man, the paternal figure of trust, who should have given advice but who instead exacted anal intercourse). And finally, in both cases, this legal narrative of betrayal produces an antiportrait of the dead gay man. Where in *Green*, however, this specular image belonged to the defendant and was recognized by the judges, in *Andrew and Kane*, the sentencing judge himself participated in the perception of the victim as embodiment of infective abuse. Sully J considered the event described by Andrew and his phantasy of infection as being significant in understanding the 'objective criminality' of Andrew (p. 7).

This objective criminality is measured against an imagined portrait of the dead man. As with many cases of homophobic murder, the judge noted that the dead cannot speak; others speak to the court on their behalf. Sully J characterized this 'body of material' representing the deceased as 'damaging as it inevitably was in its illumination of the character and lifestyle of the dead man' (p. 7).[18] The oral tales told by witnesses were transformed into a judicial image of the identity of the victim. In this conversion, law attaches an intention or desire to the dead. Tonks was described by Sully J as having 'a clandestine but active homosexual lifestyle' and 'a particular attraction towards teen-aged boys and young men. He actively sought out homosexual encounters with such partners, doing so by a number of methods of which one was to solicit, in effect, by leaving appropriate invitations and personal details inscribed on the walls of public toilets' (pp. 6–7). Sully J glossed this 'lifestyle' as follows:

> It could scarcely be doubted that there are many people – and, more probably than not, a clear majority of people – in contemporary Australian society for whom the kind of lifestyle that the late Mr. Tonks is shown to have followed would be morally reprehensible, physically repellent and socially subversive. All the more reason to emphasize in the strongest and most uncompromising of terms that a person who follows that lifestyle, even if that lifestyle entails the committing of serious criminal offences, does not become on that account an outlaw whose life is simply forfeit to anybody who feels strongly enough to take it in fact. The paramount purpose of the rule of law is to uphold in principle and to

shield in practice the absolute and fundamental sanctity of human life: all human life. (p. 7)[19]

A compromise is being effected here, evidenced in the acceptance of the defence of provocation, the leniency recommended by the jury, and the judge's endorsement of leniency in a reduced sentence of six years' imprisonment. The compromise is between the moral principle of the sanctity of all human life (which has no exceptions, which cannot be sacrificed in ideal or in practice) and the subjective legitimacy, for law, of killing those who are its practical exceptions: the abusive and infectious outlaws whose necessary and contradictory inclusion within legal discourse shores up the moral principle of the legal sanctity of life.

Bleeding wounds

Enthusiastic judicial participation in the phantasy of a gay man as an embodiment of abuse is also found in a civil case involving a discrimination suit brought against the Australian Army by a recruit who was discharged when he tested HIV positive. The case begins as *X* v *Department of Defence* and becomes *X* v *The Commonwealth* in its later stages.[20] X served as a signaller in the Signals Regiment of the Army Reserve for two years, then applied to enlist in the Australian Defence Force (the army proper). He began recruit training in November 1993. Blood was taken from him to screen for HIV; this was military policy for all new recruits.[21] On 21 December, the army discovered that X was HIV positive; on 24 December, he was discharged. He complained to the Human Rights and Equal Opportunity Commission that his discharge was unlawful discrimination under the Disability Discrimination Act 1992 (HIV being categorized as a disability under that Act). The Department of Defence argued that, by virtue of being HIV positive, X could not fulfill an inherent requirement of military employment, namely 'deployment as required' in any field of army service, including combat or field training. If X were to be 'deployed as required', the Army claimed that this would risk the infection of other soldiers (who are assumed to be HIV negative).

The Commission agreed that there was a risk, varying in the circumstances of combat or training, 'that a soldier may be infected with HIV by another who is HIV positive'.[22] This risk did not mean, however, that X was unable to carry out the inherent requirements of his employment and thus the discharge of X had been unlawful discrimination. The Department of Defence promptly appealed the decision to the Federal Court, which dismissed the appeal; the Department then appealed to the Full Court of the Federal Court, which set aside the Commission's decision, allowing the appeal. X then appealed to the High Court of Australia.

The High Court accepted the army's contention that it was necessary for a soldier 'to "bleed safely" in the sense of not having HIV . . . [as] an inherent requirement of the employment'.[23] Although this was discriminatory (meaning that no HIV positive person could be recruited into the Army in any capacity), the High Court found that the Army's 'specialness' did indeed allow it exemption from discrimination law.[24] What makes the Army special is the effect of a phantasy shared by the army as the civil defendant and the majority judges in both the full Federal Court and the High Court.

This shared phantasy centres on the figure of blood, the blood spilled by soldiers in battle and the blood that signifies the transmission of HIV.[25] The Army had argued as follows:

> [D]eployment is not available to [X] because in the course of service with the ADF a soldier, whether in training or in combat, may suffer an injury, be it a major or minor one, which may involve the discharge of bodily fluids including blood which may be transferred to the body of another by some form of physical contact . . . rang[ing] from, on the one hand, an urgent blood donation or a major blood spill because of serious injury incurred in combat to, on the other, any accidental contact with even a small blood deposit, e.g. on an obstacle used for training purposes by another who may have even a minor skin lesion.[26]

From the gift of blood to an injured soldier, through the rubbing of blood on equipment, to the flowing of blood out of wounds, the Army imagines a spilling pool of infected blood which threatens to engulf it. Although X's preference for deployment was the Signals Unit where he had served before and where the risk of blood flow would be minimal, the Army argued that soldiers were required to be deployable in all fields, not simply in some. Medical evidence was admitted, estimating the risk of transmission in the field as 'not zero' and 'not fanciful'.[27] In response to X's suggestion that soldiers could routinely use protective devices such as plastic gloves, the Army countered that they would be unlikely to 'take appropriate care that such protective equipment was maintained in good order and condition', an ironic claim given the fetishization of care and order commonly associated with other Army equipment such as guns, uniforms and the like.[28]

The Army did not want to admit that it should issue protective devices to its personnel because of its own self-image as a protective device (a kind of rubber glove or condom for the nation). To concede the need for protection within its own protectiveness would admit that something had got past it, had insinuated itself through its borders. To that extent, then, the HIV positive recruit is to be screened out in much the same way that a rubber glove is thought to prevent HIV, in flowing blood, from getting access to the body within. For the Army, the virus constitutes X as the mark of exclusion.

Such a phantasy of flowing viral blood is shared by the judges. In the High Court, Callinan J described his view of the Army:

> By an Army . . . I mean a class of men set apart from the general mass of the community, trained to particular uses, formed to peculiar notions,

governed by peculiar laws, marked by particular distinctions, who live in bodies by themselves, not fixed to any certain spot, nor bound by any settled employment, who neither 'toil nor spin'; whose home is their Regiment; whose sole profession and duty it is to encounter and destroy the enemies of their country wherever they are to be met with.[29]

In the Army's successful appeal in the Federal Court, Burchett J began his judgment as follows:

This appeal . . . has much to do with blood. Modern warfare may seem less brutally physical than such a struggle as that of Horatius and his companions to hold the bridge, depicted by Lord Macaulay in his *Lays of Ancient Rome*, which cumbered with corpses – '*the narrow way / where, wallowing in a pool of blood, / The bravest Tuscans lay.*' But the big and small wars of the twentieth century, the [defendant] contends, have shown clearly enough that the science of slaughter still inflicts physical wounds, from which soldiers bleed, perhaps copiously. Realistic training exercises, too, may entail injuries. Bleeding, for today's army, involves a soldier's comrades in dangers unknown to Horatius, or to those American Indian warriors who were accustomed to seal their brotherhood in mutual blood. For the deadly viruses Hepatitis B, Hepatitis C and HIV have become prevalent, which infect through transmission of blood and other bodily fluids.[30]

The Army is configured as a fraternal order, entrusted with the safety of the nation, and trusting in each other. That mutual fraternal trust is endangered by the spectre of the HIV positive man, whose blood cannot be used as the life-giving transfusion for the injured and whose blood may put at risk his fellow soldiers. His status, as the embodiment of infection, means that he can no longer be part of the fellowship of soldiers; he must be put out of its ranks.[31]

    In the judicial discourse, we can read a validation of the military imagin-ation of the HIV positive as an uncontrollable danger to other soldiers, a kind of enemy agent or weapon within the ranks. The Army envisages soldiers bleeding on equipment during training, bleeding on the field of battle due to injury, having to give blood transfusions in the field when a fellow soldier has lost blood, or having the partially healing wounds of training or injury come into contact with the flowing blood of another soldier. However, in the military body, it is not simply that blood flows freely. In addition to 'bleeding safely', soldiers are required to be 'deployed as required', sent anywhere, receiving any orders. X wanted to be contained, he wanted only a semiotic function, to be an Army signaller, to stay in one place, sending and receiving signals, transmitting only messages. The Army, however, saw him as indiscriminate and peripatetic, moving all over the place, signifying the viral weakening of the military body from within. X is thus figured as indiscriminate in the same way as the victim in *Andrew and Kane*: a man who left his name and phone number on toilet walls inviting sex, 'soliciting' as the judge put it, and thus indiscriminate in his seduction of strangers. It does not matter that X did not want indiscriminate military mobility: since HIV infection is part of a catachresis conjoining gay sexuality, risk and promiscuity, the HIV positive individual is narrated in law as peripatetic, prolific, unfixable, and in perpetual motion, flowing like blood around, under and through the military shield.

'Into the blue': the aesthetics of disappearance

My reading of these three cases has shown that judgment in legal texts is predicated upon an aesthetics of *appearance* – a conversion of writing into a specular image. Moreover, that aesthetics subjects the appearance of gay sex and HIV positivity to the horizon of 'our values': the values of the 'ordinary' person, of the territorial nation state, the values and law of the living. In reading these three cases I have sought to show the *carceral* effects of imagination: the image of the gay man conjured in each judgment freezes and frames the victims Gillies, X and Tonks. And at the same time, the defendants – Green, Andrew, the Australian Army – are retrospectively empowered to act in response to that image, to act without the constraints which normally enjoin against killing or against discrimination. My aims in this second part of the chapter are to reject the law's judgment of the gay man or the HIV positive gay man through an invocation of appearance (of the *image*) and to argue instead that we might look towards the aesthetics of *disappearance* achieved in certain cultural texts. These texts – artworks and cinema – help us forestall the closure of community effected by the legal aesthetics of appearance and open the processes of judgment to the proximate others dwelling in law. In the written texts of law HIV is *made to appear* through a phantasy of abuse (leading to the legitimated annihilation of the personae of infection), while the visual texts of culture approach the representation of HIV through *an image of disappearance*, or disappearing images.

A comparative reading of the legal and cultural texts of HIV allows us to ask what understanding of *judgment* could take account of the suffering and fleshly body. In *Andrew and Kane* and *X*, judgment proceeds from the sense of betrayal imagined in the transmission of HIV. The judge projects anger and vengeance in response to such an imaginary event, and makes it an *a priori* condition for any judgment of the gay man. In the cultural texts that I will go on to examine, HIV transmission is more than any phantasy, it is bodily reality. In both artworks and cinema, the artists offer an approach to the lover and a means to approach the image as if it were the body of the other, without vengeance or anger. In contrast to the self-righteously violent judgment of law, in these cultural texts can be found a means for the compassionate judgment of the other.

Touch the body of the lover

In the art of Felix Gonzalez-Torres, the art object is always about to disappear.[32] His installations are organized around certain formal modalities: some works are *word lists* (seemingly random recitations of personal and public events fixed to particular dates but listed out of chronological order);[33] *billboards* (photographs or word lists produced as billboards and installed at multiple locations around a city);[34] *puzzles* (letters or photographs reprinted as jigsaw puzzles and sealed within plastic bags);[35] *spills* (sweets or candies piled in a corner or spread across the floor);[36] *stacks* (identical sheets of paper, sometimes with an image or words printed on them, forming a solid cube composed of hundreds of separate sheets);[37] and *drapes* (curtains, beads or strings of light bulbs arranged around doorways, window frames and walls).[38] In this chapter, I will be concentrating on the spills, stacks and drapes: each of these forms rejects the idea of a static artwork and, indeed, creates the artwork on the basis of its continual movement, always on the verge of vanishing.

Gonzalez-Torres – who died of AIDS in 1996, five years after his lover also died of AIDS – produced many works which deal explicitly with HIV and AIDS: for example, the spectator passes through a doorway draped with blue beads in *'Untitled' (Chemo)*, and through another doorway laced with red beads in *'Untitled' (Blood)*. As Spector notes (1995: 171), the works' titles make direct reference to AIDS and its treatment, 'but the sheer tactility of these interactive and appealing objects . . . foregrounds the body, *your* body, by the experience of moving through them' (emphasis in original). The reductivism effected by HIV upon the body is foregrounded in *'Untitled' (21 Days of Bloodwork – Steady Decline)*, a work which shows how the scopic regime of the medical gaze dismembers the corporeal self in favour of an abstracted geometry (the graphs of declining T-cells uncannily similar to the cool abstractions of Minimalist art). He participated in AIDS activism, making a billboard work for the Day Without Art in 1990 (*'Untitled'*).[39] The works on which I wish to dwell, however, approach the subject of AIDS more obliquely, through the vanishing self, the vanishing lover.

In *'Untitled' (Loverboy)*, a stack of sheets of blue paper is placed on the floor against a white gallery wall (Figure 9).[40] It is the space of the imaginary. Gonzalez-Torres has said of it:

> The beautiful blue creates a glow on the wall when it rests on the floor . . . [I]t has a gender connotation; you can't get away from that. But I also meant it as this beautiful blank page onto which you can project anything you want, any image, whatever.
>
> (in Spector 1995: 62)

The work is a screen onto which images can be projected by the spectator, but its apparent solidity is always already fragmented and its certainties bent by refraction into reflection. Like Gonzalez-Torres' other paper stacks, it exists in a constant state of diminution and replenishment. Designed to reach a certain height, it is described as being made of 'endless copies'. Visitors to the museum or gallery are invited by the label on the wall to take a sheet or sheets. As the stack reduces, gallery staff will periodically add more sheets. As Gonzalez-Torres has stated, 'these stacks are made up of endless copies or mass-produced prints. Yet each piece of paper gathers new meaning, to a certain extent, from its final destination, which depends on the person who takes it' (in Rollins 1993: 23). Diminution, dispersal and replenishment also occurs in the spills, with visitors enjoined to help themselves to the sweet candies strewn on the floor or heaped in corners. In *'Untitled' (Portrait of Ross in L.A.)*, 175 pounds (the body weight of the artist's lover, Ross) of candies are piled in a corner of the gallery with visitors enjoined to take one (to eat or to keep). *'Untitled' (Loverboys)* involves 350 pounds of candies, the combined body weight of the artist and his lover. In *'Untitled' (Placebo)* (Figure 10), thousands of candies, glinting in their metallic plastic wrappers and evoking the sugar pills of a drug trial, are spread across the museum floor and collected or eaten at random by spectators. These stacks and spills, then, are configured as always in motion and always on the verge of disappearance.

In the blue stack that is *'Untitled' (Loverboy)* and the candy spill of *'Untitled' (Portrait of Ross in L.A.)*, Gonzalez-Torres created aporetic works of art which are always fading and always returning. Gonzalez-Torres described his intentions in this way:

> I wanted to do a show that would disappear completely. It has a lot to do with disappearance and learning . . . Freud said that we rehearse our fears in order to lessen them. In a way, this 'letting go' of the work, this refusal to make a static form, a monolithic sculpture, in favour of a disappearing, changing, unstable, and fragile form was an attempt on my part to rehearse my fears of having Ross disappear day by day right in front of my eyes.
>
> (in Rollins 1993: 13)

In inviting the spectator to remove parts of the artwork, Gonzalez-Torres rehearses the death of the lover and the death of the self which will follow. The selected piece of the artwork which the spectator removes is taken away from the rest permanently, whether it is eaten or placed in drawer at home, or pinned on a wall. The artwork is always diminishing, heading towards nothingness, towards the abyss. And yet, the abyss is always held at bay, always deferred, since fragments of the artwork are transported by spectators into new places.[41] Here, the generosity of the artist is not simply about under-cutting the art market's fetishization of acquisition and ownership which operates in a closed circuit of display and ownership; it is a gift which both invokes the transmission in HIV infection and simultaneously rewrites it otherwise than as infection. In contrast to the abjection attached to notions of the 'exchange of bodily fluids', Gonzalez-Torres invites spectators to take part of the image representing his lover's body into their own bodies, to ingest or to secrete in a pocket or a drawer. As Weintraub comments, 'individuals who have taken a sheet of paper from his stacks are "carriers" in a metaphorical circuit' (Weintraub et al. 1996: 113). It is a gift without price or return, in a circuit which is open and unending. An artwork about HIV transforms the circuit of transmission from the criminalized, abjected and reviled archetype condensed around HIV infection into a rehearsal of loss *and* an act of giving, a positive positivity.

In the later version of *Lover Boy*, wherein sheer blue fabric is draped across a window, forming a transparent curtain, Gonzalez-Torres evokes the evanescence of the amatory relationship and the mutability of the body of the object of desire (Figure 11). With an opened window behind the curtain, the fabric moves with every breath of air, rarely at rest, an artwork which is never still, always in motion, impossible to fix. The fabric provides a screen onto which desire is projected and interpreted; yet the fabric's sheerness creates a screen that does not attach the gaze of the spectator to the surface of the object: it points to a beyond, an other side, a further horizon. It veils, but does not mask. As with the spills and stacks, it bespeaks loss. And for Gonzalez-Torres, in its selected blue colour, whether in stack form or fabric, *Lover Boy* enacts 'a memory of a light blue. For me, if a beautiful memory could have a color, that color would be light blue . . . an innocent blue' (in Rollins 1993: 15, 17).[42] In the chromatic hues of judgment – where blood colours the law's phantasy of the gay man – here blue is the colour of memory, the rehearsal of a loss yet to come, the loss of a lover, the loss of the self.[43] And like the stacks and spills, *Lover Boy* establishes a relation with the spectator which is prior to vision, operating instead through *touch*. The papers in each stack, the candies spilled on the floor, the curtain moving in the breeze: each exists to touch and be touched by the spectator. As Irigaray (1993: 187) comments: 'Touch makes it possible to wait, to gather strength, so that the other will return to caress and reshape, from within and without, a flesh that is given back to itself in the gesture of love'.

The works project a past experienced through the touch of memory into a future prefigured through evanescence. The mobile artworks of Gonzalez-Torres succeed in precluding the grounds for visual judgment, reinstituting judgment instead as a re-hearing, a past re-membered and a future imagined, a moving image oscillating on the border of appearance and disappearance. Where the judgments in the cases of legal phantasy of HIV and gay sex turn loss towards the self of law (the self of the Army, the self of the accused), these artworks are concerned to respect absolute alterity through an act of compassionate judgment that brings self and other into proximate, tangible relation.

Hear the voice of the lover

The liminal moment between appearance and disappearance also structures a film made by Derek Jarman, the British artist, filmmaker, writer and gardener, who died of AIDS in 1994. The film is entitled *Blue*, and it is at once a meditation on colour and also a film without a moving image.[44] For 75 minutes the screen is filled with cobalt blue, while voices, sounds and music enact scenes, read poems, toll bells and provide an aural landscape for that which cannot be seen. *Blue* gives up the glamour and the visual charge of cinema, in much the way that Gonzalez-Torres' artworks eschew expressionism or pictorial figuration. *Blue*'s abstractions, however, are still rooted in narrative: a narrative of pleasure (sunshine on a warm summer day, sex with a good looking stranger, dancing in nightclubs),[45] of anger (at AIDS activism, at the double bind of AIDS drug trials),[46] of grief (for lost friends already dead from AIDS),[47] of mourning and the contemplation of one's own death. Of the film, Lombardo writes:

> With a violent leap, the most bodyless film ever produced projects the human body in its most cruel and unspeakable presence: pain, illness, suffering at the borderline between the physical and the mental, the conscious and the unconscious, life and death.
>
> (Lombardo 1994: 133)

Like the artworks of Gonzalez-Torres, *Blue* is a judgment of death, of the inscription of bodily pain: the pain of radical otherness, of the loss of self and the loss of the other. The object of judgment, in the film like the artworks, is death.

Death is preceded by blindness. Jarman was losing his sight as a result of cytomegalovirus (CMV).[48] *Blue* allows us to imagine sightlessness and the rehearsal of imminent but still uncertain death. Rehearsal, as with Gonzalez-Torres, becomes the main modality of existence: 'The worst of this illness is the uncertainty./ I've played this scenario back and forth each hour of the day for the last six years' (p. 109). Rehearsal and repetition: with every opening succeeded by a moment of closure, as the narrative plays on and out towards its end.[49]

'Blue' is not only the colour of the screen that captivates the gaze of the spectator; it also names and marks the site to which the oral speech is destined or transmitted (in a juridical terminology, it is *justice*). And just as Gonzalez-Torres' artworks tend always towards disappearance, *Blue* always moves towards death. The film's key motifs are given a melancholic finality in Jarman's final poetic lines:

> Our name will be forgotten
> In time
> No one will remember our work
> Our life will pass like the traces of a cloud
> And be scattered like
> Mist that is chased by the
> Rays of the sun

For our time is the passing of a shadow
And our lives will run like
Sparks through the stubble.

I place a delphinium, Blue, upon your grave.
(Jarman 1995a: 123–4)

In some ways, the film makes literal the difficulties inherent in the struggle to portray the unpresentable that is HIV, the virus that cannot be seen, the illness that for years has no symptoms other than invisible antibodies present in the blood. As Haver evokes, the struggle to represent the relation of the self to the loss of self occasioned by AIDS 'signals what will henceforth be the impossibility of language, communication, and sociality' (Haver 1996: 124), an impossibility inscribed as a narrative of melancholia, desire and mourning. David Wojnarowicz, another artist who died from AIDS, spoke angrily of the pain of being frozen in the image:

> Sometimes I come to hate people because they can't see where I am. I've gone empty, completely empty and all they see is the visual form . . . I'm a xerox of my former self . . . I am disappearing. I am disappearing but not fast enough.[50]

Blue engages with the paradoxical acceleration of invisibility in the image imposed upon marginal groups (often those who have become synonymous with the transmission of HIV): gay men, injecting drug users, whiteness's racial others, prisoners. Jarman's film can thus be understood as an activist intervention, from an artist who for years had been sickened by the endless parade of stereotypes deployed by the British media when depicting gay sexuality and when depicting HIV/AIDS.[51] As Jarman asks in *Blue*: 'How are we to be perceived, if we are to be perceived at all? For the most part we are invisible' (p. 113).[52] Jarman is all too aware that visibility can be a projection, an image constructed around a condensation of fearful signifiers.[53] He notes that HIV infection invokes: 'All the old taboos of / Blood lines and blood banks/ Blue blood and bad blood / Our blood and your blood / I sit here and you sit there' (p. 121), linking social class, racial and sexual segregation, and homophobia in the overcoded signifier of blood which works to effect a paradoxical visual invisibility.

Both intensely figurative (representing blue as sexual desire, sadness, melancholy, serenity and so on) and also utterly literal in that it presents to us no image other than a blue screen, *Blue* is a cinematic work that rejects *kinesis*, the moving image. It has no personae in the sense of actors or characters, places or scenes. It thus removes the object of the gaze by providing instead a visual object which remains unmoving. *Blue* is thus strangely paradoxical: film is the art of the moving image, while *Blue* is a film whose image does not move. Where Gonzalez-Torres interrupts attachment to the image by setting the artwork in motion, for Jarman, attachment to the image is interrupted by the immobile image of blue. While the spectator seeks in vain for *something to look at*, the film insists rather that we *listen* and *remember*. Jarman tells us: 'In the roaring waters / I hear the voices of dead friends . . . My heart's memory turns towards you / David. Howard. Graham. Terry. Paul' (p. 108). *Blue* detaches the spectator from the screen and attaches the viewer to the voice. In this process, we are re-moved into an audience of voices, into an ethical relation that allows a response to the suffering other.

The scene of another judgment

Jarman's displacement of visual personae is not simply a consequence of film-making after the advent of blindness; rather: 'In the pandemonium of image / I present you with the universal Blue / Blue an open door to soul / An infinite possibility / Becoming tangible' (p. 112). Caught in the tension between the tyranny of the image ('a prison of the soul' (p. 115)) and the desire to make images, Jarman enjoins us

> For accustomed to believing in image, an absolute idea of value, [the] world had forgotten the command of essence: Thou Shalt Not Create Unto Thyself Any Graven Image, although you know the task is to fill the empty page. From the bottom of your heart, pray to be delivered from image.
>
> (pp. 114–15)

Thus Jarman uncovers the attachment to the visual order that is entailed when phantasy seizes the imagination. His injunction – 'pray to be delivered from image' – substitutes 'image' for 'evil' in the conventional invocation. A plaintiff before the court was archaically said to 'pray' to the court for relief. One of my aims in this chapter has been to trace this indelible, if illegible, prayer as the vocation of judgment. As *Green*, *Andrew and Kane*, and *X* make clear, judgment proceeds by means of a series of configurations, personae or images of infection which fix and immobilize the subject of HIV and gay sex. The written texts of law reconstruct the event (the 'real') of HIV in the order of vision, where judgment is governed by the desire to see, and in 'seeing', to have done with HIV.[54] The vision of law remains an aesthetic in which an inscribed image breaks the link between the eye and the pain of the other. The way that the law sees HIV is defensive, self-protective. Goodrich comments:

> The constitution, the community of doctrine and of law, had to be defended and indeed would define itself antirrhetically . . . against an outside peopled by strangers, foreigners . . . and other untouchables. Similarly, there were enemies within the constitution and against whose antiportrait the image of the upstanding legal subject could be projected.
>
> (Goodrich 1992: 207)

The visual texts of culture expose the writing of law as idolatry. They draw the event closer *to and through* an ethics of alterity, an ethics that confounds the juridical order of vision (a vision of the self, of the State). Their interventions turn our attention away from the image: they bind us to the other through oral and tangible media. Gonzalez-Torres re-stages the loss of the other in terms of fleshly touch, as the art object brushes up against and inscribes the other on the body of the spectator. Jarman interrupts the idolatry of modern textuality by reasserting the melancholy claims of speech, as the moving image inscribes the other in the ear of the spectator. The transmission of law in the moment or scene of judgment takes place, as a response to the other, through the corporeal and audible inscription of the pain and passion of the lover.

viewing (de)position
gifts

I have never eaten art before, and this occasion seems strange, wondrous, taboo. I unwrap the sweet and put it in my mouth. A fragment of an artwork enters into me, to be carried around within me as I move around the museum, to travel home with me, to let me remember its taste and glucose crunch.

I'm in the Museum of Modern Art in New York, working my way through their massive exhibition of selections of their holdings from the 1950s onwards. Warhols, Pollocks, Beuys, Janine Antoni, all of Cindy Sherman's film stills, one after the other. The exhibition occupies four entire floors. It's a smorgasbord, and I am feeling overwhelmed by art.

But then I come to a large room in which one of Felix Gonzalez-Torres' works (*Untitled (Placebo – Landscape for Roni)*) is installed. The work involves thousands of sweets (or *candies* as they say in America), in shiny silver wrappers, spread across the entire length of the room, to a width of about 12 to 15 feet. The sweets lie several deep upon the gallery floor. It's a silver sea of sweeties, opulent, extravagant in their sheer multiplicity.

I say to my friend, 'We're supposed to be able to eat them – do you think we should?' and we both bend down, and sink our hands into the sweets, coming up with a fistful each. The *shock* of the plastic wrappers as my fingers move down and through the silver river. The pleasure of rule-breaking, of flaunting the 'Do Not Touch' prohibition which governs gallery space. I'm laughing as I remove the silver layer of plastic and paper, my hands are trembling a little. I put the unwrapped sweet – it's a yellow one – into my mouth. Lemony sugaredness, the solidity of the sweet on my tongue, the sensation of a gift from the artist, of the infinitude of the giving: the artwork will never run out of sweets to be eaten, since they are to be endlessly replaced by the museum, no matter how many of us accept the artist's gift. I feel the gracefulness with which Gonzalez-Torres has made an act of generosity out of the medical trial, for which people may have struggled to be included and which may only offer them the sugar pill of the placebo. I keep two sweets in my pocket, not for eating, but to pilot out of the museum with me.

In a different room, another of Gonzalez-Torres' artworks is on display. This time it is *Untitled (Death by Gun)*, a stack of 'endless copies' of a sheet of paper which depicts with tiny passport-type photos and brief narratives all the individuals killed by firearms (in homicides or accidents) in one week, dozens and dozens of them, their faces succeeding one another in a blur of futile sorrow, victims of America's love of the gun. I walk up to the stack and remove the top sheet. It's large, almost 3 feet by 4 feet, and I have to fold it several times to make it easily portable. It's a strange feeling: lifting off the top sheet is like removing the artwork's skin. Yet, once it's done, I look down and the stack is apparently unchanged: the same faces look up at me, the stack is imperceptibly smaller. And in folding up my sheet of paper (and now it is *mine*, thanks to Gonzalez-Torres' gifting of it to me), it is so large that I'm forced to rest it against my body (it briefly covers my chest and thighs) as I turn it over and in upon itself. My hands smooth it down, the grain of the paper registers itself upon my palms. The artwork has now split itself in two (it was always offering to do so) and has rubbed against me and left its touch upon my hands, my torso, my legs. When I look at the stack now, my eyes 'see' the artwork as a corporeal sensation and as a bodily trace. It has become haptically visible to me.

And as I'm walking away from the stack, I realize that I'm being watched by two young women standing nearby. I think about what they've seen while they've been looking at me, and it dawns on me that I have been momentarily incorporated into the artwork, performing a small role as the receiver of Gonzalez-Torres' gift. As I leave the stack, they move towards it, bend down, and remove a couple of sheets. They're smiling as they do so.

*   *   *

Walking through the museum's enormous exhibition eventually becomes exhausting. The body is tired, the eyes ache. *The eyes ache*. No more art, they plead. There is no more desire to see images. But what happens when the eyes of an artist can no longer see? I thought about this the next day, while walking around a small gallery showing the work of John Dugdale, an artist losing his sight as a result of HIV/AIDS. Dugdale has improvised a series of techniques that allow him to continue to take photographs from the borders of sight. The images are melancholic, sensual, oneiric – as though the artist had printed a series of stills from the silent movie of his dreams. Washed in blue, they show scenes of quiet, troubling beauty – a glass vase reflects a building, a young man stands with bare torso in a moonlit river, a music score is refracted through a glass of water, a young man sits naked on a bed, a field of corn is visible through a window, a cup and saucer sit in close-up on a table, rumpled quilts are strewn across a bed. Dugdale's assistants position objects and figures according to his directions, as he composes the images in his head and imagines their final look. The resulting shots have a static quality, perhaps an effect of composing *at a remove* from the image, but their lack of fluidity, their frozenness, seems to me to enhance their eeriness, the sense I have of being allowed to glimpse the artist's inner landscape. For these are the images behind Dugdale's eyelids, the unsighted interiors of his desire, donated to me from the threshold of the visible and the borders of sight.

*   *   *

Some months later, I am interviewing William Yang, whose photographs encompass landscapes, celebrities, gay social culture and the gradual bio-graphical ravages of HIV/AIDS. We talk about the ethics of photography, the response of the public to his work, his role in imagining and documenting the gay scene in Sydney. At one point we are talking about artistic responses to HIV/AIDS and I mention my admiration for John Dugdale's work. When the interview is over, and I'm about to leave, William Yang hands me a small print: it is a photograph he has taken of John Dugdale in New York. The image shows Dugdale bent forward over one of his own photographs, which shows two hands grasping each other. He wears glasses, and is also holding a magnifying glass so that he might see his own work. With a pen, he is in the midst of annotating, or perhaps signing, the photograph, which glows a magnificent blue in the corner of Yang's image. He is intent, utterly incorpor-ated in his work. William Yang smiles at me and says: 'A gift'.

Figure 1 Spencer Tunick,
Melbourne 4 (2001).
Courtesy of I-20 Gallery,
New York.

Figure 2 Andres Serrano,
Piss Christ (1987).
Courtesy of Paula Cooper Gallery,
New York.

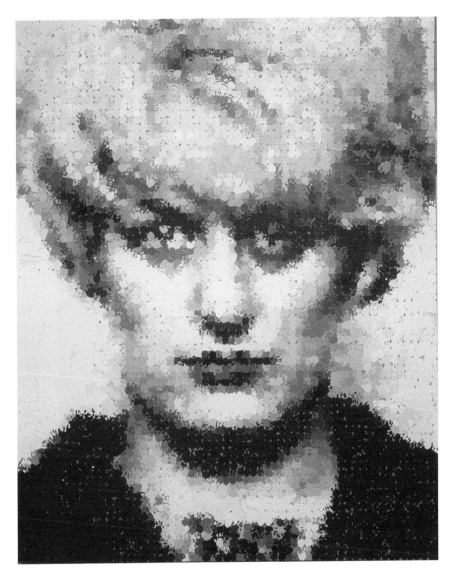

Figure 3 Marcus Harvey, *Myra* (1995).
Courtesy of White Cube Gallery, London.

Figure 4 Graffiti piece, Adelaide. September 2001.
Photograph by the author.

Figure 5 Graffiti throw-up, Adelaide. September 2001.
Photograph by the author.

Figure 6 Stencil and tag, Melbourne. April 2003.
Photograph by the author.

Figure 7 Stencil, Melbourne. March 2003.
Photograph by the author.

Figure 8 Stencil, Melbourne. May 2003.
Photograph by the author.

Figure 9 Felix Gonzalez-Torres, *'Untitled' (Loverboy)* (1990).
© The Felix Gonzalez-Torres Foundation. Courtesy of Andrea Rosen Gallery, New York.

Figure 10 Felix Gonzalez-Torres, *'Untitled' (Placebo)* (1991).
© The Felix Gonzalez-Torres Foundation. Courtesy of Andrea Rosen Gallery, New York.

Figure 11 Felix Gonzalez-Torres, *'Untitled' (Lover Boy)* (1989).
© The Felix Gonzalez-Torres Foundation. Courtesy of Andrea Rosen Gallery, New York.

Figure 12 Spencer Tunick,
New Jersey (1998).
Courtesy of I-20 Gallery,
New York.

Figure 13 Ground Zero, New York (May 2003).
Photograph courtesy of Andrew Kenyon.

Figure 14 Section of a memorial wall at Ground Zero, New York (May 2003).
Photograph courtesy of Andrew Kenyon.

5   The art of injury and the ethics of witnessing

> The body can only become sayable if it makes itself into an image . . . Once in the grip of the image, the body can be captured by language.
>
> (Legendre 1997: 212)

A man crawls naked on his stomach through broken glass.
A man is nailed – crucified – to the roof of a Volkswagen car.
A man is shut into a locker for five days.
A man is found lying under a tarpaulin at the side of the freeway.
A man is pinioned to the floor with copper wire.
A man's head is plunged into a basin of water until he chokes.
A man is shot in the arm.

The name of this man is Chris Burden and each injury was done to him as an aesthetic event, in front of a small number of spectators, and documented in the form of photographs and video.

The artistic enterprise engaged in by Chris Burden and similar artists is located at the intersection of the aesthetic and the forensic. This intersection has become a site of great interest in recent art practice and art criticism.[1] The art critic Ralph Rugoff wrote of a fascination with

> the forensic investigator who, working with the leftover rubble of an explosion or a few drops of dried blood on a car seat, attempts to answer the seven classic questions of any investigation: who, what, where, with what, why, how, and when?
>
> (Rugoff 1997: 17)

In 1997, Rugoff curated an exhibition in Los Angeles called 'The Scene of the Crime', which aimed to 'highlight artistic practices that suggest links to a forensic approach or address the art object as if it were a kind of evidence' (Rugoff 1997: 17).

The works in the exhibition were selected in order to 'emphasize the viewer's role as investigator while underscoring the cluelike and contingent status of the art object' (Rugoff 1997: 17–18). Conversely and relatedly, critics such as Peter Wollen have argued that the photographs taken at crime scenes can be read as aesthetic works. Wollen (1997: 25) writes: 'the photographer's camera is not simply a recording device but an officiant's ceremonial object, and photography itself can be regarded as a kind of icon or relic'. In his account of the aesthetic forcefulness of the crime scene photograph, Luc Sante states that these images 'like the voiceprint of a scream ... extend death, not as a permanent condition in the way tombstones do, but as a stage, an active moment of inactivity' (Sante 1992: 60).[2] And the artist Ross Gibson has used an archive of police photography to claim that crime scene images, 'as ordinary and wondrous as they are awful', show how 'citizens have left marks and stories in the physical environment and you come along later to divine some sense lurking in the clues' (Gibson 1999: unpaginated).

In all of these examples, it is the crime scene image which is central. These images are usually of empty rooms or desolate stretches of highway. There may be glimpsed a corpse, covered with a sheet. There may be signs of a struggle: upturned chairs or broken glass. Some images are generated later at the police station: victims' injuries being documented for a future investigation or prosecution. There is a sense of 'having been', of departure and the departed, of vacancy – all that remains is an image of the *aftermath* of the crime. Hence the affective charge to these images, which Wollen describes as follows:

> There is the mesmerising anxiety produced by contact with the abject and the uncanny, the awareness of a scene, haunted by degradation and terror, which is insistently fascinating, which suspends time and freezes the spectator into immobility yet, in the final analysis, remains safely removed from reality.
>
> (Wollen 1997: 24)

Crime scene images contain time in a permanent past, preserved in the forensic process. Whatever has happened in these scenes is past, over, completed as an event. As spectators – whether forensic or aesthetic – we are forced to approach the scene only in order to construct a retrospection, to narrate an event that exists in a past tense. The crime scene image thus functions as a record, an archive, a collection of traces which depends upon the viewer's deductive acumen in explicating its meaning. As Rugoff (1997) put it, they 'emphasize the viewer's role as investigator'.

The artworks which are the concern of this chapter conjoin the aesthetic with the forensic in a somewhat different manner. They exist on the borders of legitimacy, often either representing wounds and injuries, or, indeed, performing injury as part of the artwork. The crimes within their scenes are not past: on the contrary, they exist very much within the present of the image, holding out to the viewer the spectacle of an injury that is happening before their eyes. The images do not contain and suspend time; the spectator is not 'frozen into immobility'. The viewer is not asked to function as a detective, or construct a retrospective account of a crime. Rather the viewer is *required* to *witness* the actuality of injury as it takes place and takes hold on the body.

In some ways, the artworks and performances I will be examining look like crime scene images, and there are indeed generic affiliations, but they operate through very different modes of address to the spectator. The works of the three artists under consideration here insist on spectatorship as a form of witnessing rather than as an aspect of investigation and proof. Crime scene images invite the spectator's engagement as a forensic investigator, albeit an aesthetic one. Such a detective is exercising a probative function (demonstrative or indicative). The artworks I have selected engage the spectator in a testimonial relation with the artwork rather than a probative or forensic one. To reiterate: the distinction I am making is between an image that demands *observation* (the forensic crime scene image become art object) and an image that demands *witnessing* (the art practice that interrupts the law and testifies to the injured, the dead, the forgotten).

The artworks, artistic practices and aesthetic performances which are the subject of this chapter constitute a departure from those considered in earlier chapters of this book, where I investigated the effects of the oscillation between the spectator's desires as spectator and the address of the artwork imputed to it by the spectator. In this chapter, I will examine the consequences for the spectator of artworks incorporating an explicit demand made upon the viewer. That demand is for the spectator to interrogate the implications of spectatorship and to prosecute their participation in the artwork or performance as *spectators*, as *bystanders* and as *witnesses*.

In what follows, I will be looking at the work of three artists, Chris Burden, Ron Athey and Jenny Holzer. Each enforces a testimonial relation between the artwork and the spectator, but each enjoins a different modality of witnessing in their address *to* the spectator. Subsequent sections of the chapter will elaborate this in detail, but at the outset it is worth naming these modalities as follows. Chris Burden's work speaks thus to the spectator: 'my body is injured in the place where the artist is dead'. Ron Athey's performances address the spectator as follows: 'I am living on in the place where the spectator suffers'. And for Jenny Holzer: 'I am awake in the place where women die'.

'What it feels like to be shot'

Chris Burden's artworks frequently involved harm occurring to his body (suddenly or gradually), in front of a small group of spectators. Burden originally studied architecture in California in the late 1960s, but quickly transferred to art, with a strong interest in sculpture. Although he is often cited as a performance artist, Burden himself considers the various performances for which he is most famous to be examples of his extending the boundaries of sculpture, producing what he calls 'sculpture without an object'.[3] Burden justifies the term as follows:

I was suddenly struck by the way sculpture is something you have to move around in order to see all its aspects . . . What I picked up on is the fact that the body in motion around a sculpture is as much a part of the art experience as the object being looked at. So from this point on, I incorporated my body in my work not just as a material thing but as something alive that people immediately identify and sympathize with.[4]

Burden thus identified two key aspects in the experience of the spectator: first, that the spectator is physically implicated in the viewing space, circling and orbiting around the sculpture; and second, that the involvement of a living body in the sculpture would implicate the spectator in a process of identification and desire.

His first such work, *Five Day Locker Piece*, was done as a graduate student in 1971, when he had himself imprisoned in a locker measuring 2 feet by 5 feet for five consecutive days. Water was available to him through a pipe from a bottle kept in the locker above him; he urinated into a pipe that led into the locker below. In that year, he also created the piece *Back to You*, in which he shut himself in a lift for four days, during which time assistants pushed drawing pins into his chest. That Burden contained his body within the sculpture was typical of his early works, and soon came to be seen by him as problematic. He complained: 'people kept seeing these objects as the art itself, so the next step was to eliminate the object so there wouldn't be any confusion; then [people] would deal with just the manipulation of my body'.[5]

Burden therefore set about destroying the distinction between subject (artist) and object (artwork). Subsequent works involved him placing his body in situations which involved the endurance of various ordeals and the suffering of various injuries. For example, in *Trans-Fixed* (1974), in evocation of the crucifixion he was nailed to the roof of a blue Volkswagen, while it stood with engine idling in a Californian street. In *Through the Night Softly* (1973), he crawled naked on his stomach across shards of glass on the ground of a vacant car park. *Doorway to Heaven* (1973) saw him grasping live electrical wires in each hand and pressing them to his naked chest, risking electrocution (Burden was burned but not electrocuted). In 1974 at the Art Institute of Chicago, Burden plunged his head into a basin of water and inhaled it until he choked. *Prelude to 220, or 110* (1971) saw him pinned by copper bolts to a gallery floor, and the audience invited to electrocute him. Live electrical lines dangling in a bucket of water were provided: one kick would have overturned the bucket and injured or killed the artist. No-one in the audience took up the invitation.

It is interesting to compare *Rhythm 0*, the performance piece by Marina Abramovic, performed in 1974 in Naples, in which she stood in a gallery and invited the audience (comprising artworld aficionados and individuals randomly selected from the street) to do anything they liked to her for six hours (from 8 p.m. till 2 a.m.), using implements that she had provided (including a pistol, an axe, a fork, a bottle of perfume, a bell, a feather, chains, nails, needles, scissors, a pen, a book, a hammer, a saw, a lamb bone, a newspaper, grapes, olive oil, a rosemary branch, a rose, and other things). The performance was stopped by the gallery when one audience member held a loaded gun to her head. By this time, Abramovic had been stripped, painted, cut, and a crown of thorns had been fashioned and placed on her head.[6]

In Abramovic's performance, what caused the audience members to act on her invitation to 'do things' to her? The fact that she was a woman may have made it easy for some spectators to actualize any imaginings they may have had of her as a victimized or injured person. The fact that she provided an array of implements, some of which could be used without harming her, may have facilitated the audience's moving out of the frame of spectatorship and into the role of actors in the performance, gradually moving up the scale of harmfulness in their actions towards her. With Burden's artwork, audience members were provided with only two options: do nothing and watch, or intervene and cause his likely death.

Burden continued to suggest his own death in several artworks. One of them was *Sculpture in Three Parts* (1974). At the Hansen Fuller Gallery in San Francisco, Burden sat motionless on a chair, which had been placed on a pedestal, until he collapsed forty-three hours later. The event, including the moment of his fall, was recorded by photographers. As it lay on the floor, his body was outlined in chalk, in an explicit evocation of the corpse at a crime scene.[7]

Death and the corpse were again evoked by Burden in *Deadman* (1972). A small crowd had been invited to view an artwork by Burden at the Riko Mizuno Gallery in Los Angeles. The gallery walls were bare, with no sign of the artist or gallery staff. Time passed, and viewers began to speculate on Burden's whereabouts. One spectator recalled seeing a strange lumpy object lying under a tarpaulin, near a parked car and some traffic warning flares. The spectators moved outside the gallery to investigate, at the same time as a police car pulled up, alerted by a passing motorist that the tarpaulin-covered heap was lying dangerously close to the busy roadway. Burden was discovered lying under the tarpaulin and was arrested by the police officer and driven away to the police station, where he was charged with 'causing a false emergency to be reported'.[8] When Burden later stood trial, the case had to be dismissed when the jury was unable to reach a verdict.[9]

For most critics and commentators, however, the artwork which most clearly demonstrated Burden's determination to transform his body into a mutable and destructible object was *Shoot*. At 7.45 p.m. on the 19th of November 1971, the date and time as carefully reconstructed and noted as for any crime, Burden stood alone in an empty gallery in Santa Ana, California, and was shot in the left arm by a friend using a 0.22 calibre rifle. The rifle was fired from a distance of approximately 15 feet. The event was recorded by a shaky single camera and Burden was photographed after the shot had been fired. Imagine: the film is approximately 25 seconds long; it is grainy, black and white. It starts running: a man is standing alone in the corner of a large white room. A loud bang is heard. The man clutches at his arm, and then walks quickly, jerkily, out of the frame. It is astonishingly banal – almost nothing happens, at odds with the spectator's knowledge of the momentousness of what *has* occurred. Just a figure, a sound, then a grabbing at the arm, a walking away. And yet – a man has been shot in the arm.

The piece was praised by some as an anti-war gesture (the Vietnam War was at its height in 1971); as a challenge to the pristine 'white cube' of gallery space; and as a means of rendering the audience 'voyeurs at one remove'.[10] Burden commented later that the piece 'keyed into a fear we all share, which is of being shot. You can't read about the shooting at the local market without realizing it could have been you'.[11] He explained his motivations for the piece as follows:

> It was like a scientific experiment. *I was trying to examine what it feels like to be shot.* It's about controlling fate, trying to manage the unmanageable and the unthinkable. It's about turning towards the dragon, as opposed to turning your back on it . . . *It was horrific to look at my arm and see a smoking hole* (my emphasis).[12]

With *Shoot*, therefore, Burden identified three key elements of our responses to violence. The first is that any account of violence is experienced by the reader or spectator as an instance of possibility avoided or fate averted: that is, each story of violent injury says to the spectator 'this could have been you'. Second, Burden correctly surmised that part of that fascinated revulsion involves a desire to experience that which is feared. For each account of injury to others, the spectator momentarily imagines the sensations of injury. *Shoot* sidestepped any metaphorical investigation of that abject desire and represented it in its actuality.

Suddenly the body becomes the scene of a crime (and for the spectator it is the *seen* of the crime), with the smoking wound the evidence of an act of violence. The photograph or film of his wounded arm, however, is both the same as and very different from the generic crime scene image. The spectator's relation to the crime scene image is contingent and occasional, whereas the image of Burden, shot, always already constitutes a demand on and for the spectator to witness Burden's dissolution within its frame. The deductive process has also been dislocated: whodunit? Chris Burden and a friend. Why? As a sculpture. The result is a crime without a criminal; a crime without responsibility – except the responsibility enforced by the spectator's acceptance of witnessing.

Finally, experience brings knowledge, and with it horror ('it was horrific to look at my arm and see a smoking hole'). Burden is as appalled by the wound in his flesh as if it had been inflicted upon him without his prior consent. And the source of Burden's horror – shared by the spectators in their imagining what has happened, what it feels like – derives from seeing the bullet's penetration into flesh: there is now a hole where there should be smooth surface; that which should be closed is now open; that which should be inside comes leaking out as smoke. Injury, therefore – no matter how desired or sought – wounds the flesh, flays the psyche, and leaves a scar.

Deadman and *Shoot* together became the artworks for which Burden was notorious, works which were said to have 'really peeled people's brains'.[13] Most critical responses to Burden's work demonstrated profound ambivalence towards it – an ambivalence which equated the experience of viewing Burden's art with the experience of being wounded.[14] That the artist has generated painful feelings in the viewer is interpreted as an act of aggression against the spectator, a punishment, perhaps, *for being there* and *for looking*. The power given to spectators by Burden – the power to injure him if they chose – is resented as burdensome, an unlooked-for dissolution of the line that separates the viewer from the performance or the artwork. Even in the extremes of 'endurance art' or 'ordeal art', spectators were rarely invited to participate in the performance itself.[15]

This dissolution of the boundary between looking and participating is the singular achievement, and perhaps overwhelming purpose, of Burden's work. Just as Burden had himself shot in order to experience what it felt like, so he puts on display for the audience experiences which allow them to see someone else experiencing it, through the medium of his sculpture/body. And here 'seeing' cannot be separated from involvement. While a few works, such as *Prelude to 220, or 110*, explicitly invited the audience to participate, *all* the artworks emphasized the spectator's reaction to the display: in standing by and watching and in disseminating the account of the event afterwards. As one critic put it, 'as artworks, [Burden's performances] were experienced largely as rumor . . . When you heard about a Chris Burden performance, an image would streak through your mind like a blazing comet'.[16] It is that willingness to imagine and to see that Burden is both facilitating and indicting.

The spectator's response – and responsibility – is the key characteristic of Burden's work. Whether that response comes from divided and resentful critics or from the ambivalent jury who could not reach a verdict on the criminality on Burden's art, the response is an affective one of shock which arises from the inability of the spectator to bind themselves and so to reconcile the conflict experienced in viewing or thinking about the artwork. As one critic put it, the artwork 'leaves no room to sublimate the experience', because Chris Burden insists on his own death (as artist) and on the destruction or modification of his body (as sculpture) and folds the spectator into that process without relief. And so the spectator is left undone with no promise of reconciliation in the order of objective, rational knowledge and judgment is suspended. Unlike looking at the static retrospection of the crime scene image, here the spectator is not permitted to act as a detective, to collect evidence and to offer it up for judgment. Burden's work, then, is about viewing the experience of injury without a narrative or temporal frame to separate the spectator from that injury. It is thus about *loss* – loss of judgment in the face of corporeal agitation, and loss of the self, because there can be no subject of judgment.

'Wanting people to endure these real experiences'

In the face of such loss of judgment and loss of self, to what could the body testify, when put to work as an aesthetic performance? This question is approached in the punishing forensic theatre of Ron Athey.[17] In the mid-1990s, Athey became known as an artist whose stage performances involved corporeal scarification and bloodletting. These works met an extremely hostile reception in the mainstream and right-wing media, with the lexicons of disgust, anger and outrage being invoked to condemn his practices. In the late 1980s and early 1990s, use of these lexicons to name as disgusting works by artists such as Andres Serrano, Karen Finley, Robert Mapplethorpe among others had facilitated the erosion of institutional support for controversial artwork (as discussed in Chapter Two). Similarly, media condemnation of Athey's performances attracted attention from Christian associations and right-wing politicians, and was eventually used in 1994 to justify a reduction in the annual budget of the National Endowment for the Arts.

Such a crisis point resulted from the panic generated by newspaper accounts of one of Athey's performances at the Walker Art Center in Minnesota in early 1994. It took place in a small cabaret theatre, in conjunction with the Fifth Annual Minneapolis/St Paul Lesbian, Gay, Bisexual and Transgender Film Festival. The Walker Art Center receives funding from the NEA, and approximately US$150 of these funds was made available to Athey in relation to his expenses for the event. About a hundred people attended the performance (it was sold out). The Walker's calendar of events had advertised Athey's show with a note stating 'Due to the nature of this material, viewer discretion is advised'. The show was described as incorporating 'ritual-like' practices, 'erotic torture' and 'religious iconography, medical paraphernalia and bondage and discipline techniques'. A few audience members did indeed leave during the show, but approximately eighty people remained for the whole performance and for the discussion afterwards.

One audience member later called the Health Department to ask whether the performance had put him at risk of HIV infection. Why? At one point during the show, Athey made several cuts in the skin on another man's back. The resulting blood flow was blotted on absorbent paper towels, and pinned to a clothesline strung above the audience's heads. Health Department officials informed the audience member that no-one in the audience appeared to have been endangered by the activities; they also contacted the Walker and asked what safety precautions had been taken. The Walker stated that stage crew members had been provided with latex gloves for all contact with performers and items used on stage, that the stage area was cleaned with bleach after the performance, and that theatre staff were on hand to make sure that no audience member could get near the stage (and in contact with any blood) after the event.

A number of weeks later, the story was taken up by a local paper, the Minneapolis *Star Tribune*:

> A Walker Art Center member has complained to state health officials about a Walker-sponsored event in which a performer sliced an abstract design into the flesh of another man, mopped up his blood with towels, and sent them winging above the audience on revolving clotheslines. The informal complaint expressed concern that people in the theater could have contracted the AIDS virus if blood had dripped on them.[18]

The article represented the activities in the performance as more vigorous and violent than they were: the cuts are 'sliced' into the man's back; the towels sent 'winging' through the theatre. It is also made to seem as though a great deal of blood had flowed when Athey made cuts in his co-performer's back: words like 'mopped' implied a considerable quantity of blood, and 'towels' evoked the commonplace fabric items used to staunch large amounts of flowing liquid rather than the paper towels actually used. The author also claimed that audience reaction had been highly negative: 'At least one member of the audience fainted during the performance. Others left as it progressed'. One spectator was quoted as saying that 'The bloody towels were most upsetting to the audience . . . It appeared that the towels were going to drip or fall apart . . . People knocked over the chairs to get out from under the clotheslines'.

The author of this article, Mary Abbe, followed it up with another piece five days later, in which she stated: 'By presenting Athey, [the Walker] has, in effect, endorsed mutilation as an art form'.[19] Although admitting that she did not see the performance, Abbe called it 'grotesque' and 'a horror to most people'. She linked Athey to Chris Burden, calling the latter 'Athey's most-cited predecessor', and allowed an audience member to connect Athey with another controversial artistic figure, in saying: 'This made . . . Robert Mapplethorpe look like *The Sound of Music*'. Abbe speculated fetishistically on how much blood there had actually been:

> Reports differ as to how much blood oozed from his incisions – some say lots, others say not much. One says it appeared the towels used to mop up the blood were going to drip or fall apart; another says they looked almost dry, 'like art prints'.

She criticized the Walker for failing to disclose the performance's element of 'ritual mutilation' as 'shirk[ing] its responsibility to let its audiences decide for themselves what risks they will run and what brutalities they will endorse as art'.

Abbe's articles defined the terms of the furore that was to follow. Defenders of Athey's work and of the Walker Art Center found themselves having to deny that large amounts of blood had flowed; Athey and Walker officials were quoted refuting the implied violence and vigour of the activities, asserting instead the meditative, silent nature of the scene that had become the centre of controversy. The Walker was forced to publicize the safety precautions it had taken (thus appearing to concede that it had identified *some* risk that needed to be averted), and discussions took place about modes of HIV transmission and its likelihood in circumstances such as a theatrical performance. Despite prohibitions in Minnesota law on revealing any individual's HIV status, Athey and the Walker were compelled to state that while Athey is HIV positive, the man whose blood was on the paper towels hanging over the audience members' heads is HIV negative.

Within a number of months, the performance had been firmly cast by the mainstream media in the language of disgust and vertiginous outrage.[20] The Walker event was also used by conservatives to further the push for the reduction in federal funding of contemporary 'controversial' art, and as such was taken up as a cornerstone of the revived debate about public funding and freedom of expression.[21] When, in June 1994, the House of Representatives in Washington DC voted on the renewal of federal funds for the NEA, Athey's work was cited as a reason for the reduction in overall budget, and for the abolition of the NEA's programme which awards funding directly to individual artists (despite Athey never having received an individual grant in this way).

The performance art of Ron Athey thus forms part of the contemporary 'chilling effect' in US governmental support for controversial artwork, and demonstrates, once again, the point made in Chapter Two that the 'crisis' in contemporary art and its reception in conventional politics is never completed or 'over', and that the intermittent invocation of disgust and outrage now seems an entrenched part of the public discourse on contemporary art. However, Athey's work deserves attention for many other reasons than its exploitation by the political right or the mainstream media. In the account above, I have deliberately written little about what Athey's work actually involves. I will now turn to the nature of Athey's performance and its address to the audience – its invocation of the spectator in a forensic relation with the artist and his injury. To make sense of Athey's art practices, it is helpful to appreciate some biographical details, particularly since the performance pieces are inextricably bound up in Athey's life story.

Athey was born in California into a strict Pentecostal family; his grandmother had prophesied that he would become an evangelist. His childhood was filled with intense religious fervour: church meetings regularly involved participants fainting, or appearing to speak in tongues, and he developed a fascination for Christian iconography, especially the stigmata, and for stories of martyrdom and sacrifice.[22] As a teenager, Athey came out as gay, abandoned Pentecostalism and his family, and later became a heroin addict. He made several suicide attempts. At the age of 20, he developed a collaborative performance piece (*Premature Ejaculation*), then became involved with the Modern Primitives art movement and fascinated with tattooing and body modification. Athey is now in his early forties, tattooed from neck to knees (with additional tattoos on parts of his face), no longer uses drugs and has been HIV positive for a number of years. He has also developed a considerable body of work, mainly group theatrical pieces for his company, Ron Athey and Co. Much of this work draws directly from his experiences as a child in a deeply religious family, as gay man, as a drug user and as HIV positive. As Athey puts it:

> In my performance material, I am guilty of enhancing my history, situation and surroundings into a perfectly depicted apocalypse, or at least a more visual atrocity . . . It's a stretch to call the delusions of fanatical religion glamorous. Not to say that living my adult life through a time of AIDS has been disappointing as far as a drama goes; it's taken very little work for me to parallel my experiences with the jeweled doomsday prophecies from the Book of Revelations.
>
> (Athey 1997: 430–1)

In the early to mid-1990s, Athey developed what he calls the 'holy torture trinity' of works: *Martyrs & Saints*, *4 Scenes In A Harsh Life* and *Deliverance* (Athey 1997: 433). All three pieces combine elements of religious imagery, medical treatment, sexual fetishes and an inevitable progression through injury towards death.[23] Of the three performances pieces, it was *4 Scenes In A Harsh Life* which became the centre of the political furore around Athey. The work lasts one hour and involves four vignettes and an introduction in which Athey (dressed as a woman evangelist) explains to the audience his childhood fascination with religious fanaticism (for example, in his longing to receive the stigmata, he cut his and his sister's hands with a razor blade).[24] In the various scenes which follow, Athey either depicts through group action or narrates events from his experiences as a drug user (for example, describing his suicide attempts and heroin addiction as he inserts hypodermic needles in his arm from wrist to shoulder and then jabs a spinal needle through his scalp, causing blood to flow down his face), and as a gay man in a straight culture (Athey presides over a wedding of three women, each pierced with several fish hooks, inserting a long needle in one cheek and out the other for each woman; they then dance until their skin bleeds from its piercings). And, as became notorious, Athey cuts the skin on a man's back several times, blotting the blood with paper towels, and then attaches them to a clothesline over the audience members' heads.

It is worth noting briefly that Athey's performances bear some similarity to the early work of the Australian artist Stelarc.[25] In recent years, Stelarc has concentrated more upon the manipulation of his body through prosthetic limbs and electrical signals; however, in the 1970s and 1980s he came to prominence as an artist through his 'stretched skin' suspension pieces. In these works, Stelarc inserted fish hooks through his skin, in sufficient number to support the weight of his body, thanks to cords running through the hooks. His body was then allowed to hang suspended for a set period of time. He performed these suspensions in a range of locations, including over rocks next to the ocean, in a studio and over a New York street.[26]

Just as in Athey's performances, the pain experienced by Stelarc is real, and is an integral part of the performance (for himself, and for the audience). As one observer of a suspension piece noted: '[Stelarc] suddenly gasped with pain. "No worse than usual," he winced. "I just keep forgetting how bad it is"' (Carr 1993: 10). Just as in Athey's performances, there would be bleeding, and bandages were required afterwards. Like Athey, Stelarc's interest was in the body *in extremis*. He stated: 'During a suspension . . . the body was always at the threshold of catastrophe' (quoted in Carr 1993: 12).

And, just as with Athey's work, the body in suspension was transformed in ways that were unsettling for the observer. Athey's bodies would bleed as needles were inserted, bringing to the outside surface (skin) that which is supposed to be inside (blood). In seeing the confusion of exterior and interior, the eyewitness trembles and experiences nausea, discomfort, anxiety, and fear. Stelarc's body was similarly altered in the performance: the smooth surface of skin was rendered a hilly landscape of dips and peaks, as the hooks raised his skin, and gravity pulled his body downwards. Metal is thus permitted to go inside the body, inserting within it that which should remain outside. His observers experience similarly confounding emotional responses to the transformed body: Carr (1993: 12) recounts feeling 'nauseous' simply inter-viewing Stelarc, and how spectators' reactions included a woman covering her eyes in shock, and others shouting out 'Holy shit!' and 'THAT GUY'S FUCKIN' CRAZY!' (Carr 1993: 13–14).

However, unlike Stelarc, who deliberately depersonalized his perform-ances and who eschewed any attempt to read biography, sexuality or personal predilections into his work, Athey proclaims his work to be an extension of his life. His linking of gay sexuality, HIV infection and illness, injecting drug use, body mortification and Christian iconography therefore challenge those who would seek to separate those elements, to quarantine them from each other. Not only an extension of Athey's biographical past, these behaviours and beliefs are presented by Athey as extensions of himself (of his *self*). Although what is seen on the stage is a performance, Athey portrays it as real, removing any quality of inventedness and any space in which the viewer can safely believe it is 'only' a performance. Viewers do not see Athey 'acting' injury; they see Athey injuring himself and others, and in so doing issuing a procla-mation to the audience that such injury is not an image – it is his life, it is *their* life, it is *their injury*.

Whereas Chris Burden's work directs the question of suffering upon himself as performer, asking the audience to observe the consequences of his self-injury and their implication in the process of his suffering, Ron Athey parcels the phenomenon of suffering out towards the audience for their shared experience of it – he has said that his work is about 'wanting people to endure these real experiences'. As I noted above, Chris Burden's work effectively stated: 'my body is injured in the place where the artist is dead', turning his body into sculptures which sit quietly and passively awaiting injury or harm. The artist's sovereign control over the artwork is abandoned by

Burden, who repetitively staged and re-staged his own injury at the hands of others, so that the spectator could witness someone experiencing injury or pain.

Ron Athey, on the other hand, bases his work around the premise of survivorship (of trauma) through suffering (a suffering deflected onto the spectator). The aim of Athey's work, then, is to state: 'I am living on in the place where the spectator suffers'. Suffering animates Athey's work; the spectator's suffering is its aim. In response to criticism his work, Athey has said: 'when I get told *4 Scenes* contains too much suffering, what can I say? What comes to mind is the voice of Patti Smith . . . "Those who have suffered know suffering"' (Athey 1997: 435). Living on, surviving, continuing, enduring, in an autobiography of trauma, re-enacting injury in order to tame its effects and insisting that there be an audience to witness the process. For all injury has its audience (although not every bystander or spectator notices that they are an audience to injury).

Athey's objective, therefore, is to make the spectators aware of their implication in the demands of watching and to take responsibility for watching (a responsibility which is experienced as suffering). What end does this serve? Athey has commented:

> Sometimes I question the meaning of my performance work, I'm still not exactly sure what the reasons are to keep doing it . . . Why the fucking bloodbath? The shit? The vomit? All performed on a well-lit stage so that, hopefully, no details will be missed. To take a stab at it, using these bodily functions, assisted by the voice, words, and sound, *I'm testifying*.
>
> (Athey 1997: 432, my emphasis)

In this last phrase ('I'm testifying'), Athey neatly incorporates the twin axes of his performance's charge upon the audience. The notion of testimony evokes the Pentecostalist fervour of his childhood; as he recounts his experiences and acts out their consequences, it gives his work the *frisson* of autobiography and of the real ('this was his life, this really happened to him'). The notion of testimony also evokes the forensic: he is re-enacting injury and making juridical witnesses of everyone in the audience. In court, a witness can answer the demands of testimony with the certainty that the event belongs to the past. A crime scene image can be approached by the spectator with the comforting knowledge that its events are over, and any interpretation of its scene must necessarily be retrospective, disengaged from the present. Athey's work, however, transports the viewer into the present tense of a crime scene. Retrospection is impossible; instead, spectators must acknowledge that this injury is actually happening, right now, before their eyes. Aesthetic spectatorship becomes the witnessing of actual injury; viewers are made part of the crime scene, left to endure their ethical implication in the process of injury.

'I am awake in the place where women die'

'This is not as simple as reading (about war) in the newspaper . . .
[B]ecause this is a crime against the body, it made sense to somehow insist
on the fact that this is alive in the world. To have evidence. Almost.[27]

To testify; to bear witness. Where Chris Burden demonstrates his disappearance in the face of injury and Ron Athey puts on display the demands of
bearing witness, Jenny Holzer's artworks address the problem of testimony in
the face of suffering.[28]
    Since the 1970s, Holzer has made art out of text. She has created series of
short sentences which have been variously printed on paper and posted on
street walls; made into T-shirts; carved into stone benches; engraved in
marble floors; and incorporated into LED (light-emitting diode) electronic
light displays and installed both in galleries and in public space. Her work has
dealt with issues of consumerism, gender difference, motherhood, loss and
mourning.[29] In 1993, Holzer was commissioned by the German newspaper,
Suddeutsche Zeitung, to create an artwork which would be published in a
magazine supplement to the newspaper. She was already working on a text
relating to war (in the aftermath of the first Gulf War): the invitation
generated a European context for her ideas at the same time as news reports
were beginning to appear concerning the mass rape, torture and murder of
women in the former Yugoslavia.
    Holzer re-oriented her writing and the result was *Lustmord*.[30] 'Lustmord'
translates as 'sex-murder' or 'lustful murder'. It is an archaic German word
dating from the *fin-de-siècle* fascination with sexuality and perversion, falling
out of common use after the mid-twentieth century.[31] '*Lust*' in German is
specifically out-of-control desire and when conjoined with '*mord*' connotes a
sadistic, pathological derivation of sexual pleasure from killing. *Lustmord* was
conceived by Holzer as partly about atrocity (the mass rape and murder of
women in Bosnia) and partly about violence, death and trauma more
generally and more individually (Holzer also drew on her recent experience of
bereavement following the death of her mother after a protracted illness).[32] In
the context of wartime rape, 'lustmord' would indicate the unleashing of
archaic or primal drives or forces, an overwhelming tide of violence used for
sexual pleasure.[33]
    For the magazine publication, Holzer had a graphic designer photograph
her text written on women's skin. The effect, as one commentator noted, is like
turning the pages of a book of flesh (Weir 1998: 18). On the front cover of the
magazine, a card was attached, upon which was printed DA WO FRAUEN
STERBEN BIN ICH HELLWACH, which, in translation, states: 'I AM
AWAKE IN THE PLACE WHERE WOMEN DIE'. Holzer calls this the
'thesis sentence' of the work and stated that she envisaged the work as slipping
unheeded into people's homes, bringing with it its accounts of brutality and
terror (quoted in Weir 1998: 18). The text was printed in red ink mixed with

blood. There was a fierce outcry in the German tabloid press against Holzer: some criticized the use of blood (calling it a health risk, even though the blood, donated by German and Yugoslav women, had been pasteurized and rendered 'safe' before its use); others criticized Holzer for exploitation of the women who were victims of rape and murder.[34]

For subsequent installations of *Lustmord*, although the details of the setting vary according to the location, the basic components are the same. Let me describe the installation that I saw.[35] A narrow passage opens into a larger space. Lighting is very dim throughout. Both walls of the passageway are lined with the photographs of skin, inscribed with Holzer's text. One photograph shows only bruised skin, with no words. In the larger space at the end of the passageway, eight of Holzer's characteristic boxes with LED displays run vertically up and down the walls. The same text flashes red and yellow and green in dizzying repetition. Four tables are arranged neatly around the space. On each table, laid out in orderly rows are human bones of different sizes. Soft spotlights shine on them. Around some of the bones are silver rings, engraved in German and English with the same texts as in the photographs and LED displays.

As with all of Holzer's works, the words are paramount. Johnson writes that they are 'awful, painful, repellent. They give the piece its meaning . . . The words conjure up images no photograph, painting or movie could capture'.[36] *Lustmord* is conceived as spoken by three voices: the perpetrator, the victim, and the observer (perhaps a journalist, or a UN official, or, as Holzer has indicated, a relative of the now-dead victim, or the person who is required to remove the body).[37] The voices appear in no particular order, but can be distinguished from each other through varying linguistic ordering.[38] The voices speak from the photographed ink on skin, from the delirious LED lights, and out of the engravings on the silver bands around the bones. In order to read the text on the silver bands, the bones must be lifted and handled by the spectator. (In some versions of the installation, the darkened room is lined with leather panels, with the text tooled into the leather.) The text reads, for example:

> I TAKE HER FACE WITH ITS FINE HAIRS. I POSITION HER
>   MOUTH.
> MY NOSE BROKE IN THE GRASS.
> MY EYES ARE SORE FROM MOVING AGAINST YOUR PALM.
> SHE STARTED RUNNING WHEN EVERYTHING BEGAN
>   POURING FROM HER BECAUSE SHE DID NOT WANT TO BE
>   SEEN.

The perpetrator speaks in short, choppy sentences which tend to follow the grammatical pattern subject-verb-object, with the subject of the statement alternating between the described woman (as in SHE HAS A URINE SMELL or HER BREASTS ARE ALL NIPPLE) and the omnipotent perpetrator himself (I WATCH HER WHILE SHE THINKS ABOUT ME and I TELL HER TO SOAP HERSELF). A terrible acceleration occurs throughout the perpetrator's account, discernible even as it is jumbled with the other voices. Excerpts show its development thus:

> I SWIM IN HER AS SHE QUIETS.
> I SINK ON HER.
> I SING HER A SONG ABOUT US.
> I STEP ON HER HANDS.
> I SPLAY HER FINGERS.
> SHE ROOTS WITH HER BLUNT FACE.
> HER SWALLOW REFLEX IS GONE.
> SHE ACTS LIKE AN ANIMAL LEFT FOR COOKING.
> I WANT TO FUCK HER WHERE SHE HAS TOO MUCH HAIR.
> THE COLOR OF HER WHERE SHE IS INSIDE OUT IS ENOUGH
>   TO MAKE ME KILL HER.

For the spectator, the perpetrator's text is enormously disturbing, its first-person narration providing an ineluctable window into a brutal worldview. The language is, as Ruf (1997: 111) puts it, 'ruthlessly detailed' with 'frighteningly normal descriptions [which] allow us to participate in the events'. The spectator is not allowed to be separate from the account: it is one which is narrated in the spectator's head as if it were a confession, a memory or an experience.

In the victim's narration, the first person pronoun is still in use, but where the perpetrator reduced the victim to a third person or thing (SHE, HER), the victim addresses the perpetrator as YOU. Much of this account is a litany of injury, inflicted by a clearly identified individual and with its consequences upon the victim's body and spirit relentlessly accumulated:

> MY NOSE BROKE IN THE GRASS. MY EYES ARE SORE FROM
>   MOVING AGAINST YOUR PALM.
> WITH YOU INSIDE ME COMES KNOWLEDGE OF MY DEATH.
> I HAVE THE BLOOD JELLY.
> YOUR AWFUL LANGUAGE IS IN THE AIR BESIDE MY HEAD.
> HAIR IS STUCK INSIDE ME.
> WHAT IS LEFT ON THE BLANKET IS CLEAR AND THE COLOR
>   OF HELL.
> I AM AWAKE IN THE PLACE WHERE WOMEN DIE.

In the perpetrator's account the spectator is consigned to the place of violator, reinforced by the victim's words which repeatedly address the spectator as if they were the agent of her suffering. In its quietude and deliberation, this voice 'talks and talks, naming the things, listing the pain . . . yet leaving behind an enormous void of silence' (Volkart 1997: 117).

When I saw *Lustmord* as an installation, I believed there to be only two voices (victim and perpetrator). Subsequent reading of commentaries on the work revealed a third. I had diagnosed the voice of the observer as the perpetrator's, perhaps indicating that to me the observer is as implicated in the violence as the person committing the crimes. However, there are distinct characteristics in the observer's narration which do separate it from that of the perpetrator. The language is more distanced, bespeaking failure, loss, refusal or resignation. It is an apathetic account, which holds out no hope of change or willingness to indict the perpetrator. The victim's injuries, culminating in her death, are registered with a flat acceptance:

> SHE ASKS ME TO SLEEP IN THE HOUSE BUT I WILL NOT
>   WITH HER NEW BODY AND ITS NOISES AND WETNESS.
> SHE SMILES AT ME BECAUSE SHE THINKS THAT I CAN
>   HELP HER.
> I FIND HER TOWELS SHOVED IN TIGHT SPOTS. I TAKE THEM
>   TO BURN ALTHOUGH I FEAR TOUCHING HER THINGS.
> SHE STARTED RUNNING WHEN EVERYTHING BEGAN
>   POURING FROM HER BECAUSE SHE DID NOT WANT TO
>   BE SEEN.
> SHE IS NARROW AND FLAT IN THE BLUE SACK AND I STAND
>   WHEN THEY LIFT HER.

The observer can only watch without acting, has no agency to effect change or to achieve justice for the now-dead victim. For the spectator, this third voice, speaking again with the first person, provokes considerations of the ethics of watching and the role of the observer: this is looking as witnessing. As in the work of Burden and Athey, the spectator is *held* before the work as witness to atrocity.

The incorporation of the spectator into the artwork is achieved through more than the words of the text. The architecture of the installation, with its long narrow passageway and the darkened room at its end, physically and completely surrounds the viewer. When looking at *Lustmord*, there is no 'outside' that can be glimpsed: the spectator is within the entire artwork. Holzer states: 'I wanted the installation to be enveloping, because it is about the body . . . It's crucial to this piece that it be literally around you and it work on your whole being'.[39] The artwork thus covers the viewer like skin, the words of the three participants imprinting themselves upon the spectator in the same way as the ink sinks into the women's flesh.

More than that, the spectator is enjoined to move within the artwork and thus render it as a performative: in the act of reading the text, and in picking up and handling the human bones placed so delicately in rows upon the tables. The experience of handling the bones, according to Avgikos, impels the viewer

> to imagine a death, perhaps a violent one, as if it were their own; to engage
> in the perversity of holding someone's bones, as though they were art; to

remember their own sublime moments of fear or terror or alienation, as though they belonged to another.

(Avgikos 1994: 102)

Lustmord thus institutes a sequence of exchanges: in that, first, the spectator moves through the positions of perpetrator, to victim, to observer; and second, the spectator also registers, through the experience of being enveloped in the installation, an echo of the force that the artwork embodies. But, finally, the spectator is encouraged to exchange their sense of a transcendent, inviolable self for the possibility of reduction to a mere totemic memento or trace: a bone, a piece of skin, a silver bracelet or tag, words floating in the air.

Forensic aesthetics and the ethics of witnessing

There is an extensive history of artists deploying the bodies of themselves or others within their artworks. Vito Acconcci lay under the floorboards of a gallery masturbating while visitors walked around above him. Bob Flanagan turned his experience of cystic fibrosis into the platform for intensely maso-chistic performances (for example, nailing his penis to a block of wood). Cindy Sherman incorporates her endlessly mutable body into her photographs to create a seemingly infinite series of characterizations. Orlan has undergone repeated surgical operations in order to transform her face, the operations captured on film and some broadcast on satellite television. Tilda Swinton, as part of a collaborative work with Cornelia Parker, lay in a glass coffin in an art gallery, for seven days, eight hours a day. Joseph Beuys sat in a gallery reading to a dead hare. Gilbert and George, as 'living sculptures', have made their lives into continuing artistic performances and have also incorporated their bodily waste (semen, blood and faeces) into their images (as have many artists from Andres Serrano to Helen Chadwick).[40] What distinguishes Burden, Athey and Holzer from these other 'body artists'?

With Burden, it is the dissolution of the boundary between looking and performing. From the initial recognition that the spectator should be regarded as physically implicated in the viewing space and that the spectator's involvement with an artwork is intensified if a living human body is contained within it, Burden raised the stakes of spectatorship to include the possibility of doing harm to another, whether by looking and doing nothing or by choosing to act against them. He saw that violence fascinates through a complex process of identification, fascination and repulsion, with a tendency for the viewer to imagine themselves as potential victim. Burden's artwork flips the viewer out of the category of potential victim, by presenting the artist in that position, and into that of perpetrator or injurer, by showing them the effects of violence.

In the forensic autobiography of Ron Athey, the address to the spectator is both more and less incriminating than in Burden's artworks. At one of Athey's performances, the spectator can initially take distancing comfort in the idea that this is a performance of a life experience that belongs to Athey alone – Athey's highly wrought identity politics provide a screen behind which the spectator can shelter. However, the uncompromising physicality of the performance insinuates itself behind this screen and creates a continuous present tense and a universality of implication through the spectacle of inflicted injury. The viewer is thus metaphorically *charged* with participation in the injury. Whereas with Burden the spectator could watch to see if something *might* happen, Athey removed all such uncertainty: something will and does happen before the spectator's eyes, and it involves injury, it holds up to the audience the spectacle of blood flowing, and faces flinching in pain. The spectator is thus taken directly to the scene of the crime.

Holzer's work is perhaps less didactic, in that the spectator is allowed the small comfort of enforced oscillation between speaking positions (from victim to perpetrator to observer).[41] However, each voice indicts the spectator through its address and resultant identificatory effects. The viewer must think as the I/eye of the perpetrator, as the helpless victim, and in shared inertia with the observer. Thus violence is carried out, without respite, without any spectatorial fantasy of separation from it. Further, the physical incorporation of the viewer into the artwork shares with Burden's and Athey's work a desire to question the alibi of 'just' looking. To leave on display a crime where the criminal will not face trial.

And yet: *someone* is put on trial. At the scene of a crime where injury occurs with only the artist as perpetrator, the trial, then, is directed *at the spectator*. In the profoundly prosecutorial works of Athey, Holzer and Burden, straightforward identification of victim and injurer is not possible, with these categories repeatedly eviscerated and reorganized within the artwork. Instead of the comfort of compassionate identification with the suffering of the victim, the viewer is incorporated into both the body of the victim and the body of the injurer and required to take responsibility for the ethics of looking – to become a witness.

The question that this leaves for us is whether and how the witness can move beyond the screen of the spectacle of suffering, rather than be transfixed by the image. Perhaps the last word should be given back to Jenny Holzer and the line which is both the 'thesis sentence' of *Lustmord* and also a summary of the modality of address undertaken by Holzer: '*I am awake in the place where women die*'. To be awake: to do more than simply see. To see, and to take cognizance, to remain aware, to be conscious. To abandon the comfort of just looking, to acknowledge that there can be no justice in looking without an ethics of witnessing. To accept the burden of testimony. To be put on trial. To face the charges of art.

viewing (de)position

'is there anything you wish to ask me?'

Prague. I'm in Josefov, the Jewish Quarter. During the Second World War, 80,000 of Prague's 90,000 Jews were killed. In Josefov, only six synagogues, the Town Hall and the cemetery were left standing – and then only due to Hitler's desire to establish, after the war, an 'Exotic Museum of an Extinct Race'. Today, these buildings have indeed become tourist attractions. The Ceremonial Hall is now the Muzeum Terezina, both museum and monument to the 140,000 people who were taken to Theresienstadt (Terezin), the insincere, public face of the annihilation of the Jews. Much of the museum is devoted to a display of the artworks done by children in Terezin. The synagogues too can be visited: the Staronova (or Alt-Neu) synagogue is the oldest; the Maisel synagogue contains a display of the impact of the Holocaust on Prague's Jewish community. And to visit the cemetery, we have to queue, and then file through it at a slow shuffle. The gravestones grow askew out of the ground, like snaggleteeth: over the centuries, people were interred in layers since the Jews were forbidden to expand the size of the cemetery.

It is the Pinkas Synagogue, standing on eleventh century foundations, that has been chosen to house Prague's Holocaust memorial, designed by Václav Boštík and Jiří John. The names of the 77,297 Bohemian and Moravian Jews who died have been painted on the synagogue's interior walls.

The memorial was closed in 1968, purportedly for restoration, and remained closed for over twenty years, during which time the names faded as the walls crumbled. In 1991, the memorial was reopened and the names repainted, a task which took five years to complete in full.

In the entrance hall, there is an inscription on the wall, from *Lamentations* I, 12: 'Let not it come unto you, all ye that pass by! Behold, and see if there be any pain like unto my pain'. The visitor is thus immediately being addressed by an individual – a victim of genocide speaks in a memorial voice.

But this conversation with the dead cannot take place with any singular interlocutor, any one individual whose name might be painted upon the memorial's walls. Entry into the synagogue reveals that *there are thousands of names*. Banal to say that, of course, because there is one name for each person who died, and I know that 77,297 people died. The name of each is inscribed on the walls. But this phrase is what runs through my head as I enter the synagogue and gaze around: *there are thousands of names.* The creamy-coloured walls and vaulted ceilings of several rooms are entirely covered in tiny capital letters, in red, black and ochre paint. The writing is in a uniform script, as though the same hand has written all the words.

I move closer to the walls, to read some of the text. It includes not only the names of people, but also the names of towns, villages, cities. These place names in fact are the organizing device: in alphabetical order, the memorial lists places, beginning with A and working through the subsequent letters, where victims lived. The place name is in ochre, and is followed, red-lettered in alphabetical order, by the names of the dead; surname first, then given names. Place names and the names of the dead are lettered slightly larger than the lists of dates, painted in black, which follow them. The listing only of an asterisk followed by a surname denotes that the whole family has been killed. In some instances, dates of births and of deaths are given. Where the precise date of death is not known, the date given is that of the individual's deportation to the ghettos and camps in the east. Many names are not accompanied by a date of death, transportation to the camps standing in its stead. As far as recorded history goes, their deaths took place *out of time*, beyond the calendar.

The wall tells me:

DODAIKY: * ABERBACH MAX 19.X 1877 – 15.IV 1939 * ADLER OTA 4.I 1870 – 25.IX 1943 * BOZENA 20.IV 1884 – 7.II 1943 * OTOKAR 9.IV 1892 – 15.XII 1941 * ALT LEO 12.VIII 1916 – 26.X 1941

It's dizzying: my eyes waver between looking at the memorial as a whole – with the names blurring into an indistinct pattern on the walls of its rooms – and zeroing in on one name after another. The general scale of the extermination is attested to by the building as a whole, while each individual victim is acknowledged in a minute place upon a wall.

And on either side of a deconsecrated Holy Ark are listed the names of some of the ghettos and camps to which Bohemian and Moravian Jews were deported:

Terezin	Oswiecim
Majdanek	Treblinka
Lublin	Zamosc
Christianstadt	Kaufering
Warszawa	Maly Trosinec
Nisko	Chelmno
Izbica	Lodz
Riga	Schwartzheide
Flossenburg	Minsk
Dachau	Sachsenhausen
Bergen-Belsen	Mauthausen
Hamburg	Sztutowo

Between this list of camps and the recitation of towns and the names of the dead, an unstated narrative recounts the removal of each and every one of these people and their deaths in all of these places. That the synagogue contains nothing else – a building of empty rooms – seems completely appropriate. All that remains is brick, paint, names and empty air in between.

* * *

The Holocaust Memorial in Budapest (another city whose Jewish population was almost eradicated during the war). Not a building this time, but a sculpture. In 1991, around the time that Prague was beginning the renovation of its damaged Holocaust memorial in the Pinkas synagogue, Imre Varga's sculpture was installed in a courtyard garden on Wessenlyi *utca*, at the rear of the Great Synagogue. It is an enormous, metallic weeping willow. It stands on a stone slab in the middle of the courtyard, set a little back from the street. Its branches grow upwards then arch down towards the ground. Each branch bears dozens of metal leaves. On many of the leaves there is a name inscribed – the names of families who were killed during the Holocaust. More names. Unlike in Prague, here the names are not made the dominant motif of the memorial. The names are present but incorporated into a larger symbol: the willow, which reaches upwards and downwards simultaneously, which evokes mourning and grief even as it symbolizes life.

The branches wave in the breeze. I walk around the willow, and finger its silvery leaves. Some visitors have walked up to its stone slab (they must have stooped over in order to step under the waving branches) and left small pebbles, following the Jewish custom – marking it as if it were a grave. In front of the sculpture is a broken marble slab, inscribed with the solitary injunction, 'remember'. But closer to the railings that divide the memorial from the street there is a plaque, bearing words from the Talmud:

Whose pain can be greater than mine?

The memorial imperative (*remember*) lies in quiet relation to this unanswerable question.

* * *

Names and questions. Slide back a few years, to 1996, during a visit to Los Angeles, and to the Simon Wiesenthal Museum of Tolerance. I had expected a museum similar to the more famous Holocaust museum in Washington DC. But the Museum of Tolerance is very different, mainly as a result of its determination to be an interactive experience for the visitor. In the leaflets I collect at the ticket office, it describes itself as 'a high tech, hands-on experiential museum'. Although it contains a floor featuring documentary records and relics from the Holocaust (camp uniforms, a camp bunk bed and so on), its main aim in relating the story of the Holocaust is for visitors to be 'led back in time to become witnesses to the events of World War II'.

It does this by means of a walk-through exhibit, whereby events and scenes from everyday life in 1930s and 1940s Germany are re-enacted for the visitor. A succession of dioramas lights up in turn, with recorded voices dramatizing the increasing grip of Nazism and the relentless movement towards the Final Solution (the Wannsee conference is one of the featured events). At the start of the exhibit, before beginning the walk through, the visitor is given a 'passport', upon which a child's identity is imprinted. At various stages throughout the exhibit, the child's story is updated. As the museum's leaflet ominously promises, at the end of the exhibit 'the ultimate fate of the child is revealed'. The moment of revelation comes as the visitor is reaching the final scene of the exhibit. But this time, instead of seeing a staged diorama, the visitor is brought *into* an imitation gas chamber. Instead of looking at the exhibited scene, I am suddenly *in it*. It's disorienting, and profoundly affecting. What was previously something to look at is now something to inhabit. I'm trying to get used to the discombobulating shift, when a figure detaches itself from the darkness and walks towards me. A tall, thin man, with a serious face. He is in his early seventies. He speaks quietly and soberly: 'I am a survivor of Auschwitz. Is there anything you want to ask me?'

This is the ultimate experiential moment for the visitor, who is expected at this point to question the survivor about life in the camps, about liberation, about trauma. Just as the museum also provides 'testimony' sessions, in which survivors 'share their unique experiences' with visitors, here the museum offers the visitor the opportunity to participate in the *aftermath* of the Shoah by listening and asking questions. Standing in a simulated gas chamber, one is supposed to question the chamber's survivor.

How? I had no questions for this man. As the Budapest memorial asks, 'whose pain can be greater than mine?' As the Prague memorial urges, 'see if there be any pain like unto [his] pain'. How could the language of information usurp those solicitations and replace them with an *ersatz* experience simulated for my benefit? The man's invitation seemed compelled by the setting, the museum subjecting him to a demand to speak ('speak, memory') and putting him under obligation to tell, to recount. I backed away from him, tears in my eyes, mumbling 'no, no', horrified at the obligation that had been constructed for him.

The survivor speaks for herself and for himself. He did not need my questions in order for his story to be remembered. The museum's restaging of annihilation as the culmination of an exhibit had generated a dialogue in which I refused to speak my allotted lines. It would not be until I saw the Holocaust memorials of Budapest and Prague that I would experience a conversation with the dead encompassing both the singular and the multiple, both silence and entreaty.

6   All that remains

Image in a place of ruin

The city, for the first time in its long history, is destructible. A single flight of planes no bigger than a wedge of geese can quickly end this island fantasy, burn the towers, crumble the bridges, turn the underground passages into lethal chambers, cremate the millions. The intimation of mortality is part of New York now: in the sound of jets overhead, in the black headlines of the latest edition.

All dwellers in cities must live with the stubborn fact of annihilation; in New York the fact is somewhat more concentrated because of the concentration of the city itself, and because, of all targets, New York has a certain clear priority. In the mind of whatever perverted dreamer would loose the lightning, New York must hold a steady, irresistible charm.

(White 1949: 50–1)

This emptiness will remain and cannot be obliterated by any building.
(Libeskind 2002)

Immanent ruin

Art, photography, television, architecture, posters, graffiti.

When disaster is all that remains, how can image stand in the place of ruins?

Spencer Tunick's temporary site-related installations capture their participants as both subjects and objects of art (see Chapter 1). One of his installations, *New Jersey*, coincidentally also captured within its frame a site now inescapably associated with destruction and loss. *New Jersey* depicts a nude woman, seated on rocks at the edge of the Hudson River, her body in three-quarters view, her head turned away so that her profile foregrounds the water behind her and the skyscrapers of Manhattan in the distance (Figure 12). In the film *Naked States*, a documentary about Tunick's project of photographing individuals in every American state, the woman described the experience of posing for Tunick as one of finding, for the first time in her life, a kind of 'public solitude', a respite from the physical and verbal abuse she has endured for years as a result of her considerable weight and enormous size. The resulting image is one of great beauty: a felicitous combination of contrasts between the woman's body and the rocks, the water and her flesh, the distant city and the woman in the foreground.

One of the buildings which frame the river and the woman's flowing body is the World Trade Center. Like all images in which that building appears, *New Jersey* seems fated to be viewed as an image which is now as much about the cataclysm that is yet to come. It cannot be read in its present tense. It demands an acknowledgement of its future, a reading that melds the present tense of the image with the coming disaster. When I saw *Naked States* in a cinema in Melbourne in late September 2001, at the point when the image *New Jersey* appeared, several audience members spontaneously raised their arms to point at the screen – not at the seated figure of the woman but at the two towers of the World Trade Center, an uncanny manifestation only two weeks after the September 11th attacks. On screen, September 11th had not yet taken place, and thus the image *New Jersey* seemed to hold out the promise that the attacks might never happen and yet also underscored the completeness of the World Trade Center's obliteration, like a letter only read after its author's death.

At the time of its installation, Tunick's image *New Jersey* was a reclamation of public space for and by a woman whose body had been the object of assault, abuse and humiliation. The photograph both acknowledged the injury and loss of autonomy that the woman had suffered as a result of her physical body and also displaced that sense of loss in a reconstruction of her body as the subject of art. And now, *New Jersey* is also a graven image – an image pre-figuring both monumental loss and the attempt to displace that loss into a memorial for those who died at the World Trade Center. In its uncanny representation of the recent past, the image *bespeaks loss, but it also remembers for us.*

This chapter considers the imperatives of mourning and memory in the wake of September 11th and pursues the discomfort of images located in a place of ruin, by considering some of the representations of the event of September 11th. It will also examine the public desire to memorialize the deaths of approximately 3,000 people and to console for the loss of an architectural landmark. However, while an image such as Tunick's *New Jersey* successfully accommodated its subject's simultaneous experience of injury and assertion of self in public space, in the context of the World Trade Center site, it has proved more difficult to invent an aesthetic or architectural vocabulary which will both embody and displace trauma in the midst of unbearable loss.[1] In a quiet way, *New Jersey* always recalled the small destructions and assaults that had injured its subject. After September 11th, *New Jersey* also commemorates the larger violence of the attacks on the World Trade Center and the two enormous towers now melted into air. Like *New Jersey*, any image of the World Trade Center contains that violence and destruction within it, points towards the building's disappearance, and heralds its loss. After September 11th, all concrete is also smoke, all flesh is already dust. Whoever stands proudly in any photograph may yet vanish. Whatever has been built can be destroyed. The certainty of such a possibility animates every image; ruination dwells in every building. Its immanence has become the condition of possibility of every glance.

Vision in ruins

It has become a cliché that everyone remembers where they were at the time of the World Trade Center attacks, just as everyone remembers where they were when they heard that John F. Kennedy had been shot or that Princess Diana had died in a car crash in Paris. And it is also now an accepted truism that everyone saw the September 11th attacks live on television, that the images of those attacks generated a global media community of grief and disbelief.[2] In the face of this apparent worldwide participation in the event it seems somewhat unlikely to have to provide a confession: of *not having seen*. That evening (due to the time difference it was night-time in Australia when the attacks occurred), I was watching *The West Wing* on television. Towards the episode's end, a preview for the late news was featured (as is the network's usual practice). The announcer said: 'Coming up on *Nine News*, a plane has crashed into the World Trade Center in New York'. I turned to my partner and said, 'Wow, one of those little tourist planes that fly so close to the skyscrapers in New York must have crashed.' The episode of *The West Wing* resumed, and when it ended, as is our habit, we switched off the television without waiting for the news.[3]

If I had continued watching, I would have seen the effects of the first plane's crashing into the North Tower of the World Trade Center, and would have seen, live, the second plane hitting the South Tower. If I had remained watching, as thousands did, late into the night, I would have seen the World Trade Center's collapse. As it was, I had no idea, until I opened the newspaper at breakfast the next day, of what had occurred. At that point I did switch the television back on, and then, subject to a time lag of several hours, experienced the astonishing glut of images and the seemingly endless replaying of the event. It quickly became apparent that, as Virilio (1994: 9) puts it, 'the series of visual impressions become meaningless. They no longer seem to belong to us, they just exist, as though the speed of light had won out, this time, over the totality of the message'.

Repetition, replay, representation: it took several days before most television channels were able to arrest their compulsion to re-view the attacks, by which time video footage from innumerable amateur cameras had been broadcast. Survivors' accounts had made frequent reference to popular American blockbuster films in their efforts to describe the event, likening their flight through the streets of lower Manhattan to scenes from *Independence Day*, *Die Hard*, *Godzilla* and *The Towering Inferno*. One eyewitness said of her reactions to the first tower's collapse:

King Kong could swing from the remaining tower and I wouldn't be surprised. It's like a bad movie, I keep repeating. I struggle with this cliché but can draw on nothing else in my experience to define what is happening.[4]

Actor Bruce Willis, the star of the *Die Hard* movies, was in Manhattan on the day of the attacks and described walking down Fifth Avenue in a group of friends: 'Someone made the comment, "Where's John McClane [the protagonist of *Die Hard*] when you need him?".'[5] And film critic Anthony Lane wrote of the event:

> the fireball of impact was so precisely as it should be, and the breaking waves of dust that barrelled down the avenues were so absurdly recognizable – we have tasted them so frequently in other forms, such as water, flame, and Godzilla's foot – that only those close enough to breathe the foulness into their lungs could truly measure the darkening day for what it was.[6]

As Žižek (2002: 15) comments on the recourse to cinematic referents, 'for us, corrupted by Hollywood, the landscape and the shots of the collapsing towers could not but be reminiscent of the most breathtaking scenes in big catastrophe productions'.

The repetition and proliferation of different segments of video footage lent the attacks an even more cinematic quality than that attested to by eyewitnesses and survivors: television viewers were shown the planes hitting the towers and the towers' collapse from multiple angles and positions, in slow motion and at normal speed, with sound and without. One eyewitness and survivor described 'watch[ing] hours and hours of CNN, seeing the towers falling so often it seems more real than what I saw'.[7] After several days of such a surfeit of imagery:

> In spite of all this machinery of transfer [the technologies of television and cameras], we get no closer to the *productive unconscious of sight*, something the surrealists once dreamed of in relation to photography and cinema. Instead we only get as far as its *unconscious*, an annihilation of place and appearance the further amplitude of which is hard to imagine.
> (Virilio 1994: 8, emphasis in original)

At the same time, newspapers, websites and television programmes repeatedly featured shots of the World Trade Center as it once was (not the Ground Zero it had become), the towers grabbing the sky, now subject to retrospective re-presentation as tragic architectural achievements fated for destruction, or as symbols of Western hubris targeted by terrorists, or as structurally flawed buildings whose construction was destined to implode under such heat and force. (In later months, television programmes and newspaper articles would sift through these alternate identities for the World Trade Center with gloomy determination.) No matter how hard one tried to resist these limited narratives being grafted retrospectively onto the World Trade Center, it was difficult to avoid looking at images of the now-obliterated towers without feeling something of what Sebald called

> a kind of wonder which in itself is a form of dawning horror, for somehow we know by instinct that outsize buildings cast the shadow of their own destruction before them, and are designed from the first with an eye to their later existence as ruins.
>
> (Sebald 2002: 23–4)

Some global media events are forgotten within weeks or even days; others persist for some time, their contours adjusting and sharpening as the months pass. In the immediate days and weeks following the event, as part of the obsessive replaying of the images of the World Trade Center's destruction, there was of course a considerable amount of emphasis on the dead and the injured. The *number* of dead ('ten thousand', 'five thousand', 'several thousands', 'approximately three thousand' and the final number of those who died in the towers and on the planes that crashed into them, 3,016) received much attention, and many types of individuals were singled out as particularly tragic figures (the tourist visiting the towers, the individual who had just started work, conference attendees, firefighters answering emergency calls and so on).[8] However, public discourse on the event known as '9/11' or 'September 11th', also features a peculiar facet: the notion that the spectator, including all those hundreds of thousands of individuals who had watched the attacks (in person, live on television or in the repetitive obsessions of the aftermath), was also victimized by the event. It was as if the *image* injured its spectators, in its abruption and redefinition of the parameters of 'image', 'liveness', death, and magnitude of destruction.

A sense of community with New York and its inhabitants had already been effected by countless fictional television and cinematic representations: as one writer put it:

> Relatively few Australians have visited New York, but thanks to television they feel they know the city. For that reason, and because the images – witnessed in real time, right there in our homes – were so graphic, the immediate impact on the Australian consciousness was immense.[9]

Fictional representations of New York had forged a sense of televisual community. And then: the attacks of September 11th both ruptured and reiterated that representational effect. As Žižek (2002: 19) puts it, 'this is what the captivating effect of the collapse of the WTC was: an image, a semblance, an "effect", which, at the same time, delivered "the thing itself"'. This notion should not be understood as an endorsement of the oft-repeated claim that September 11th saw the intrusion of reality into the culturally shuttered lives of Americans. Such a claim appears in statements such as '[the horror] occurred in what we have learned to call real time and real space' and 'last Tuesday's monstrous dose of reality'.[10] Rather, as Žižek goes on to argue, the imaginary burst through the screen of reality. He states:

> We should therefore invert the standard reading according to which the WTC explosions were the intrusion of the Real which shattered our illusory Sphere: quite the reverse – it was before the WTC collapse that we lived in our reality, perceiving Third World horrors as something which was not actually part of our social reality, as something which existed (for us) as a spectral apparition on the (TV) screen – and what happened on September 11 was that this fantasmatic screen apparition entered our reality.
>
> (Žižek 2002: 16)

That the effect of this *as representation* was violent and traumatic is self-evident. Certainly the notion that it was now possible to be injured *by watching* passed into public discourse without much query.[11] As did the sense that the world had irrevocably changed, that a momentous historical event had occurred before our very eyes, that we had all been eyewitnesses to history. This notion of witnessing history functions of course in an entirely constitutive manner: as Agamben (1993: 94) says, 'the word *historia* derives from the root *id-*, which means to see. *Histor* is in origin the eyewitness, the one who has seen'.[12] As I suggested in Chapter 5, there is a sense of ethical demand involved in witnessing. Built into the experience of watching the work of artists such as Athey, Holzer and Burden is a demand that witnesses interpret what they see. Such an interpretation makes history, faces up to the question of what sense history will make of what has been seen and of what actions have been taken by the witness, the one who has seen.

Witnessing history leads to trauma: 20 per cent of those living within a 2 kilometre radius of the World Trade Center were said, one year after the event, to be suffering post-traumatic stress disorder (PTSD), a twofold increase, affecting some 422,000 individuals.[13] Unexpected bodily senses had been redefined as mechanisms of distress: many reported that the smell in the air of the city was appalling (caused by the dust of pulverized building, jet fuel, asbestos and body parts).[14] One individual commented: 'I just feel that there are 3,000 bodies there – you can smell it'.[15] The dust lingered for several weeks and even after its dissipation local residents, traders and rescue workers were unsure as to whether unseen but noxious fumes were still present. Thus the very act of breathing became a source of anxiety and stress for thousands.[16] One writer described the sensation of pain as 'this gnawing thing that brings you to tears at unexpected times'.[17] Others would feel that they had managed to overcome the stress of the event, but would experience revisitations of distress many months afterwards:

For many, it happens on the nicest sort of days, those mornings when the sky is clear and a bold sun defies the season. On days like that, you'll step outside and the radiant blue dome above becomes a torment. It was that way on September 11, you recall, and there is no way to stop the images and the anger flooding back.[18]

'Images and anger flooding back'. The individual experiences trauma as drowning in the liquid force of representation: having 'seen too much' on September 11th, a series of commonplace images (a clear sky, a bold sun) acts as triggers for the resurgence of psychic pain.[19] Such pain has followed the violence of traumatic loss, an effect and affect of loss that goes beyond the obvious loss of life, of urban resources, of revenue and expenditure. It is a loss that cannot be readily restored (by insurance, by a country going to war, by salvage and cleanup operations). The subsequent sections of this chapter consider both the contours of traumatic loss in the aftermath of September 11th, and the endeavour to counter trauma through images that bespeak memory in the aftermath of disaster.

Loss and the ruin

The six-month and one-year anniversaries of September 11th saw a condensation of emphasis in the discourse on the World Trade Center. Six months after the event, public discourse had narrowed, on the whole, to the questions of the clearing of Ground Zero and the two temporary memorials installed at the site (the twin beams of light projected skywards every night for a month, and the sculpture known as 'The Sphere' which had previously been located in the forecourt of the World Trade Center and which had survived the collapse). One year after the event, the memorialization of loss dominated public discourse, a loss which has had two categories of victim. The first category includes the thousands of individuals who died or were injured in the event; the second relates to the visual injury effected by the attacks, thus deriving from a sense of the victimization of the urban spectator and a mourning of the loss of New York City's skyline. For this second category of victim, injury is perpetrated and perpetuated by the existence within the city of Ground Zero.

Ground Zero projects a morbidity of affect, not just through its physical appearance (from the initial unruly jumble of rubble to its subsequent excavated absences), but also through intense public awareness of its existence as a grave. Two thousand, eight hundred and thirteen people died at the World Trade Center. Most of the dead were identified through DNA technology being applied to retrieved body parts and fragments, found both at the site and at locations around it.[20] The rubble that was removed from Ground Zero was sent to a landfill site on Staten Island, where workers sifted through it, searching for body parts and items of personal property.[21]

For families and friends of the dead and perhaps for the majority of the city's inhabitants, Ground Zero is gravespace.[22] It is both gravespace and the very image of gravespace: earthy, gaping, drear. But, to be precise, it is the image of *empty* gravespace. It looks like a vacant grave, a grave that has been dug but whose occupant is not yet interred, or a grave that has been opened and its contents plundered. A significant part of the visual trauma of looking at Ground Zero, for survivors and the bereaved and witnesses, is its now obvious emptiness, as though the bodies it should hold are elsewhere. As gravespace, it is thus always already paradoxical: it is a grave without a corpse, and those who seek to construct it as memorial space must do so in the face of its obdurate emptiness and in the face of their own insistence that the bodies of countless dead do indeed lie *somewhere* within.

That the bodies of the dead are both present and vanished from their grave is not the only source of Ground Zero's painfulness. Some of those bodies fragmented into pieces, but most were instantly transformed into dust, passing into the very air of the city and thence for days and weeks afterwards into the lungs of witnesses and survivors. For those who were present in the city on September 11th, Ground Zero has acted as a visual reminder that on that day and for some time after, along with noxious fumes and toxic chemicals everyone was 'breathing the dust of the dead' (Bird 2003: 92). Ordinarily, the corpse, body parts and fragments of bodies, such as hairs and nail clippings, are regarded as abject, items to be avoided or shuddered over and rejected. Relatives of those missing in and around the World Trade Center found themselves forced to fetishize these normally abject bodily remainders (from the comparatively rare intact body down to the smallest fragment identified through DNA matching).[23] The impossibility, for most relatives, of knowing for certain that their friend or loved one had died and the impossibility of their identifying any body as their loved one, caused both enormous pain and unendurable hopefulness for many. From posting photographs of their missing relatives on city walls to waiting for a telephone call inviting their identification of a body part or personal item, thousands of individuals spent weeks and months oscillating between hope and hopelessness.[24]

In such a traumatic process, any remaining personal belongings and bodily fragments of the missing person become invested with all of the loved one's personality, identity, history and potential. From the items and body parts collected by landfill workers to the microscopic fragments that passed into people's lungs, body parts and belongings were turned into *relics*. A relic is a fragment of the body or belongings of a dead person, in which the mourning survivor invests pain and anguish. Fedida writes:

> In the private ritual practice attached to the memory of the deceased after mourning, one can bring up this habit of preserving from the deceased a fragment of the body (hair, teeth . . .), finery, or further still an object of wholly insignificant appearance which truly belonged to the deceased.

The relic is here, wholly or in part, foreign to the idea of an objective value that one would be able to discern in the object.

(Fedida 2003: 63)

Thousands of people in New York, in the immediate aftermath of September 11th, found themselves in the position of suddenly possessing tiny reliquary fragments of their beloved, or son, or sister, or parent. Photographs became totemic means of searching for the missing individual (thousands of 'missing' posters, usually featuring a photograph and text, were affixed to walls, lamp-posts, mailboxes and shop windows all over New York City in the weeks following September 11th). Prosaic items of everyday activities, such as combs and toothbrushes, became repositories of the only available pieces of the lost one's body, containing hairs or blood or mucus which could be used for DNA identification. That which would normally be regarded as everyday, as insignificant, or even as waste material, had suddenly become freighted with the value of a remnant, of *the only remnant*: 'in order to escape from the sorrow [*douleur*] of separation and to remove oneself from hallucinatory desire, the survivor constitutes the relic in a kind of enlarged reality or, as it may be better put, in a sur-reality' (Fedida 2003: 64).[25] For many, these tiny relics have never been matched with any remains found at Ground Zero, the beloved simply and cruelly vanishing.[26] Others have suffered the surreal trauma of repeated identifications. One family were notified five times that parts of their son had been discovered: one leg, part of the other leg, a piece of skin, a piece of skull bone, some muscle tissue.[27]

An individual who was until September 11th simply a lover, brother, friend is now compelled to be a *survivor*, to *live on* without the loved one. This survivor sees these remnants (clothes, hair, mucus, photographs) simultaneously as wondrous traces of the beloved's presence and as obscene and dreadful evidence of their disappearance. Ground Zero is similarly regarded: it is the appalling gravespace of the dead, every crevice and seam filled with their reliquary dust, and it is also the place in which the beloved was last alive, it is filled with the memory of their last thoughts, breath, movements.

Such a literal gravespace has also been metaphorized into the New York skyline, with Ground Zero characterized as a deep wound in the architecture of the city. Virilio writes that 'on September 11 2001, *the Manhattan skyline* became the front of the new war' (2002: 82, my emphasis). Given that far more attention was commonly paid to skyscrapers such as the Chrysler Building and the Empire State Building, it is perhaps surprising that there has been so much mourning of the *aesthetic* loss deriving from the World Trade Center's destruction.[28] Meyerowitz writes lyrically of the building as an object of architectural beauty:

The towers were by turns hard-edged and glinting, like the Manhattan schist they stood on, or papery, brooding and wet, smothered in tropical cloud banks carried up by the sea. And on other days they were pewter, or gilded, or incandescent.[29]

Individuals recounted their personal reactions to the absence from view of the World Trade Center: it is 'that great grey hole where once the Twin Towers stood', a hole 'where the great cranes moved and plucked at Ground Zero'.[30] Salman Rushdie, on a visit to Ground Zero two months after the attacks, found the experience overwhelming in its visual impact:

> My own eyes kept being dragged upward to look at the empty sky. Many people have written and spoken about the force of the towers' absence from the landscape. The eye seeks them out where once it found them, and can't believe what it doesn't see. The absence has become a presence. At Ground Zero . . . the hollow air seemed to gather and shape itself into those huge lost forms and soar upward toward the memory of billowing fire.[31]

The absence is like the after-effects of a visual amputation: 'the transformed tip of Manhattan' is 'like a familiar smile or mouth with teeth removed' (Frascina 2003: 119), while Bird, who was by chance in New York City on September 11th and witnessed the attacks, writes nostalgically and elegiacally of the World Trade Center that has been lost:

> the Twin Towers . . . were the point of reference for both spatial orientation and checking the time – the way the vertical girders trapped the sunlight, deep gold on their eastern side during early morning, turning to a shimmering silver at midday, deepening as evening fell to a pearly luminescence. At night, the 100 illuminated floors stretched impossibly upwards, a city within the city, half the population of Oxford suspended in layer upon layer of tiny bright squares piercing the night sky.
>
> (Bird 2003: 88–9)

From that nostalgically imagined glorious apotheosis of urban landmark, the World Trade Center has been forced through a series of figural and forceful transformations. The collision of the two hijacked planes into the two towers turned the buildings briefly into a precarious and perilous site of injury and horror, a place from which evacuation and rescue were immediately required. The collapse of the buildings shifted the site into a disaster area, a mass grave and a crime scene all at once. No longer the World Trade Center, tourist destination, retail centre and office building, it has become Ground Zero, a place where thousands died and where injury was imprinted upon the contours of the city. And as physical space, the World Trade Center passed through an abrupt series of visual metamorphoses: from shining glass towers pointing skywards, it was suddenly a wounded building with gashes in its sides from which smoke and fire billowed and from which people fell or jumped. It then became a thunderous plummeting cloud of dust and rubble as the towers plunged earthwards, pulsing its debris out over the city to a radius of a dozen blocks or more. Its obliteration occurred once, as the South Tower fell, then all over again with the North Tower's collapse, a ghastly repetition in which shock had been replaced by a sense of inevitability. Thus, in a period of approximately one and three-quarter hours, the World Trade Center became Ground Zero.[32]

And as Ground Zero, the site has transmuted through various forms: at first, it reached upwards, with shards of actual building piled high and still pointing to the skies.[33] As the wreckage and debris was gradually cleared, the shape of Ground Zero flattened and became briefly level with the ground. However, it quickly moved towards its current form: an enormous hole, 6.5 hectares in size, several city blocks wide and long, extending deep into the ground, with the original support wall of the World Trade Center laid bare to the eye. It has an incompleteness of look; it resembles waste ground or an excavated building site in its apparent lack of use (Figures 13 and 14). It bespeaks emptiness. It has been a mutable space (from pile to hole) and the idea that its mutation is over – that this is how it *is* – is unbearable.[34] The plan to redevelop Ground Zero thus has become invested by an urgent sense of the need to keep the site under transformation and to move it forwards toward *what it once was*: to both remember the event of September 11th that transformed the World Trade Center into gravespace and simultaneously to counter that memory with an other image that moves away from the grave and the corpse towards a radiant skyline.

Memorial spaces

The aching sense of bereavement before the visual image of Ground Zero means that the project of rebuilding has become freighted with the responsibility of restoration, of solace, of denial. The very notion of *re*-building offers comfort because it explicitly promises a return to that which has been lost (and hence a return *of* the lost). But such promises cannot be fulfilled: even if the towers were rebuilt exactly as before in exactly the same location, it would not be possible to erase the image of the previous towers' collapse. As Bird puts it, underlying the public debate on redevelopment of the site, 'the question is what counter-image could possibly impose itself, and thus deflect meaning onto other paths. Herein lies the essential "aesthetic" of the act and its legacy' (Bird 2003: 93).

Many participants in the public debates on redevelopment called for the rebuilding of the towers exactly as they once were. The attractions of such an idea are obvious. For some, the notion of building an exact replica offered a means of dispelling the sense that 'America' or 'New York' had been injured or victimized: the restoration of an identical building would thus serve to indicate that any such injury was now gone, part of the past, with 'America' and 'New York' returned to all possible potency. Goldberger notes:

Reconstructing the original towers makes absolutely no sense, but it has a curious allure for many people, as if spending billions of dollars to duplicate one of the more conspicuous architectural mistakes of the twentieth century would be the way to show Al Qaeda that [Americans] are in command of contemporary civilization.

(Goldberger 2003: 78)

And, if Ground Zero represents a wound, the re-creation of 'the World Trade Center' would seem not only to suture the wound but also to remove any sense of scar or permanent injury. Bird (2003: 93) comments: 'Thus, the suggestion that the Towers be rebuilt exactly as before has perhaps little to do with planning, but a great deal to do with the processes of unbearable loss'. The building of an identical World Trade Center would erase the sense of Ground Zero as the real, its vastness, drabness, smell, depth (indeed, its very being-ness).

This desire for an exact replica derives from the wish to return to the last place of the loved one, to deny the existence of the gravespace of the beloved's death, to cover over the wound in the city. Other proposals veered towards the opposite impulse, arguing that Ground Zero would always be and should always remain a burial ground. One suggestion for the site came from Japanese architect Tadao Ando, and was described as being:

as close to nothing as you could possibly imagine . . . Build an earthen mound about 30 metres high . . . Make it 200 metres or so in diameter. Plant it with grass. End of story . . . Mr Ando's design is reminiscent of the ancient burial mounds near his native city of Osaka.[35]

It is also strikingly similar to that urged by a relative of one victim: 'Ground Zero is a cemetery . . . Fill it in, bury the remains of the unrecovered bodies, plant grass on it, put a marker in the middle with the names of those killed.'[36] Others wanted to use the rebuilding project solely as a means to make a political statement about America's global power: 'The terrorists wiped an American landmark off the map . . . Build the tallest buildings in the world on the site. Let the terrorists know that we can't be pushed around'.[37]

In the face of such oscillating claims and desires, the process of redevelopment was always going to be burdened with competing aims and interests. The Lower Manhattan Development Corporation (LMDC) summed up the perceived public objectives for the site:

The public has reaffirmed the need for an appropriate memorial to those killed at the World Trade Center site, renewed their call for a tall symbol or symbols in the Lower Manhattan skyline, reiterated their desire for more civic amenities and public space, and lastly, confirmed the need to improve connectivity of the World Trade Center site with the existing neighborhoods.

(Lower Manhattan Development Corporation 2003: 10)

Although the need to fill the aesthetic emptiness of the skyline (a 'call for a tall symbol or symbols') and the pragmatic desires for amenities, public space and connectivity have undoubtedly been important in the public debate on rebuilding, it is the 'need for an appropriate memorial to those killed at the World Trade Center site' that has impelled the wildly divergent architectural suggestions made. This need raises questions about law and memory, violence and aesthetics. How do we remember those who died on September 11th?[38] What form should a public memorial take? How can an image – a building, a monument – provide a space for mourning and for memory?

The very absence of the buildings acts as a constant spur to begin this process of redevelopment, it is a constant visual mnemonic of the attacks. In the buildings' place, at present, only phantoms hover.[39] But the World Trade Center's destruction also raises an aesthetic problem in the projection of a future image sufficient to deflect, accommodate, or repress the architectural ghost in the skyline. *The World Trade Center became Ground Zero.* That irrevocable transformation and antonomasia has had to be the starting point for any architectural rhetoric of rebuilding. Much of the public debate has been animated both by a clear desire to use the redevelopment as a panacea for the traumatic loss sustained on September 11th and to avoid the realization that the World Trade Center had been irrevocably lost, in a loss without return or restoration. As Goldberger suggests:

> Many of the people who wrote letters to the editor or participated in the seemingly endless round of online forums and polls about the World Trade Center site didn't actually want a final resolution. The closer a design got to becoming real, the less desirable it appeared to be. For one thing, it destroyed the fantasy that the twin towers would be put back the way they were.
>
> (Goldberger 2003: 78)

To that extent, then, the rebuilding project, and its contestation, is primarily about the *affectivity* of the site (by 'site', here I mean the lost image of the World Trade Center as it was, the abyssal image of Ground Zero as it now is, and the projection of a 'something' that could occupy the wounded physical space of the city). The heavily freighted enterprise of selecting a design for the rebuilding of the World Trade Center site has been overseen primarily by the LMDC, in cooperation with the Port Authority of New York and New Jersey.[40] Once a redevelopment design had been selected, a competition was held by the LMDC to design a memorial within the redeveloped site – a memorial artefact within a memorial building.[41] As a result of the LMDC's call for proposals for the rebuilding of the site, 406 plans were submitted. These were reduced down to nine detailed designs which were then subjected to public scrutiny and feedback as well as assessment by the LMDC.[42] Two of the nine designs were then chosen for detailed consideration.[43]

The first of these designs came from a team called THINK and led by

Rafael Viñoly, which proposed a redevelopment centred around a 'World Cultural Center'.[44] The design featured a pair of latticework towers, more than 1,600 feet high. The economy of mercantilism housed in the World Trade Center was to be replaced by the 'Towers of Culture', with 'a program of innovative cultural facilities'. Viñoly described his objective as 'not just how best to remember those who perished . . . but how to make their memory the inspiration for a better future'.[45] The towers were poised around the original 'footprints' of the North and South Towers of the World Trade Center, thus preserving them within the frame of the new buildings. The plan proposed parkland, open space, museums, and a memorial not only above ground, but placed in the sky many storeys above ground level. The public response to Viñoly's plan was extremely positive: many were impressed by the notion of two tall towers in the Manhattan skyline, and many 'supported the symbolism of bringing the memorial to the sky'.[46] On the design's public appeal, Goldberger comments:

> [The concept] evoked the image of the twin towers, but subtly, and while I suspect that the allusion to the original World Trade Center is what made this design appealing to people whose primary interest was in memorializing the events of September 11th, it was a powerful image in itself, with an extraordinary transparency that made it appear to be a tower of light.
>
> (Goldberger 2003: 81)

Indeed, the very notion of a 'tower of light' echoes the suggestions of one individual struggling to respond to the visual trauma sustained in viewing Ground Zero:

> So, what if we did build a new 110-storey tower here, or even two towers; but what if the top 30 or 40 storeys of one or both the towers were left empty, filled only with light, like a giant atrium or pair of atriums, and what if that were the memorial – a memorial in the very sky-space where the assaults occurred, and which repossessed and dignified that space forever?[47]

In contrast to the skywards lift of the memorial space in Viñoly's proposal, the other plan selected for final consideration located the memorial below ground level. Studio Daniel Libeskind proposed a design called 'Memory Foundations'. Its most significant feature involved exposing portions of the 'slurry wall' that holds back the Hudson River from the World Trade Center site. This wall had been visible to the public since the clearing and excavation of Ground Zero, and had come to symbolize the idea of the United States 'surviving' the attacks, just as the wall held back the river.

The design also proposed a massive building, with a 1,776 feet high tower and radio mast that would be the tallest building in the world, providing a sense of historical echo and appropriateness, since the World Trade Center was the tallest building in the world when it was constructed. Gardens were located high in the tower (called the 'Gardens of the World');[48] at ground level there was proposed a park (the 'Park of Heroes') featuring the names of the firefighters and rescue workers who died on September 11th; and a 'Wedge of Light' – an area of public space where, every September 11th, the sun would shine without shadow from 8.46 a.m. (the time the first tower was struck) to 10.28 a.m. (the time the second tower collapsed). A museum, cultural facilities and a new performing arts centre were also included in the design.

Libeskind's design statement was strikingly different from those accompanying the other eight proposals. For example, Viñoly's design statement declaimed, in an exhortative yet distant manner: 'The issues at stake in planning the site have a local dimension as well as global repercussions; therefore the design should address the specific condition of our city from a perspective that could also transcend its limits'.[49] Libeskind, however, began his statement thus:

> I arrived by ship to New York as a teenager, an immigrant, and like millions of others before me, my first sight was the Statue of Liberty and the amazing skyline of Manhattan. I have never forgotten that sight or what it stands for. This is what this project is all about.[50]

Instead of the cognitive process of design represented by Viñoly's claim to 'address the specific condition of our city from a perspective that could also transcend its limits', Libeskind's intentions were represented as rooted in affect:

> To acknowledge the terrible deaths which occurred on this site, while looking to the future with hope, seemed like two moments which could not be joined. I sought to find a solution . . . So, I went to look at the site, to stand within it, to see people walking around it, to feel its power and to listen to its voices. And this is what I heard, felt and saw.

His tone was intensely personal, urgent, passionate: 'We have to be able to enter this hallowed, sacred ground . . . We need to journey down, some 70 feet into Ground Zero, onto the bedrock foundation'. The memorial space is contained below ground level (in 'the deep indelible footprints of Tower One and Tower Two'), while an enormous skyscraper, with a radio mast as spire, would reach 1,776 feet high.

Libeskind's design was thus a masterpiece of equipoise. Instead of seeking to erase Ground Zero in an effort to create a new building with no memory of trauma, he *highlighted* the significance of the bedrock, the bathtub and the slurry walls – all the below-ground structural features that make up Ground Zero: 'the foundations withstood the unimaginable trauma of the destruction and stand as eloquent as the Constitution itself asserting the durability of Democracy and the value of individual life'. At the same time, Libeskind's building reached skywards away from the physical remnants of disaster:

> a skyscraper rises above its predecessors, reasserting the pre-eminence of freedom and beauty, restoring the spiritual peak to the city, creating an icon that speaks of our vitality in the face of danger and our optimism in the aftermath of tragedy.
> Life victorious.

As well as balancing the aesthetic desire for an icon in the sky with the tremulous memory of gravespace below ground, Libeskind's design similarly seemed to address the demands of both those who wanted the site left as it is or turned into a funerary garden, and those who wanted a bigger, brighter, bolder skyscraper as a nationalistic statement. Its appeal is therefore easy to understand. However, as the LMDC noted, 'although the public gravitated to this treatment of the below ground memorial experience and exposed slurry wall, some expressed a desire to approach the memorial setting both below ground and a companion memorial setting at-grade'. Libeskind revised his plan to accommodate these criticisms, providing two separate areas offering, as the LMDC put it, 'a variety of memorial experiences' (LMDC 2003: 10).[51]

Most aspects of Libeskind's proposal met with public and critical approval. The 'Gardens of the World' were seen as an admirable alternative to offices in the sky, a softer use of tower space that seemed to speak of community and sustainability rather than profit. Day writes:

> The stunning part of this design is a 40-storey 'gardens of the world', which is basically a greenhouse located between levels 70 and 110, a place people can visit, a generator of sustainable servicing and a symbol for better values, held in the New York skyline like a beacon. More importantly, it shows that architecture can be expressed beyond the use of structure, glass and metal . . . It gives reason for hope out of such a calamity.[52]

While the 'Wedge of Light' was criticized by some as 'a bit forced' (Goldberger 2003: 81), others noted that it was a common device used in many memorial settings.[53] Despite its generally favourable reception,[54] the Libeskind plan was not the one initially selected; instead, on 25 February 2003, the World Cultural Center design by Viñoly's THINK team was endorsed by the LMDC.

However, on the next day both Libeskind and Viñoly made presentations on their proposals to the Mayor of New York City, Michael Bloomberg, and the Governor of New York State, George Pataki, after which the decision to select Viñoly's design was reversed, with Libeskind's design the winner. Undoubtedly, the equipoise between the earth and sky in Libeskind's plan would have contributed to its appeal and success; however, its overall charge may well derive from its affective acknowledgment of loss and its refusal to deny the physicality of the space of Ground Zero. As Goldberger (2003: 81) put it, 'There is something fitting about going into the earth to memorialize the victims of the attacks, and leaving a portion of the Ground Zero site permanently excavated, a wound deliberately left open'.

The memorial space is directed downwards, 'into the earth', and the design's very title, 'Memory Foundations', manifests its double intentions: to provide a base (a bedrock) for memory (of the event, of the victims) and to acknowledge that memory needs to be grounded, cannot be allowed to evanesce (through time, through the supervention of other events, through the eventual deaths of witnesses and survivors).[55] And yet: the memorial architecture of this design does not only move downwards, earthwards (which would have rendered it too grave, too funerary):[56] the building stretches skywards at the same time as it embeds itself in the earth. The other designs restricted themselves to a skywards reach; by exposing the slurry wall and foundation as part of the new building's memory, Libeskind allows the ground of Ground Zero to become a space both of loss and of counter-memory to the new building that will stand above it.

This duality of movement characterized Libeskind's most famous work, the Jewish Museum in Berlin.[57] Libeskind called that design 'Between the Lines':

> it is a project about two lines of thinking, organization, and relationship. One is a straight line, but broken into many fragments; the other is a tortuous line, but continuing indefinitely. These two lines develop architecturally and programmatically through a limited but definite dialogue. They also fall apart, become disengaged, and are seen as separated. In this way, they expose a void that runs through this museum and through architecture, a discontinuous void.[58]

The Jewish Museum enacted a dialogue between two lines of flight; Libeskind's design for rebuilding the World Trade Center site enacts a productive tension between two opposing movements. And just as the Jewish Museum design 'exposes a discontinuous void', so 'Memory Foundations' has at its base a space of nothingness, a void.[59] Where the other designs attempted to deny this void, Libeskind embraced the void that is Ground *Zero* (its projected vacancy embodied in its very name) as inevitable, appropriate and necessary for the work of memory and mourning. What should be an untenable paradox (that at the foundation of memory is nothing) becomes the touchstone of memory's possibility. Libeskind's design leaves exposed the void which would ordinarily be repressed, covered over: the void 'walled up in the violent structure of the founding act' (Derrida 1992: 14).[60] It is as if he has removed the glass from the front of a mirror to reveal the silvered backing that allows a mirror to reflect an image. Instead of this silvered backing, at the site of the World Trade Center what has been left visible is the grave with its traces of the corpse and its phantoms. These phantoms are not anchored there, beneath the ground: they are mobile, itinerant; they travel around the city in motes of dust, they appear fleetingly on cinema screens and in television images. They stare out from the posters of the missing in the New York streets and from pictures of the lost in the pages of the *New York Times* and on the walls lining Ground Zero. In frozen moments awaiting the coming disaster, they are subjects forever captured by and forever eluding judgment in the image.

Image in a place of ruin

After the attacks, memorial images appeared quickly around the city. You could say that the first were the posters of the missing which lined New York streets for weeks, tacked to mailboxes and shop windows and clustered together in collages, from the moment that they were no longer seen as embodying any hope that the missing beloved could return. And then there was the graffiti. Messages were written in the dust of the pulverized buildings – on car windscreens, on store windows, on the ground: 'welcome to hell', 'you are alive', 'nuke them all', 'we are not afraid', 'God bless N.Y.' As the dust was cleaned away, graffiti continued to appear – as painted images, as stencils, as messages scrawled on the walls. A stencilled portrait of Osama bin Laden was accompanied by the words 'wanted dead not alive'. In red, white and blue the letters WTC RIP appeared on sidewalks around the city.[61] New York has always imagined itself, has always made itself into an image, and the city's responses in the aftermath of September 11th continued this practice, with memorial images flooding the city (alongside the images of nation that were furiously asserted: the flags, the stars-and-striped souvenirs, the angry tattoos burned into flesh). Messages on walls, stencils on sidewalks, the 'Portraits in Grief' printed each day in the *New York Times* – thumbnail sketches of the missing and the dead.[62]

It was six months before the city generated its first 'official' memorial image – six months constituting, as one commentator put it, 'that awkward period of in-between – in which a city felt the strong pull of commemoration'.[63] This memorial image explicitly evoked the lost buildings and appeared, temporarily, to suture the wound between the vanished past and the traumatic present. Two massive beams of light, stretching skywards as if the attacks had not occurred and yet acknowledging that the attacks, in all their dreadful devastation, did occur. The memorial was initially called 'Phantom Towers', then 'Towers of Light', and finally 'Tribute in Light'. Two artists, Paul Myoda and Julian LaVerdiere, conceived of the idea for the memorial as a direct response to their own sense of visual trauma on and after September 11th: 'they spent the day looking up at a once familiar skyline and seeing something disorientingly blank'.[64] The artists had been working on a project to install a light sculpture on top of the World Trade Center; they adapted the planned sculpture in the hope of 'refilling the void left by the twin towers with incandescence'.[65] Their aim was to create 'twin white beacons of light that would rise from lower Manhattan as a symbol of strength and resiliency: a reclamation of New York City's skyline and identity' acting as a 'tribute to rescue workers and as a mnemonic for all those who lost their lives' (Bird 2003: 94). The idea was simple: two beams of light, projected skywards, perpendicular to Ground Zero (the beams of light were generated by 88 high-powered searchlights, donated by an electricity company). The beams would both imitate and evoke the vanished towers. On the day of the six-month anniversary, the installation of the memorial was described as follows:

> Shortly before 7pm, the crowds at vantage points around Manhattan grew silent, and Valerie [a 12-year old girl whose father died on September 11] stepped forward and flicked the switch. The two beams rose slowly. At first they formed one shaft of light. Then they separated, but not completely. For a while, it looked like when you cross your fingers – they were touching at the top. Later, as the beams steadied, they formed two perfect pillars in a clear night sky.[66]

The memorial was intended as 'an ephemeral monument, occupying the hole in the skyline', which would temporarily restore the missing shapes from the skyline of Manhattan. As LaVerdiere had said, 'Those towers are like ghost limbs, we can feel them even though they're not there anymore'.[67] And yet the solace that such a monument could provide would inevitably be fleeting: because the blue shimmering towers could only be seen at night, and would only be present in the city only for a short period of time, they would be spectral evocations of the vanished towers, mere hints and memories, without substance or permanence.[68]

The spectral image of the World Trade Center: it has now become one of the most unsettled and unsettling images in contemporary culture. Films and television shows that featured scenes shot at or near the World Trade Center (or contained references to it in their scripts) were heavily edited or had their release dates delayed in the wake of September 11th.[69] Television shows based in or near New York whose title sequences featured shots of the World Trade Center have had those images removed.[70] In some ways, it is as if the image of the World Trade Center has become unbearable, a heartless joke that ignores the brutal reality of Ground Zero.[71] Yet at the same time, images of the lost World Trade Center seem to have endlessly replicated and reproduced themselves. Baudrillard notes:

> Although the two towers have disappeared, they have not been annihilated. Even in their pulverized state, they have left behind an intense awareness of their presence. No one who knew them can cease imagining them and the imprint they made on the skyline from all points of the city. Their end in material space has borne them off into a definitive imaginary space.
>
> (Baudrillard 2002: 52)

At Ground Zero itself images of the World Trade Center abound: there are display plaques featuring its design plans, site history and architectural development, and innumerable photographs of the two towers have been attached to the fences and walls around the site. There are also hundreds of websites devoted to photographs of the lost towers. Online, one can view images of the towers as aerial shots, satellite photos, shots from the Empire State Building looking south, photographs taken in the plaza looking dizzyingly upwards.[72] The image of the towers is thus both unbearable and indispensable, a constitutive touchstone of that which has been lost and that which must be restored.

And at Ground Zero itself, in the midst of all the debate and politics over the rebuilding project and the selection of a memorial, the twin imperatives of mourning and memory are being carried out, every day, all the time. Walls have been put up for the purpose of attaching photographs of lost relatives and writing memorial graffiti (messages to the dead, exhortations to survivors, exclamations of community).[73] On these walls we can read:

> We will never forget.
> RIP All.
> Standing here, looking at this, knowing it took pain 2 make a country, there is a God.
> Never forgive. Never forget.
> Support our troops.
> Fuck Bin Laden.
> Make Love, Not War.
> God Bless America, September 11 will always be remembered in history. God bless.
> Heros even greater than we will ever know. May God bless each one.
> I'm so sorry, you are in my prayers.
> God Bless America – United We Stand.
> The only way to battle unconditional hate is with unconditional love.
> The sun sets, no-one forgets, a new day begins, with a tally of wins. A small but rather significant memorial from a teen of 13.
> They can break our buildings but they can't break our harts.
> RIP Heroes.

Posted up alongside these grave(n) messages can be seen hundreds of photographs and postcards of the World Trade Center. Pasted on the grey walls that run along the edge of the gaping hole of Ground Zero, these images constitute an uncanny collage of moments frozen before disaster. Looked at as a whole, they form an unlikely tapestry of bright colours and cheerful touristic souvenirs. As individual gestures, they evidence thousands of bereavements.[74] Trembling between the past that has been lost and the site of redevelopment for a building whose shape is yet to come: each performs the twin processes of memory and counter-memory, of art in the remnants of disaster, image in the place of ruin.

Notes

1 The capture of the subject

1 Tunick's photographic installations divide into two categories. In the first, nude individuals, alone or in pairs, are often juxtaposed with striking 'man-made' artefacts or buildings (such as *Maryland*, *Iowa*, *Tennessee* and *Indiana*). The subjects in these photographs often face the camera directly and engage the lens with their eyes. In the second category, groups of massed individuals (anything from 50 to 4,000 people) are posed in ways that de-individualize them: faces hidden, eyes down, bodies combining to form a completely separate 'mass' individual (see for example *Maine*, *Nevada*, *Momentum*, *Pennsylvania*, *23rd Street and Tenth Avenue NYC 1*, *New Vienna 2*). The settings are usually ones which provide a high contrast to the undulating skin on display: particularly urban locations of concrete roads and buildings, although Tunick has recently started photographing some mass groups in more rural locations. On this recent development in his work, Tunick says:

> I felt that the city makes the bodies softer, and when you bring the body into nature, the body becomes the city, and so it becomes very artificial. When I brought the bodies into nature I thought it would be like nature-and-nature, and I wasn't comfortable with doing that. But the first time I brought the bodies into nature I felt there was something unnatural about the bodies – and in those scenes, the bodies represent the city in nature.
>
> (interview with me, Melbourne, 10 October 2001)

It should be noted that, in his most recent work, Tunick has been photographing nude bodies in nature more and more often (email correspondence with me, 25 October 2002).

2 Tunick has already been the subject of a documentary film, *Naked States* (1998, dir. Arlene Donnelly), which focused on his successful efforts to photograph someone naked in every state of the United States, and to obtain his first major gallery show. The documenting of Tunick's *nudeadrift* project became *Naked World* (2003, dir. Arlene Nelson Donnelly), shown at the Melbourne International Film Festival, August 2003 and broadcast on HBO in the United States in November 2003.

3 Tunick distinguishes himself and his work from that of other artists who have orchestrated a scene or performance. In discussing Yves Klein, whom he cites as influential on his work, he separates Klein's work (commanding the use of women's naked bodies to make marks on paper with paint, in the *Anthropometries* pieces) from '[Klein's] persona, his mystique . . . I don't have that aura around me that a Matthew Barney or a Chris Burden might have' (interview with me, Melbourne, 10 October 2001).

4 Tunick himself is very aware of the dual aspect of his aesthetic practice. He speaks of 'the performance end of it . . . capturing something else to it rather than just the portraits' (interview with me, Melbourne, 10 October 2001).

5 See, for example, Buck, L. (2001) 'German heavy-weights at D'Offay and Gagosian', *The Art Newspaper*, 12 (110): 50–1; No Author (1998) 'Spencer Tunick', *New York Times*, 16 October, Weekend, p. E38; Turner, G. T. (1998) 'Spencer Tunick at I-20', *Art in America* 86 (12): 90–1.

6 Roberts, J. (2001) 'Beauty on a strip of St Kilda Road', *The Age*, *Today*, 8 October, p. 5.

7 No Author (2001) 'Fringe awards', *The Age*, *Today*, 16 October, p. 5.

8 Shuter, J. (2001) 'The naked truth revealed much', Letter, *The Age*, 9 October, p. 18.

9 Participant quoted in Bone, P. (2001) 'When women are unequal, we all suffer', *The Age*, 13 October, p. 7.

10 On, T. (2001) 'Naked emotion', *The Age*, *Extra*, 13 October, p. 5. An assertion of certain individual or social freedoms is mentioned in the documentary film *Naked World* as a reason for posing for Tunick by models in Russia and South Africa.

11 An aspect of the completed images rarely perceived by participants at the time of posing is that they sometimes suggest apocalyptic events or disasters, as if they represent mass victimization and death. This dimension has been commented on by reviewers: see, for example, Turner, who states 'Slouched on asphalt against a hard or giddy background, [the writhing, prone figures] recall the victims of a methodical catastrophe on the order of ethnic cleansing or the Jonestown mass suicide' (1998: 91). Tunick states:

> My black and white pieces of the past were more reminiscent of a natural disaster or a disaster caused by human hands, but in my new work in colour I'm trying to work more with the body as an abstraction, to work with the body as a temporary, site-related installation, and as a performance for the participants.
>
> (interview with me, Melbourne, 10 October 2001)

12 See the comments in *Naked States* (1999, dir. Arlene Donnelly) made by, respectively, participants Tanysha, Jerome and Deborah.

13 Interview with me, Melbourne, 10 October 2001.

14 Arrest would lead to Tunick being kept for hours in a holding cell in a New York City police station: on one occasion he was held from 7 a.m. until 1 a.m. (discussed in a telephone conversation with me, 22 May 2003).

15 See Tunick's account of this arrest in Wadler, J. (1999) 'Assemble 150 nudes. Don't forget permit', *New York Times*, 30 April, Metro p. B2.

16 See No Author (1999) 'For nudity, a 1 in 100 shot', *New York Times*, 19 July, Metro p. B5.

17 Judge Guido Calabresi, quoted in Drew, C. (2000) 'Suits against city burden courts, judges say', *New York Times*, 28 March, Metro p. B4.

18 Judge Robert D. Sack, quoted in Drew, C. (2000) 'Suits against city burden courts, judges say', *New York Times*, 28 March, Metro p. B4.

19 The cases are reported as follows: *Tunick v Safir* 99 Civ. 5053 (HB); *Tunick v Safir* 209 F.3d 67; *Tunick v Safir* 94 N.Y. 2d 709, 731 N.E.2d 597, 709 N.Y.S.2d 881; *Tunick v Safir* 228 F.3d 135; *Safir v Tunick* 530 U.S. 1211. And see the accounts of the litigation in, for example, Dewan, S.K. (2000) 'Live! Nude! Legal! Artist gets his naked photograph', *New York Times*, 5 June, Metro p. B3; Lebowitz, C. (1999) 'Artist fights back', *Art in America*, 87 (11): 41; Lebowitz, C. (2000) 'Another Tunick reprieve', *Art in America*, September, p. 35; Riley, M. (2000) 'A brave nude world wins court approval', *The Age*, 6 June, p. 13; Sullivan, J. (2000) 'Court rules nude photos can be taken on the street', *New York Times*, 20 May, Metro p. B4.

20 Many thanks to Spencer Tunick for providing me with this information by telephone, 22 May 2003.

21 In interview with me, Melbourne, 10 October 2001.

22 Quoted in Riley, M. (2000) 'A brave nude world wins court approval', *The Age*, 6 June, p. 13.

23 Quoted in On, T. (2001) 'Naked emotion', *The Age*, *Extra*, 13 October, p. 5.

24 Quoted in Dewan, S. K. (2000) 'Live! Nude! Legal! Artist gets his naked photograph', *New York Times*, 5 June, Metro p. B3. The reference to 'pinkness' hints at a little remarked feature of Tunick's work, at least where the massed images are concerned: the overwhelming majority of participants appear to be white. The documentary film *Naked World* does, however, show several people of colour posing for Tunick in South Africa.

25 Quoted in Bayliss, S. (1998) 'Naked ambition', *World Art*, 18: 22–3, at p. 23.

26 Quoted in Dewan, S. K. (2000) 'Live! Nude! Legal! Artist gets his naked photograph', *New York Times*, 5 June, Metro p. B3.

27 See *R* v *Hicklin* (1868) LR 3 QB 360.

28 On the iconography of justice, see Douzinas and Nead (1999b); Goodrich (1990); Haldar (1999); Jay (1999) and the short poetic documentary film *Thick Skin* (2000, dir. Peter Rush).

29 As Douzinas and Nead note, law is 'an aesthetic practice that denies its art' and at the same time 'the power of . . . icons is celebrated in every courtroom' (1999a: 5, 9). Other texts which have investigated the repressed conjoining of law and the image include Gearey (2001); Goodrich (1990, 1995); Hachamovitch (1994); Hutchings (2001); Manderson (2000); Sarat and Kearns (1998); Sarat and Simon (2003); Sherwin (2000); J. B. White (1990); A. Young (1996, especially Chapters 1 and 5, 2000).

30 See, for example, texts such as Tiefenbrun (1998) and Merryman and Elsen (1998). The latter contains a chapter entitled 'What happens when the art world encounters the law, and vice versa?'

31 To a certain extent, this should not be surprising, as Murphy elaborates:

> For the common law tradition, phronesis and experience are the genius of being at home in the play of connectives and associations which is the metaphorical architecture of contiguity and resemblance. It is a 'science' of the mobilization of virtual orders, a realism of the 'as if'. Its 'traditional' guarantee, at its core, was based on the insinuation and contiguities lived in close proximity to the nature of things.
>
> (Murphy 1994: 91)

And, indeed, the notion that law might learn by analogy from aesthetics is in a sense nothing new. For example, Cicero describes the jurist as a painter, distinguishing the positions of objects by modifying their shapes: see Hachamovitch (1994: 43); Haldar (1999). And Quintilian writes:

> We sensibly call visualisations through which the images of absent things are represented in such a way that we seem to see them with our eyes and have them present with us. Whoever has mastered these things will be very powerful in his appeal to the emotions.
>
> (quoted in Hachamovitch 1994: 41)

32 For an exemplary reading of this fundamental tenet of legal reasoning, education and practice, see Goodrich (1994), especially pp. 113–20. The operation of resemblance and substitution is highlighted in the conceptual art of John Baldessari, one of whose works proclaims 'This Not That'.

33 Gearey begins his arguments, which take on poetry rather than art, at a similar point, one that he calls a point of disturbance: to 'sketch a more problematic and disturbing relationship [between law and aesthetics]' (2001: 1).

34 As Hachamovitch puts it, fiction underwrites truth, the image founds the legal sensibility:

> The images of judgement are forms of fealty, forms of faith in an originary experience, the originary scene of sense, of the fantasm; the original scene authenticates the image and puts into play a logic of the as-if . . . a logic which authorizes a juridical and political notion of truth whose foundation lies in fiction, in the life-world as a fiction.
>
> (Hachamovitch 1994: 44–5)

35 Dubin's perspective would make varying interpretations of an artwork the result of different spectator's different histories or constitutions. I would rather follow Bal's approach in emphasizing that differences in interpretation are a necessary condition of the image (of the image's undecidability) and the spectator's relation to it. Bal speaks of 'a process of meaning-production in which subject and object become two mobile, correlated subjectivities' (1999: 36).

2 Aesthetic vertigo: disgust and the illegitimate touchings of art

1 For varying critiques of the organizing principle of beauty in art, see Donoghue (2003); Foster (1993); Steiner (2001).

2 I do not mean to suggest that there is no value in these perspectives. On the contrary, I have benefited from reading many excellent texts within each tradition. For example, on censorship, see Childs (1997); Dubin (1992); Hoffman and Storr (1991a, 1991b); Post (1998); on freedom of speech, see Carmilly (1986); Dubin (1992); Fiss (1998); Gurstein (1996); on transgression in art, see (the highly varied accounts of) Foster (1996); Freeland (2000); hooks (1995); Julius (2003); La Placa (2003).

3 On Serrano's artworks, see, variously, Bal (1999); Carr (1993); Hagen (1991); Hess (1991); Lippard (1990); Phelan (1990); Todd (1995); Weintraub (1996).

4 On the Culture Wars, see Ault et al. (1999); Bolton (1992); Cossman (1995); Devereaux (1993); Dubin (1992); Frohnmayer (1993); the essays in Hoffman and Storr (1991a, 1991b); Marquis (1995); A. L. Morgan (1996); Post (1998); Schauer (1998); Stychin (1995); Vance (1989); Wallis (1991); Zeigler (1994).

5 In 1988 Serrano was awarded a fellowship by the Southeastern Center for Contemporary Art, one of ten artists selected from 599 applicants. He had first exhibited *Piss Christ* at the Stux Gallery in New York in 1987: initial responses to the work were favourable, with no hint of the controversy to come. Hobbs (1994: 31) describes how the wife of a minister of religion told Serrano that both she and her husband were 'very moved' by *Piss Christ*. A travelling exhibition of artwork by all ten fellowship holders displayed *Piss Christ* without any difficulties at the Los Angeles County Museum of Art and at the Carnegie-Mellon Art Gallery in Pittsburgh.

6 The line of cases is as follows: the four artists, Karen Finley, John Fleck, Holly Hughes and Tim Miller, sued the NEA in the District Court, resulting in a settlement by the NEA (*Finley et al.* v *NEA*, 795 F. Supp. 1457, CD Cal. 1992); the District Court's summary judgment in favour of the artists was affirmed in the Court of Appeals (100 F. 3d 671, CA9 1996); whereupon the Supreme Court of the United States reversed these findings in favour of the NEA (*NEA* v *Finley et al.*, judgment delivered 25 June 1998, reported at http://laws.findlaw.com/US/00097-371.html, and as *NEA* v *Finley* 522 US 991; 118 S. Ct. 554.

7 Boreham, G. (1997) 'Crucifix art image outrages State MPs', *The Age*, 29 September, p. 3.
8 Burn, G. (1997) 'The height of the morbid manner', *Guardian*, 6 September, p. T14. Hindley's police photograph has been referenced in another artwork: artist Douglas Gordon appeared in a photograph wearing a poorly fitting blonde woman's wig. The work is titled *Self-Portrait as Kurt Cobain, as Andy Warhol, as Myra Hindley, as Marilyn Monroe* (1997).
9 On Hindley's life and death, see Stanford, P. (2002) 'Moors killer Hindley dies', *Sunday Age*, 17 November, p. 18.
10 See Waugh, P. (1997) 'Outrage over Myra painting made from children's handprints', *Evening Standard*, 25 July, p. 15; and Highes, D. (1997) 'Lords boost Hindley', *Daily Mail*, 25 July, p. 2.
11 Packer, W. (1997) 'What sensation?', *Financial Times*, 20 September, p. 7.
12 From the transcript of judgement in the matter between the Most Reverend Dr George Pell, Archbishop of Melbourne and The Council of Trustees of the National Gallery of Victoria (hereafter *Pell* v *NGV*), delivered on 9 October 1997 by Harper J in the Supreme Court, p. 2. Subsequent page references to this transcript will be given in the main text.
13 Cited in Pegler, T. and Usher, R. (1997) 'Row on crucifix art heads to court', *The Age*, 8 October, p. 1.
14 The Office of Film and Literature Classification recommended restricted viewing of the catalogue. Prior to this decision, the catalogue had been on open access in bookstores. After the decision, the catalogue was seal-wrapped in plastic, bore a warning sticker and was no longer shelved openly in stores.
15 413 US 15 (1973).
16 458 US 474 (1982).
17 491 US 576 (1989).
18 The subsequent outcry was to lead to the resignation of the Corcoran's director.
19 On Mapplethorpe's seductive aesthetic, see Koch (1986); S. Morgan (1987); on the baroque, see Bal (1999).
20 See Alberge, D. (1996) 'Child charities attack gallery's explicit display', *The Times*, 9 September, p. 3; Moore, S. (1996) 'Photography and the New Censorship', *The Independent*, 12 September, p. 11. The conjunction of children, nudity and aesthetics has frequently proved legally and socially troubling. The American photographer Jock Sturges was subject to an FBI investigation into child pornography after being contacted by a photo lab processing Sturges' prints of children in nudist families: see Coleman (1993); Stanley (1991). Alice Sims, another American artist, superimposed nude photos of her one-year-old daughter over images of water lilies (the *Water Babies* series). Again, a photo lab employee contacted police, believing that the images related to child pornography. Sims was investigated, her materials confiscated and her two children taken into emergency protective custody (details in Dubin 1992: 138). Sally Mann is best known for her large haunting photographs of her three children. Their frequent nudity in the images had led to a fierce debate about the propriety of the works. For example, Gordon writes: 'we must question the ethics of an art which allows . . . the mother . . . to place them in a situation where they become the imagined sexual partner of adults . . . It is inevitable that Sally Mann's photographs arouse the sexual imagination of strangers' (1996: 145). Moore is more equivocal: 'I would defend [Mann's] right to take [the photographs] but I would not deny that there are sexual elements to the pictures . . . and, yes, I would be extremely uncomfortable if anyone other than the children's mother had taken them', in Moore, S. (1995) 'A testing time for innocence', *Guardian*, 9 November, p. 6. Solnit (1997: 39) claims that Mann's great achievement may be to 'remap the territories of the American family whose much vaunted crisis might be . . . a crisis of representation'. British

artist Graeme Ovenden (whose work includes a series entitled *Aspects of Lolita*) was arrested on charges relating to child pornography, after the Obscene Publications Squad seized materials from his home: the charges were eventually dropped. For a rather sceptical assessment of the artistic value of Ovenden's oeuvre and the surrounding controversy, see Walker (1999: 176–80). See also Higonnet (1998) for a thorough and thoughtful survey of images of children in art (including discussions of the work of Mapplethorpe and Mann). In 2001, the Crown Prosecution Service considered prosecution of the Saatchi Gallery in London, after complaints relating to its exhibition of American photographer Tierney Gearon's images of her own children, who are depicted nude or semi-nude and often masked. Proceedings were dropped since there seemed to be no realistic prospect of conviction under the Protection of Children Act 1978.

21 See comments by Serrano in interview with me, October 1997.
22 Serrano's comments that

> this aversion to piss probably has more to do with the aversion that we have to our own bodies than it actually has to do with piss – because it's very difficult to me, personally, to think of putting a value system on these fluids and saying that they're either good or bad.
>
> (quoted in Guthrie 1989: 45)

23 On interesting aspects of the place of urine and urination in art practice and art history, see Weinberg (1994).
24 On *Piss Flowers* and other works by Chadwick, see Hall (1994).
25 Rickett states: 'The women pissing could signify some sort of marking of territorial boundary, but there's a very down to earth, pragmatic sense to the work that's liberating simply because they dared to do it'. Quoted in Brittain (1997: 33).
26 Editorial (1997) 'Viewing the art of offence', *The Age*, 10 October, p. A18.
27 For example, Serrano has said: 'If I didn't indicate by the titles of the pieces [such as *Piss Christ* and *Piss Discus*] that it was piss, most people would be completely seduced by them.' Quoted in Hobbs (1994: 30).
28 For an account of the history of and euphemisms ('cripes', 'crikey', 'jeepers creepers' and so on) for 'Christ' as a swear word, see Hughes (1998: 14).
29 On the matter of blasphemous libel, Pell's suit also failed. Harper J concluded: 'There is no evidence before me of any unrest of any kind following or likely to follow the showing of the photograph in question' (p. 9), as required to establish the 'ancient misdemeanour' (p. 6).
30 All quoted comments from Haywood are taken from Naidoo, M. (1997) 'Vandal says he won't repent', *The Age*, 14 October, p. A6.
31 Archbishop Pell commented that although, of course, he could not condone violent protests, he understood the sense of outrage which had led to the acts. Quoted in Faulkner, J. (1997) 'Serrano show axed: NGV acts after hammer attack', *The Age*, 13 October, p. 1.
32 See the account in Cauchi, S. (1998) 'Man gets bond for role in art attack', *The Age*, 17 April, p. 6.
33 The term 'young British artists' has more or less passed into the contemporary lexicon, often shortened to 'YBAs'. On young British art and artists, see, for example, Collings (1997); Corris (1997); Maloney (1997); Roberts (1996); Stallabrass (2000). At the time of writing, *Myra* is exhibited in the Saatchi Gallery in London, which showcases Charles Saatchi's collection of works (including many of those in the 'Sensation' exhibition).
34 The charity director was quoted as saying: 'This is done purely for shock value and without any sensitivity to the very alive relatives of the dead children or the public in general. How sad that an artist has to resort to sick exploitation of dead children

to get noticed.' In Waugh, P. (1997) 'Outrage over Myra painting made from children's handprints', *Evening Standard*, 25 July, p. 15. The role of the media here is comparable to its production of a furore surrounding the exhibition of works by artist Jamie Wagg relating to the murder of James Bulger. See Walker (1999: 192–7).

35 Editorial (The Voice of the *Mirror*) (1997) 'Art of order', *Mirror*, 26 July, p. 6.
36 Editorial (*The Sun* Says) (1997) 'Myra Hindley is to be hung in the Royal Academy', *Sun*, 26 July, p. 2.
37 No Author (1997) 'Readers slam Myra picture by 42 to 1', *Sun*, 28 July, p. 2.
38 Hindley, M. (1997) 'Myra Hindley's portrait plea', *Guardian*, 31 July, p. 18.
39 Mouland, B. (1997) 'Invitation to an outrage', *Daily Mail*, 17 September, pp. 1–2, at p. 1.
40 Mouland, B. (1997) 'Invitation to an outrage', *Daily Mail*, 17 September, pp. 1–2, at p. 1.
41 Quoted in Mouland, B. (1997) 'Double assault on the Hindley horror', *Daily Mail*, 19 September, p. 11. In one photograph of the damaged *Myra*, it looked as though Fisher had tried to write on the image: the letters P and E were clearly visible (perhaps the start of 'PERVERT'?). See the image accompanying Hartley-Brewer, J. (1997) 'Academy defiant as damaged Hindley portrait stays on view', *Evening Standard*, 19 September, p. 6. No mention was made in any chapter of Fisher using the ink to write words or letters.
42 One of *Piss Christ*'s attackers in Melbourne also attended the show twice and thus paid its entrance fee twice.
43 For an analysis of a comparable attempt to portray representational objects as if they were the things depicted in the theatrical context, see Merck (1999).
44 See Editorial (*The Sun* Says) (1997) 'Myra Hindley is to be hung in the Royal Academy', *Sun*, 26 July, p. 2.
45 Another linguistic innuendo paralleled the anxiety over Hindley's possible release from prison. An editorial in the *Mirror*, after the two attacks of vandalism upon *Myra*, stated: '*The Hindley picture must never be put back on show. It should be put where it belongs – in the bin*' (double emphasis in original). In the Editorial (Voice of the *Mirror*) (1997) 'Sick at art', *Mirror*, 19 September, p. 6.
46 Burn, G. (1997) 'The height of the morbid manner', *Guardian*, 6 September, p. T14.
47 Quoted in Burn, G. (1997) 'The height of the morbid manner', *Guardian*, 6 September, p. T14.
48 In many ways, the furore surrounding *Myra* bespeaks a desire for an effective memorial for the victims of the Moors murderers. Chapter 6 notes the imperative, when commemorating violent crimes, of constructing a monument that refers only to the victims and not to the perpetrators. Part of *Myra*'s discomfort for the viewer is its insistence on including the perpetrator within a potentially memorial image.
49 Size also matters in Serrano's images (which are large). *Piss Christ* is 60 x 40 inches.
50 Quoted in Burn, G. (1997) 'The height of the morbid manner', *Guardian*, 6 September, p. T14.
51 See for example *Blood Patterns/Forensic Archives/Racism* (1997) by Australian artist Sally McClymont (now Jaguar Lacroix). On other artistic evocations of the crime scene, see Rugoff (1997). For a critical interpretation of the forensic aesthetic, see my comments in Chapter 5 and, especially, Scott Bray (2002).
52 See for example Waugh, P. (1997) 'Outrage over Myra painting made from children's handprints', *Evening Standard*, 25 July, p. 15.
53 One letter writer commented: 'How do you know it's urine? What if it were revealed that it's actually jasmine tea? How would that affect the way it's received?' See Laurie, J. (1997) 'Perhaps it's a hoax!', *The Age*, 9 October, p. A14. Germaine

Greer stated: 'There's nothing to say that *Piss Christ* was actually in piss . . . It was probably, you know, in Budweiser. Well, that's just piss anyway'. See Shiel, F. (1997) 'Greer shoots from the lip', *The Age*, 14 October, p. 1. Serrano stated (in an interview with me, 21 and 22 October 1997) that it is important to him that the images *are* made with the fluids (urine, blood, semen, milk) as described by the works' titles.

54 See the comments in Burn, G. (1997) 'The height of the morbid manner', *Guardian*, 6 September, p. T14.

55 Anthony Green, quoted in Reynolds, N. (1997) 'Royal Academy divided over Hindley portrait', *Daily Telegraph*, 11 September, p. 17.

56 All quoted in Vogel, C. (1999) 'Chris Ofili: British artist holds fast to his inspiration', *New York Times* online, 28 September. In a news conference, Giuliani also called the exhibit 'disgusting', claiming that it featured 'dung being thrown at the Virgin Mary', as quoted in Bashinsky, R. and Finnegan, M. (1999) 'Rudy blasts art show, but Museum's mobbed', *New York Daily News* online, 4 October.

57 Kimmelman, M. (1999) 'Of dung and its many meanings in the art world', *New York Times* online, 5 October.

58 Walsh (2000: 1) calls elephant dung Ofili's 'trademark'. Ofili himself states of the dung:

> There's something incredibly simple but incredibly basic about it . . . It attracts a multiple of meanings and interpretations . . . [The balls are] a way of raising the paintings up from the ground and giving them a feeling that they've come from the earth rather than simply being hung on a wall.
>
> > (quoted in Vogel, C. (1999) 'Chris Ofili: British artist holds fast to his inspiration', *New York Times* online, 28 September)

Ofili has also explained: 'The paintings themselves are very delicate abstractions and I wanted to bring their beauty and decorativeness together with the ugliness [of the dung] so that people can't ever really feel comfortable with it', a comment that very clearly echoes the effects of *Piss Christ* and Serrano's conceptualization of *Piss Christ*. Quoted in Kimmelman, M. (1999) 'Of dung and its many meanings in the art world', *New York Times* online, 5 October.

59 Ofili's sculpture *Shit Head* involves a piece of elephant dung mixed with resin and decorated with baby teeth and clumps of his own hair.

60 The painting was described thus: 'dung-dappled', in Birnbaum, G., Seifman, D. and Hardt, R. (1999) 'Sides seek Museum "peace"', *New York Post* online, 28 September; 'dung-stained', in Kuntzman, G., Seifman, D., Topousis, T. and Geller, A. (1999) 'Defiant Museum: the show goes on', *New York Post* online, 29 September; 'dung-smeared', in Haberman, M., Barrett, D. and Hardt, R. (1999) 'Senate pulls federal funding as City slams Saatchi "shills"', *New York Post* online, 30 September; 'festooned with elephant dung', in Kifner, J. (1999) 'Culturati view controversial art exhibit in New York', *New York Times* online, 1 October 1999. Giuliani stated: 'If they think it's important to *throw faeces at national and religious symbols* then they should pay for it themselves', in No Author (1999) 'Hillary backs Britart show that New York seeks to ban', *Guardian Weekly*, 30 September, p. 1 (emphasis added).

61 The critical reception of the artworks was somewhat cool: one critic stated that the exhibition 'isn't really exceptional among private collection shows' (in Kimmelman, M. (1999) 'In the end, the "Sensation" is less about the art than the money', *New York Times*, 3 November, p. B1) and commented that *Holy Virgin Mary* 'doesn't deserve much attention . . . Visually speaking, there's not a lot to it' (in Kimmelman, M. (1999) 'Of dung and its many meanings in the art world', *New York Times* online, 5 October).

62 The lawsuits did, however, force the museum to reveal its financial dealings with Charles Saatchi and with Christie's auction house. A morass of deals lay behind the 'Sensation' exhibition in Brooklyn: for example, a Christie's executive suggested in a memo that sponsorship of Saatchi's artworks, through the Brooklyn exhibition, might tie him into selling his artworks through the auction house. The director of the Brooklyn Museum persuaded Christie's to sponsor 'Sensation' with promises of selling some artworks through the auction house. Saatchi did indeed hold a sale of works with Christie's, and Christie's did indeed pledge a donation to the Brooklyn Museum for 'Sensation' (the largest donation for an exhibition in the United States that it had ever made). This and other behind-the-scenes dealings are set out in Barstow, D. (1999) 'Sense, sensibility and sensation', *The Age, Today*, 13 December, p. 5.

63 See the slightly differing accounts given in Witheridge, A. (1999) 'US protester pours paint on Ofili's Virgin Mary', *The Scotsman*, 18 December, p. 9 and in McFadden, R. D. (1999) 'Disputed Madonna painting in Brooklyn show is defaced', *New York Times*, 17 December, p. A1.

64 Given Giuliani's lengthy campaign against graffiti in New York City, it is supremely ironic that he should be linked, through a shared dislike of an artwork, with an individual facing 'graffiti'-related charges. Giuliani took pains to distance himself from Heiner, disavowing any suggestions that he may have inspired the attack on the painting: 'I haven't said anything [about the exhibition] for about a month or a month and a half. So that would be a real stretch'. Quoted in Feuer, A. (1999) 'Man is arraigned in defacing of painting', *New York Times*, 18 December, p. B3.

65 Quoted in McFadden, R. D. (1999) 'Disputed Madonna painting in Brooklyn show is defaced', *New York Times*, 17 December, p. A1.

66 Quoted in Santiago, R., Claffey, M. and Hutchinson, B. (1999) 'Virgin Mary canvas defaced in Brooklyn', *Daily News*, 17 December, p. 7, and in Broughton, P. D. (1999) 'Catholic defaces "Virgin"', *Daily Telegraph*, 18 December, p. 18.

67 One miniature culture war took place in Australia, in connection with a plan to exhibit 'Sensation' at the National Gallery of Australia in Canberra. 'Sensation' was scheduled to travel to Australia in June 2000; however, in late 1999, Brian Kennedy, the gallery director, announced that the exhibition had been cancelled. He gave varying reasons during the following days. These included the exhibition was too large for the gallery (an excuse which sounded fatuous); its possibly dubious sponsorship as revealed through Giuliani's suits against the Brooklyn Museum; and the input of the Australian Federal Minister for the Arts (a conservative member of a conservative government) in the wake of the 'Sensation' controversy in New York.

68 'Handle' appears in Kifner, J. (1999) 'Culturati view controversial art exhibit in New York', *New York Times* online, 1 October 1999; 'Heavey' in Kimmelman, M. (1999) 'After all that yelling, time to think', *New York Times, Weekend*, 1 October, p. B31.

69 Both the repetition of disputes and the repetition of artistic 'transgressions' are lampooned in the story by the online satirical news organ, the *Onion*, 'Some genius juxtaposing religious iconography and bodily waste yet again', at www.theonion.com, 13 October 1999. The *Onion* writes:

> The ultimate taboo was broken for the 856th time Monday when the controversial art exhibit 'Doo-Doo Messiah' opened . . . The shocking series of sculptures . . . has sparked outrage among Christian leaders, many of whom flew straight from the Brooklyn Museum of Art's 'Sensation' exhibit to begin work on protesting this latest shocking installation.

70 As exemplified in Dubin's account of seeing Serrano's artwork *Milk, Blood*

('a pleasant enough symmetrical design of one white square placed immediately next to a red square'):

> it is only with the addition of the title that you understand this is one of his early experiments with bodily fluids . . . As the grandson of a kosher butcher, my immediate reaction was 'You don't do this; you don't mix milk and meat. It *just isn't* done!' Categories which I long ago rejected intellectually, I suddenly desired to uphold emotionally; they seemed natural and inviolable. But not only had they been juxtaposed, they seemed to bleed into one another down the middle of the photo. Unthinkable, and yet here was the record of this transgression.
>
> (Dubin 1992: 5, emphasis in original)

Dubin writes further:

> While I had one reaction [to the artwork], it was not difficult to realize that, had it been another day, were I another person, or had the artist used symbols that I was more securely and immediately attached to, my reaction could just as easily have been anger or fear or contempt.
>
> (Dubin 1992: 6)

71 Kristeva (1982) calls disgusting, or 'abject', the skin that forms as warm milk cools, a wound in flesh, waste products, vomit and hypocrisy. The most thoroughly phenomenological account of disgust is provided by Miller (1998), whose 'anatomy of disgust' recounts the vicissitudes of repulsion in all its sensory fullness (covering bodily substances such as vomit, faeces, pus, things such as rotting food, bacteria and garbage, and moral states such as cowardice and evil).

72 See McAuliffe, C. (2003) 'The shock of the taboo', *The Age, Review*, 22 February, p. 5.

73 On vandalism and artworks more generally, see Cash and Ebony (1998); Cordess and Trucan (1993); Dornberg (1988); Gamboni (1997); Schama (1998); Schwartz (1998).

74 The phrase derives from Adams (1996).

3 Written on the skin of the city

1 Note that Stephen J. Powers, the other artist in the exhibition, also faced separate graffiti-related charges. In November 1999, police raided Powers' apartment, seizing artworks, art supplies, photographs and material for a book about graffiti (Powers 1999). Some of Powers' photographs included shots of Lazcano and James carrying out graffiti, and were used to authorize the arrests outside the gallery. Powers has been indicted in the State Supreme Court in Manhattan on four graffiti-related felony charges, and in the State Supreme Court in Brooklyn on two such charges. Each charge carries a maximum sentence of four years' imprisonment. Powers' tag is ESPO (standing for 'exterior surface painting outreach') and his idiosyncratic method of tagging is to paint over heavily tagged metal grates and then etch his tag into the painted surface. For a detailed discussion of Powers' case, and the arrests of James and Lazcano, see Siegal, N. (2000) 'Exhibit becomes opportunity for arrest', *New York Times*, 10 October, p. B4.

2 This might include walls, fences, train seats and windows, bus shelters and so on. In New York, police officers seized a writer's self-made videotape, showing him tagging a sleeping subway passenger's head. See Marzulli, J. (2000) 'Teen tagged in subway vandal video', *Daily News*, 15 January, 7. Chalfant and Prigoff (1987: 42) state that tagging was being carried out first in Philadelphia by Cornbread and

Top Cat, appearing in New York after the latter moved there in 1969 (although it was Taki 183 in New York who first achieved 'fame' through the practice).

3 Banksy's work was on display at the 'Turf Wars' exhibition in a warehouse in the East End of London. See Weaver, C. and Leitch, L. (2003) 'Hottest artist around', *Evening Standard*, 18 July, p. 21. Misty Bar in Melbourne in 2003 exhibited the work of local stencillers. For a representative selection of stencil art on the Internet, see www.stencilrevolution.com, www.cleansurface.org.au, www.wooster collective.com and www.banksy.co.uk/4stencil.html. On stencil art see Dawson (2003: 94–111); Hattenstone, S. (2003) 'He's always got something to spray', *Guardian Weekly*, 7–13 August, p. 18; Lucas, C. (2003) 'High art meets street art', *Melbourne Times*, 16 July, pp. 8–9; Manco (2002); Nader, C. (2003) 'Could street stencils be the artful answer to graffiti?', *The Age*, 3 November, p. 7; Norman, J. (2003) 'Graffiti goes upmarket', *The Age, Review*, 16 August, p. 7; Norman, J. (2003) 'Street art's political expression', *The Age, A3*, 3 November, p. 9.

4 British Home Secretary Jack Straw on graffiti, quoted in Bennett, C. (1996) 'Why the writing's on the wall for graf art', *Guardian*, 3 July, p. 15.

5 For the purposes of this chapter, I will be examining mainly examples taken from newspapers in Australia, the United Kingdom and New York City.

6 In Adams, P. (1997) 'Painted into a corner', *The Weekend Australian, Features*, 8–9 February, p. 2.

7 Adams, P. (1997) 'Painted into a corner', *The Weekend Australian, Features*, 8–9 February, p. 2.

8 Haberman, C. (1999) 'New vandals scratching up the subways', *New York Times*, 26 January, p. B1.

9 No Author (2000) 'Down the line', *The Age*, Today, 19 May, pp. 1, 3, at p. 3.

10 Hunder, E. (1997) 'Local knowledge', *The City Weekly*, 1(39): 3.

11 Nancarrow, K. (1996) 'Graffiti gets sprayed, then wiped', *Sunday Age*, 1 September, News, p. 9.

12 Adams, P. (1997) 'Painted into a corner', *The Weekend Australian, Features*, 8–9 February, p. 2.

13 Bennett, C. (1996) 'Why the writing's on the wall for graf art', *Guardian*, 3 July, p. 15.

14 Note that municipal removal strategies run parallel to criminal justice interventions, which often require apprehended writers to clean off their own or other writers' graffiti as part of a formal or informal punishment.

15 Haberman, C. (1999) 'New vandals scratching up the subways', *New York Times*, 26 January, p. B1.

16 Adams, P. (1997) 'Painted into a corner', *The Weekend Australian, Features*, 8–9 February, p. 2.

17 Johnston, C. (2000) 'Last train', *The Age*, 17 July, Today, pp. 1, 3, at p. 3.

18 Miller, E. (1995) 'Jail for train spray vandals', *Herald Sun*, 4 October, p. 3.

19 Das, S. (2000) 'Harry Connex's trains hit the button for safety', *The Age*, 25 July, p. 5.

20 Das, P. (2000) 'Tram cameras to boost security', *The Age*, 14 July, p. 5.

21 Adams, P. (1997) 'Painted into a corner', *The Weekend Australian, Features*, 8–9 February, p. 2. That 'Jackson Pollock'd' suggests a condemnatory rhyming slang is not, I would contend, coincidental.

22 See for example the views of this police officer: 'It is all criminal damage . . . and is no different from slashing seats or breaking windows and offenders are prosecuted accordingly'; 'It may be artistic but if it costs somebody money to remove it, it is vandalism'. Quoted in Sill (2000: 144–5).

23 Damage to property such as breaking windows or slashing train seats is not the concern of this chapter. On vandalism, see Geason and Wilson (1990); Levy-Leboyer (1984); Vernon and McKillop (1989).

24 In the Australian context, graffiti is classified as damage to property and a range of statutory provisions in the various States covers most aspects of the activity. For example, the South Australian Summary Offences Act 1953 s.48 sets out the offences of 'posting bills and marking graffiti': with 'marking graffiti' defined as 'defac[ing] property in any way' and 'property' defined to cover 'a building, structure, road, paved surface or object of any kind' (s.48(5)). Specific legislation exists to deal with graffiti on public transport. In Victoria, for example, the Transport Act 1983 s.223B(1) prohibits injuring, damaging or defacing property of the Public Transport Corporation, or adjacent property, by marking graffiti (with a possible punishment of up to six months' imprisonment). Being found on Public Transport Corporation property in possession of a 'graffiti implement' 'with the intention of using it for the purpose of marking graffiti' is also an offence (s.223B(4)). Marking graffiti is defined as 'writing, painting, spray-painting . . . scratching or burning' (s.223A(1)). Thus the Act aims to criminalize graffiti, written in any manner and with any possible implement, at or on trains, buses, bus shelters, train stations, and also on the property abutting the train lines or stations. In the United Kingdom, graffiti is classified as criminal damage, and is one of the activities categorized as 'anti-social behaviour' in a recent government initiative. Graffiti writers can now be subject to an 'Anti-Social Behaviour Order'. For an earlier instance in which persistent graffiti writing on trains resulted in a custodial sentence for a young offender, see *R* v *Hurren* (1989) 90 Cr App R 60. New York City is often cited as the most famous example of the criminalization of graffiti writing: in the 1990s Mayor Giuliani classified graffiti as a 'quality of life offence', a notion which has much in common with the British definition of graffiti as 'anti-social behaviour'.

25 Both 'graffiti vandals' and 'graffiti vandalism' are used in Weir, S. (1998) 'Tiny camera pinpoints vandals', *Adelaide Advertiser*, 2 July, p. 11.

26 Lerner, J. (2000) 'When is graffiti art? Never', *The Age*, 11 August, p. 14.

27 Sabini, J. D. (1999) 'Graffiti as vandalism: "quality of life" is no cliché', *New York Times*, 12 September, p. 17.

28 In Hammond, G. (2000) 'Train wrecker web braggarts', *Herald Sun*, 6 August, p. 11.

29 Haberman, C. (1999) 'New vandals scratching up the subways', *New York Times*, 26 January, p. B1.

30 As Todd notes:

> To many people at the time the news of the fall of Rome to the northern invader seems to herald the end of the world, or at least the end of their world, and later generations up to the present have taken the same view. In actuality, the capture of Rome was a relatively minor event in the political and military fields of Romano-Germanic relations. But its psychological impact was tremendous.
>
> (Todd 1972: 20)

31 For example, see the deployment of this notion in the realm of the corporate leveraged buyout (Burrough and Helyar 1990) and its more poetic elaboration in Coetzee (2003).

32 Hammond, G. (2000) 'Train wrecker web braggarts', *Herald Sun*, 6 August, p. 11.

33 Adams, P. (1997) 'Painted into a corner', *The Weekend Australian*, Features, 8–9 February, p. 2.

34 Schofield, L. (1998) 'My week', *The Age*, News Extra, p. 10.

35 In Das, S. (2000) 'Art attack', *The Age*, 7 August, p. 13.

36 Heinrichs, P. (2000) 'How to stop teenage alienation', *Sunday Age*, 14 May, pp. 10–11, at p. 11.

37 Chivers, C. J. (2000) 'Graffiti leads police to 2 boys, who are charged with arson at a school', *New York Times*, 15 March, p. B3.

38 Wilmoth, P. (1997) 'Our heroin children', *Sunday Age*, 18 May, pp. 10–11, at p. 11.

39 Das, S. (2000) 'Harry Connex's trains hit the button for safety', *The Age*, 25 July, p. 5.

40 Adams, P. (1997) 'Painted into a corner', *The Weekend Australian*, Features, 8–9 February, p. 2.

41 Castleman (1982: 91–2) points out that graffiti writers in New York City, because of their interest in writing their name on a wide scale, were rarely satisfied with the limitations imposed on writing by gang membership, which restricts graffiti to the declaration of territorial limits.

42 For a detailed ethnographic study of graffiti culture in the gangs of Los Angeles, see Phillips (1999).

43 Quoted in Bennett, C. (1996) 'Why the writing's on the wall for graf art', *Guardian*, 3 July, p. 15. Graffiti in Britain is now considered 'anti-social behaviour', along with abusive language, excessive noise, littering, drunken behaviour and drug dealing. See the Home Office publication 'A Guide to Anti-Social Behaviour Orders and Acceptable Behaviour Contracts' (2002).

44 For example, in New York City, in a speech given on 11 July 1995, the then Mayor Giuliani asserted:

> Some commentators would have us believe that graffiti is art. It is not. Graffiti is vandalism. Where graffiti flourishes, communities suffer. Graffiti intimidates residents. It encourages street gangs. It discourages tourists, lowers property values and invites other kinds of crime. Graffiti painted New York City into a corner, but we don't have to stay there.

To that end, the Office of the Mayor of New York City justified its strict stance on graffiti by citing the 'Broken Windows' theory, popular in criminology since the early 1990s:

> the 'Broken Windows' theory – that unaddressed disorder is a sign that no one cares and actually invites further disorder – has been a cornerstone of the Mayor's governing and crimefighting strategies . . . [O]n July 11 1995, Mayor Giuliani . . . [established] the Mayor's Anti-Graffiti Task Force as a vital part of the Administration's effort to improve the quality of life for New Yorkers.

Graffiti in New York City was, from then on, known as a 'quality of life' crime. See the press release at www.ci.nyc.us/html/nograffiti/html/aboutforce.html.

45 Quoted in Donald, A. (2000) 'Writing is on the wall for vandals', *The Herald*, 25 March, p. 14.

46 Adams, P. (1997) 'Painted into a corner', *The Weekend Australian*, Features, 8–9 February, p. 2.

47 Schofield, L. (1998) 'My week', *The Age*, News Extra, p. 10.

48 Haberman, C. (1999) 'New vandals scratching up the subways', *New York Times*, 26 January, p. B1.

49 Writer X, in interview with me, July 2000.

50 Much of this section derives from interviews conducted by me with graffiti writers, from 1999 to 2003, as part of a research project, funded by the Australian Research Council, on the experience of graffiti, its representation in media discourse, and its socio-legal regulation. My thanks to all the writers who participated in interviews with me.

51 Comments made on WataRush website on 19 May 2000, at http://watarush.cjb.net/.

52 Writer quoted in Das, S. (2000) 'Art attack', *The Age*, 7 August, p. 13.
53 One news article on the problem of retaining young people above the age of 16 in school was illustrated by a photograph showing two teenaged boys sitting on a wall, with two frowning girls in the foreground. A graffiti piece and a number of tags are written on the wall. At first glance it readily appears as though the image is linking school drop-outs with graffiti. Close inspection reveals that the piece and tags actually read 'Laverton Secondary College': the graffiti is clearly sanctioned by the school. The effect of the photograph, however, is to link drop-outs with graffiti. See Jones, C. (2000) 'Inquiry to look at rise in drop-outs' and Viljoen, S. (2000) 'Plan keeps pupils keen and in school', both in *The Age*, 14 January, p. 7.
54 D says:

> Everybody loved *Beat Street*. The good thing about it was like they had everything, they had like graffiti by Brim, who was like an old school master from New York, they had the New York City Breakers in it, they had um the Furious Five and Afrika Bombaata, who were like hip hop pioneers.

55 A useful survey of stylistic variations in the 1980s can be found in Chalfant and Prigoff (1987); Cooper and Chalfant (1984).
56 Another writer also emphasized the aesthetic dimensions of graffiti: 'all the aspects of good art go into graffiti: use of colour, shading, shape, positioning, perspective etc., most graffiti artists are extremely good artists'. Comments posted on 18 May 2000, on the WataRush website at http://watarush.cjb.net/.
57 The DSG, or District Support Group, is a community relations group within the Victoria Police.
58 It is certainly hard to imagine the phrase as a self-naming device in the way that the hip hop writer's tag is. It is also interesting to imagine whether any passer-by would read the phrase and feel named by it (it seems more likely that most passers-by would imagine the phrase as applying to someone else).
59 Quoted in Nader, C. (2003) 'Could street stencils be the artful answer to graffiti?', *The Age*, 3 November, p. 7.
60 In interview with me, 17 December 2001.
61 Both quoted in Norman, J. (2003) 'Street art's political expression', *The Age*, A3, 3 November, p. 9.
62 In interview with me, 19 June 2003.
63 This view was shared by another writer, who stated: 'I think a lot of people in the community just see graff for its destructive value and don't actually consider how much time and effort went into it'. Comments posted on 18 May 2000, on the WataRush website at http://watarush.cjb.net/.
64 See Chalfant and Prigoff (1987); Collins (1995: 2–3); Lachmann (1988).
65 As documented in Cooper and Chalfant (1984: 38). 'Stuck – no cap!' is an apology I spotted on a train-line fence in Queens, New York, September 2000.
66 See also the recent practice of using pieces to memorialize victims of street violence in New York City, documented in Sciorra and Cooper (2002), while memorial graffiti is becoming increasingly common in cities such as Melbourne, Sydney and London. For example, see the graffiti by relatives of the dead memorializing sites in the centre of Melbourne where drug users fatally overdosed. One legal graffiti site in Sydney, at Bondi Beach, features piece after piece commemorating the lives of deceased graffiti writers. And it must be remembered that memorial graffiti has been prominent in New York after the attacks of 11 September 2001, with dedicated graffiti walls provided at the viewing sites for Ground Zero (see further my discussion in Chapter 6).
67 Writers of political slogans are usually not interested in declaring their names, real or assumed. Exceptions to this include grr, who tagged the crew name on all

their slogans, and the prolific Melbourne sloganist known as 'Shut Up and Shop', whose favoured topics included mass consumption, Third World Debt, Aboriginal politics and state-organized violence.

68 Quoted in Siegal, N. (1999) 'From the subways to the streets', *New York Times*, 22 August, *New York Report*, p. 1.

69 Among New York City writers, for example, Peo, also wrote Cisco; Movin 2 also tagged TI 149. Of the writers interviewed in Melbourne, D had more than one tag.

70 Writers will sometimes tag their crew name, rather than their own. In New York City, famed crews include The Fantastic Partners, the Death Squad and The Fabulous Five. The initials of a crew may be understood by its members and other writers to refer to more than one thing: thus 'CWN' means both 'Cops' Worst Nightmare' and 'Communities' Worst Nightmare'. Crews, just as individual writers, may have more than one tag: a large and celebrated Melbourne crew is known both as 'WCA' (Wild Child Artists) and 'DMA' (Da Mad Artists), while another crew uses both 'CW' (Crime Wave) and 'STR' (Stands To Reason).

71 For a discussion of masculinity in graffiti culture, see Macdonald (2001).

72 Writer Iz the Wiz quoted in Austin (1996: 274–5).

73 Teenaged boys' experiences of appearing to be figures of risk are related in Guilliatt, R. (1997) 'Hey you . . . boy!', *Good Weekend*, 22 November, pp. 16–20. In this article, the journalist relates an encounter between a group of boys sitting in a public park in Hurstville (a suburb of Sydney) and a police officer, who moves them out of the park, saying 'Well as far as I'm concerned, if you're hanging around this park you're either dealing drugs or doing graffiti, right?', while the boys respond: 'This is a park, isn't it? . . . Aren't we the public, too?' (p. 16). On young people's negotiation of public space, see also White (1999).

74 The phrase 'official graffiti of the everyday' belongs to Hermer and Hunt (1996); the term 'corporate tagging' was created by Mark Halsey, see Halsey and Young (2002); the expression 'sign wars' is taken from Goldman and Papson (1996). On the depth of advertising's penetration into the urban sphere, see Meyer's account of the colonization by advertisers of any available space, such as the handles of petrol pumps, the backs of cocktail napkins, the reverse side of supermarket and road toll receipts: in Meyer, C. E. (2000) 'It's becoming a mad ad world', *Guardian Weekly*, 1–7 June, p. 35.

75 As discussed in Duerksen and Goebel (1999).

76 Thus '[sandwich boards] have been criticized as unsightly, ugly and dangerous – and now they are set to be banned from some city streets . . . The movable A-frame advertising boards have been criticized for cluttering streets and creating hazards for pedestrians'. In Michelmore, K. (1997) 'Waiting for a sign', *Adelaide Advertiser*, 3 November, p. 31.

77 Cited in Adams, D. (2000) 'Signs of the times for a city', *The Age*, 17 June, p. 6.

78 See Hughes, G. (1998) 'Plan change allows giant signs to stay', *The Age*, 25 June, p. 7.

4 Disappearing images and the laws of appearance

1 For other evocations of ethical or compassionate judgment, see Glass (1997); Goodrich (1990).

2 *Green* v *R* (1997) 148 ALR 659 (High Court of Australia) (hereafter *Green*). Judgments for the majority are given by Brennan CJ, McHugh and Toohey JJ; judgments for the minority are given by Gummow and Kirby JJ.

3 See Australian cases such as *R* v *Pritchard* (1990) A Crim R 67; *R* v *Stiles* (1990) 50 A Crim R 13; *R* v *Grmusa* (1990) 50 A Crim R 358; *R* v *Preston* (1992) 58 A Crim R 328; *R* v *Whittaker* (1993) A Crim R 476. The homosexual advance defence has received much attention, judicial and academic, in Anglo-American jurisdictions:

for example, see Howe (1997, 1999); Johnston (1996); Lunny (2003); Mison (1992); Moran (1996). An attempt to establish the homosexual advance defence was made in the trial of Aaron McKinney, one of the two men charged with killing Matthew Shepard in Laramie, Wyoming, in 1998. The trial judge ruled that any evidence as to an alleged homosexual advance could not be led, because it would point towards the defenses of diminished capacity or temporary insanity, neither of which are available in Wyoming law. See the discussions of the case in Ellison, M. (1999) 'Roofer beat gay student to death', *Guardian*, 4 November, p. 21; Estrich, S. (1999) '"Homophobia" defense rests', *Denver Post*, 6 November, p. B7.

4 For example, between 1993 and 1995 in New South Wales, thirteen murder trials saw the homosexual advance defence invoked. Of those trials, two resulted in acquittals; two in jury verdicts of murder; three in verdicts of not guilty of murder by guilty of manslaughter; eight resulted in pleas being accepted to a lesser charge such as manslaughter; and one case was dismissed. See Attorney-General's Department (New South Wales) (1996: 10). Successful attempts to enter evidence about a homosexual advance can be seen in the following cases. For example, one accused said an elderly man invited him for a drink in his house; he accepted. The old man grabbed his buttocks and made an indistinct comment. The accused beat him with a garden gnome, then stabbed him to death. He was found guilty of manslaughter rather than murder and received a three-year sentence of imprisonment. In another case, the defendant, while riding his bike along a cycle path, saw a man in a dress waving his penis and shouting at him. The defendant beat the man to death. He was found not guilty of murder and guilty of manslaughter, as discussed in Marr (1999).

5 57 F. Supp. 2d 1151.

6 171 F. 3d 270.

7 2000 Colo. J. C.A.R. 6455.

8 Discussed in Ellison, M. (1999) 'Roofer beat gay student to death', *Guardian*, 4 November, p. 21.

9 All page numbers in the main text refer to citations from the High Court of Australia's judgement.

10 In respect of the homosexual advance, the prosecution did not concede that there had been such an advance. At most, there had been amorous or sexual touching by Gillies which the accused could easily have rebuffed. As Kirby J remarked in his dissent in the High Court,

> if every woman who was the subject of a 'gentle', 'non-aggressive' although persistent sexual advance . . . could respond with brutal violence rising to an intention to kill or inflict grievous bodily harm on the male importuning her, and then claim provocation after a homicide, the law of provocation would be sorely tested and undesirably extended. (p. 719)

11 Application for special leave to appeal to the High Court of Australia, transcript of oral argument, *Malcom Thomas Green* v *The Queen*, unreported, per defence counsel and Gummow J, p. 9. Transcript on file with author.

12 Application for special leave to appeal to the High Court of Australia, transcript of oral argument, unreported, p. 30.

13 McHugh J (p. 683) also described Gillies as 'a person whom the accused looked up to and trusted'. In the Court of Criminal Appeal, Smart J commented on 'the deceased's betrayal of the relationship of trust, dependency, friendship and the abuse of his hospitality' (quoted in Kirby's judgment, p. 704). In applying for special leave to appeal to the High Court, defence counsel contended during oral argument:

> He said . . . there were flashes of his father over his two sisters, at the time he lost self-control, that he kept hitting him because he felt trapped. The evidence . . . would establish a clear connection between his relationship with the deceased as a father figure and his own sense of betrayal in relation to his relationship with his father.

In application for special leave to appeal to the High Court, p. 2.

14 In contrast, see the provocation cases *R* v *Moffa* (1977) 13 ALR 225 (High Court of Australia) and *R* v *Tuncay* [1998] 2 VR 19 which emphasize that words must be of a violent or extreme character in order to be provocative.

15 See, for example, the comments of Smart J in the Court of Criminal Appeal, where he states: 'Some ordinary men would feel great revulsion at the homosexual advances being persisted with in the circumstances . . . They would regard it as a serious and gross violation of their body and their person'. Quoted in the judgment of Brennan CJ in *Green* (p. 665).

16 On phantasy and the structure of attachment more generally, see Laplanche and Pontalis (1986).

17 *Benjamin Bruce Andrew and Peter Clive Kane* [1999] NSWSC 647, unreported, Supreme Court of New South Wales, 2 July 1999. Internet version held by Australian Legal Information Institute (Austlii) at www.austlii.edu.au/. All subsequent page numbers refer to the Internet version and are given in parentheses in the main text.

18 See also Sully J's comments at p. 14.

19 This echoes the comments of Smart J in the Court of Criminal Appeal in *Green*, when he describes the 'great revulsion' that 'some ordinary men' would feel at a homosexual advance: quoted by Brennan CJ, *Green* (p. 665).

20 *X* v *Department of Defence* [1995] HREOCA 16, unreported, Human Rights and Equal Opportunity Commission of Australia, 29 June 1995; *Commonwealth of Australia* v *Human Rights and Equal Opportunity Commission (HREOC)* (1996) 70 FCR 76, Federal Court, Cooper J; *Commonwealth of Australia* v *HREOC and Another* (1998) 76 FCR 513; and Internet version at [1998] 3 FCA 1 (13 January 1998); *X* v *The Commonwealth of Australia* [1999] HCA 63, unreported, High Court of Australia, 2 December 1999. All page numbers cited in notes and in the main text refer to Internet versions of the decisions available at www.austlii.edu.au/ and on file with author.

21 Clause 12 of their Service Policy states:

> Applicants are to be informed, before entry, that such testing will take place . . . and they are to be given the option to refuse and to withdraw their application. As with newly inducted entrants in whom other potentially serious diseases have been detected, personnel with HIV infection are to be discharged.
>
> (cited in *X* v *Department of Defence*, p. 5)

22 *X* v *Department of Defence*, p. 8.

23 *X* v *The Commonwealth*, p. 6.

24 The majority of the High Court found in favour of the Army, sending the case back to the Commission for further adjudication by a different Commissioner. Compare *Green*: in the judgment of the High Court, as also in the argument of defence counsel, the phantasy of paternal abuse is characterized as giving rise to a 'special sensitivity to a history of violence and sexual assault within his family': *Green*, per McHugh J, p. 682.

25 Further on blood, see McVeigh et al. (2001).

26 *X* v *Department of Defence*, p. 6

27 *X* v *Department of Defence*, p. 8. These calculations of risk are strikingly vague in comparison with the usual epidemiological calibrations which occur in other cases concerning the possibility of HIV transmission, such as *Mutemeri* v *Cheesman* (1998) 100 A Crim R 397; and *Hall* v *Victorian Amateur Football Association* (1998), unreported, Administrative Appeals Tribunal of Victoria (Internet version available at www.austlii.edu.au/ and on file with author). On the calibration of risk in relation to HIV transmission, see Grimwade (1998); Lupton (1994); Neveldine (1998); Waldby (1996). On risk more generally, see Beck (1992); Giddens (1999).

28 *X* v *Department of Defence*, p. 8.

29 *X* v *The Commonwealth*, p. 36.

30 *Commonwealth of Australia* v *HREOC and Another*, pp. 5–6 (emphasis in original).

31 Note that an impassioned dissent is provided in the High Court (*X* v *The Commonwealth*) by Kirby J (who also dissented in *Green*, and who is the only 'out' gay man on the High Court Bench). He states:

> It would be as well . . . if the courts were to avoid the preconceptions that lie hidden, and not so hidden, in tales of . . . soldiers wallowing in blood (however vivid may be the poetic image), or in descriptions of regimental life and soldierly duty in the heyday of the British Empire (however evocative may be the memories). (p. 34)

He also notes the persistent difficulty of obtaining legal recognition of discrimination and victimization:

> the field of anti-discrimination law is littered with the wounded who appear to present the problem of discrimination which the law was designed to prevent and redress but who, following closer judicial analysis of the legislation, fail to hold on to the relief originally granted to them. (p. 24)

32 On Gonzalez-Torres' work generally, see Amor (1995); Avgikos (1991); Demos (1995); Princenthal (1994); Spector (1995); Storr (1996); Watney (1994).

33 See, for example, the work which lists: 'People with AIDS Coalition 1985 Police Harassment 1969 Oscar Wilde 1895 Supreme Court 1986 Harvey Milk 1977 March on Washington 1987 Stonewall Rebellion 1969'. In another work, the list reads: 'Red Canoe 1987 Paris 1985 Blue Flowers 1984 Harry the Dog 1983 Blue Lake 1986 Interferon 1989 Ross 1983'. Finally, a third list cites: 'Alabama 1964 Safer Sex 1985 Disco Donuts 1979 Cardinal O'Connor 1987 Klaus Barbie 1944 Napalm 1972 Bitberg Cemetery 1985 Walkman 1979 Capetown 1985 Waterproof Mascara 1971 Computer 1981'. Reproductions of these and other works by Gonzalez-Torres discussed in this chapter can be found in the comprehensive accompaniment to his 1995 Guggenheim retrospective, published as Spector (1995).

34 See, for example, *'Untitled' (The New Plan)*, a photograph of undulating denim displayed in one location; *'Untitled' (For Jeff)*, a photograph of a man's hand, displayed in thirty locations; *'Untitled' (Strange Bird)*, a photograph of distant birds against a cloudy sky, displayed in twenty locations; and *'Untitled'*, a photograph of a rumpled bed, with the imprints of two heads still visible on the pillows, displayed in twenty four locations.

35 See, for example, *'Untitled' (Ross and Harry)*; *'Untitled' (Lover's Letter)*; *'Untitled' (Klaus Barbie as a Family Man)* and *'Untitled' (Waldheim to the Pope)*.

36 See *'Untitled' (Portrait of Dad)*, 175 pounds of white candies piled into a corner; *'Untitled' (USA Today)*, a corner pile of red, white and blue candies; *'Untitled'*

(Welcome Back Heroes), hundreds of Bazooka bubble-gum chews spread across the floor.
37 See, for example, *'Untitled' (NRA)*, a stack of sheets of red paper edged in black; *'Untitled'*, two stacks placed side by side: each sheet in one stack reads 'Somewhere better than this place', while each sheet in the other stack reads 'Nowhere better than this place'; and *'Untitled' (Death by Gun)*, which reproduces on each of its sheets the names, ages and faces of the 464 people who were killed by gunshot wounds in the United States in a one-week period.
38 For examples of drapes using light bulbs, see *'Untitled' (March 5th)* and *'Untitled' (Ischia);* for drapes using beads, see *'Untitled' (Chemo)* and *'Untitled' (Blood);* for fabric drapes, see the various versions of *'Untitled' (Lover Boy)*.
39 The full text of the billboard reads: 'HEALTH CARE IS A RIGHT. A government by the people, for the people, must provide adequate health care to the people. NO EXCUSES.' The billboard was simultaneously displayed in ten locations around New York City.
40 Gonzalez-Torres states: 'Around 1989 everyone was fighting for wall space. So the floor space was free, the floor space was marginal' (in Rollins 1993: 13). Note that another version of *Lover Boy* drapes sheer blue fabric as curtains, perhaps because the window space in galleries is also marginal. In his placement of the art object within the gallery, then, Gonzalez-Torres metaphorizes the marginality awarded to the gay man, the racial other, the HIV positive person.
41 Gonzalez-Torres said: 'I wanted people to have my work. The fact that someone could just come in and take my work and carry it with them was very exciting' (in Rollins 1993: 13).
42 Note that, for the artist, the colour evokes the erotic relation: 'Ross and I would spend summers next to a body of blue water or under clear, Canadian skies' (in Rollins 1993: 17).
43 For similarly evanescent artworks evoking the loss of friends to AIDS, see the blurred and indistinct photographs of Bill Jacobson, reproduced in Jacobson (1998) and discussed in Aukeman (1995); see also *'Untitled' (Hujar Dead)* by David Wojnarowicz (reproduced in Scholder 1999: 60).
44 *Blue* (1993, dir. Derek Jarman), Basilisk Communications. See also Jarman, *Chroma* (1995a [1988]). The chapter 'Into the Blue' represents the text of the film *Blue*. Subsequent quotations of lines from the film are from *Chroma* and are given in parentheses in the main text. The film's image is motivated by Jarman's admiration of Yves Klein, of whom Jarman writes: 'The great master of blue – the French painter Yves Klein. No other painter is commanded by blue' (1995a: 104). On the film, see Lombardo (1994); Schwenger (1996); Smith (1993).
45 Jarman says, variously: 'Lost in the warmth / Of the blue heat haze' (p. 108); 'Kiss me again / Kiss me / Kiss me again / And again / Never enough / Greedy lips / Speedwell eyes / Blue skies' (p. 118); 'The smell of him / Dead good looking / In beauty's summer / His blue jeans / Around his ankles / Bliss in my ghostly eye' (p. 124); 'Dance in the beams of emerald lasers . . . What a time that was' (p. 116).
46 On AIDS activism, Jarman states: 'I shall not win the battle against the virus – in spite of the slogans like 'Living with AIDS'. The virus was appropriated by the well – so we have to live with AIDS while they spread the quilt for the moths of Ithaca across the wine dark sea' (p. 110). Jarman's ambivalence about the AIDS Quilt (also known as the Names Project) is also expressed elsewhere: 'When the AIDS quilt came to Edinburgh during the film festival I attended out of duty. I could see it was an emotional work, it got the heartstrings. But . . . I shall haunt anyone who ever makes a quilt panel for me' (1995b: 91). Of drug trials, he says in *Blue*:

Oral DHPG is consumed by the liver, so they have tweaked a molecule to fool the system. What risk is there? If I had to live forty years blind I might think twice . . . The pills are the most difficult . . . I'm taking about thirty a day, a walking chemical laboratory. (p. 120)

47 Of lost friends, he laments 'The virus rages fierce. I have no friends now who are not dead or dying. Like a blue frost it caught them' (p. 109).
48 Note also the artwork of John Dugdale, photographer, who is also losing his sight to AIDS. His blue-washed images are now made with the help of assistants, and can be seen in Dugdale (1995).
49 To that extent, *Blue* has a perfectly circular, or perhaps spiralling, structure. The opening lines of *Blue* evoke an awakening to vision: 'You say to the boy open your eyes / When he opens his eyes and sees the light / You make him cry out. Saying / O Blue come forth / O Blue arise / O Blue ascend / O Blue come in' and mark 'blue' as the space of subjectivity and relationality: 'Blue of my heart / Blue of my dreams / Slow blue love / Of delphinium days' (pp. 107, 108). In *Blue*'s closing lines, having moved through details of illness, treatment and decline, Jarman rewrites 'blue' as the space of subjectivity, relationality *and death*: 'I place a delphinium, Blue, upon your grave' (p. 124).
50 Text from the artwork *'Untitled'* (1992) by David Wojnarowicz.
51 See the account in Peake (1999), especially in Chapter 27, and in Parkes (1996: 137).
52 See also the discussion of visibility, nationality and queer politics in the 'cinema of AIDS' (including Jarman's *Blue*) in Smith (1993).
53 As Neveldine writes,

> [O]nly an accumulation, an overaccumulation, of representations will make AIDS, and the bodies of persons with AIDS, radically *visible* and therefore *viable*: granted life, authorized to be written and read, allowed to mingle, or condemned to wither away, or condemned *for* withering away.
> (Neveldine 1998: 150, emphasis in original)

Further on the metaphorization of HIV/AIDS, and its consequences, see, variously, Sontag (1991); Waldby (1996); Watney (1989); A. Young (1996).
54 The Aristotelian account of the will to knowledge as a desire to see constructs the juridical moment of metaphysics as the pronunciation of judgments on the correctness of the world. Minkinnen notes the aporetic and agonizing nature of this will or desire when remarking that

> Justice constitutes the desired object (*to orekton*) of a 'first philosophy' of law, but in the judgments of correctness that a mortal man is capable of, such justice is forever delayed./ For the ownmost essence of things, that is, justice in itself, or the future that will come to be, is a matter fit only for infinite gods.
> (Minkinnen 1999: 47)

5 The art of injury and the ethics of witnessing

1 For a detailed and sophisticated reading of the forensic turn in art criticism and practice, see Scott Bray (2002).
2 For an interesting reading of *Evidence* from a legal perspective, see Friedman (1995).
3 Quoted in Herman, J. (1988) 'Burden takes art form from crucifixion to re-creation', *Los Angeles Times*, 26 April, p. 9.
4 Quoted in Lewinson, D. (1987) 'He risks his life for art – literally', *San Diego Union-Tribune*, 23 April, p. C2.

5 Quoted in Harrington, R. (1982) 'Portrait of the artist as a young snake: the loose reins of Chris Burden's imagination', *Washington Post*, 27 March, p. C1.
6 See the discussion in McEvilley (1995).
7 Rugoff comments:

> Besides testifying to a feat of endurance, these ghostly artefacts were posed as polemical evidence that a certain conception of art and of the artist's role had been knocked off its pedestal. As the trace of a physical action, Burden's piece harked back directly to Pollock, yet the chalk outline . . . added an ominous note. It seemed to imply that once the art object was linked to the artist's prior physical process, it became inextricably tangled with his mortality and so was banished from the timeless platform of traditional art.
>
> (Rugoff 1997: 78)

8 A detailed account of this event can be found in Wilson, W. (1988) 'Chris Burden – a daredevil's new expressions: realism makes his work tick', *Los Angeles Times*, 24 April, p. 93.
9 One critic noted: 'Burden's most insidious menace to the world was his tendency just to lie there, doing nothing. He increasingly drifted towards total passivity in performances, and, in the most extreme instance, played dead in a LA street': Jones, J. (1999) 'The man who used water as the oxygen of publicity', *Observer*, 21 February, p. 7.
10 These reactions are summarized in Rugoff (1997: 70). It was also criticized as demonstrating a lack of talent and direction: see Jalon, A. (1988) 'Chris Burden – a daredevil's new expressions; . . . and inquiry is his guiding principle', *Los Angeles Times*, 24 April, p. 93.
11 Quoted in McKenna, K. (1992) 'Unmasking Chris Burden', *Los Angeles Times*, 29 November, p. 36.
12 Quoted in Alberge, D. (1999) 'Suffering artist sees career take off', *The Times*, 12 January, p. 6.
13 A commentator and friend of Burden's, quoted in McKenna, K. (1992) 'Unmasking Chris Burden', *Los Angeles Times*, 29 November, p. 36.
14 For example, works like *Shoot*, *Deadman* and *Trans-Fixed* were described as 'infused with a Jesuitical purity combined with a diabolical aggression', in McKenna, K. (1992) 'Unmasking Chris Burden', *Los Angeles Times*, 29 November, p. 36. Furthermore, one critic complained:

> There was always something bothersome about these performances. In part, they seemed like a narcissistic enterprise, in which the artist simply tested his threshold of pain and tenacity. And in some cases, they taunted viewers, as in *Prelude to 220, or 110*, where spectators possessed the power to electrocute him.
>
> (in Pincus, R. L. (1988) 'Burden's performance pieces never fail to fascinate', *San Diego Union-Tribune*, 8 May, p. E8)

And another stated:

> The greatest strength and most pulling weakness of [Burden's] work lies in its realism. It provokes actual gut emotions . . . the ability to create such vivid and specific reactions is remarkable, but it leaves no room to sublimate the experience so you just wind up aggravated at the artist . . . [T]he work is so self-centered you always leap back to the imaginary person of the maker jerking your feelings around in a way that appears sadistic.
>
> (in Wilson, W. (1988) 'Chris Burden – a daredevil's new expressions: realism makes his work tick', *Los Angeles Times*, 24 April, at p. 93)

15 Most artists working in 'body art' or 'performance art' rigorously maintain a line of distinction between the performer and the audience. However, Marina Abramovic and her collaborator Ulay forced spectators to push between their naked bodies in order to enter the gallery at one performance (a performance entitled *Imponderabilia*, which took place at the Galeria communale d'arte moderna in Bologna in 1977), and Abramovic in *Rhythm 0*, as discussed above, invited the participation of audience members in her performance, with gallery visitors told they could do anything they liked to her passive body for six hours.

16 McKenna, K. (1992) 'Unmasking Chris Burden', *Los Angeles Times*, 29 November, p. 36.

17 Athey says of his work: 'it's more of a controlled experience than it is theater. The blood, pain and exhaustion are real', in Tillotson, K. (1994) 'Athey pushes taboo envelope', *Star Tribune*, 1 November, p. 4A.

18 Abbe, M. (1994) 'Bloody performance draws criticism', *Star Tribune*, 24 March, p. 1A.

19 Abbe, M. (1994) 'Walker seems surprised at reaction to mutilation show', *Star Tribune*, 29 March, p. 1E.

20 Examples from public discourse include the following: 'there are those who see taking a knife to someone's back as more an assault than art', in Hentoff, N. (1994) 'On the cutting edge in Minneapolis', *Washington Post*, 21 May, p. A23; 'even the sympathetic have been known to become weak of stomach when faced with some of [Athey's] onstage endeavors', in Breslauer, J. (1994) 'The body politics', *Los Angeles Times*, 2 July, p. F1; '[Athey's presentation] will . . . be a shocker, and some will find it sickening', in Armistead, C. (1994) 'Piercing thoughts', *Guardian*, 6 July, p. T4; and 'the inhumane activity which characterizes Athey's brand of lunatic sensationalism' and 'a show in which convulsive self-loathing is made so horrendously graphic', in Constanti, S. (1994) 'On ritual pain and abuse', *Financial Times*, 6 August, p. XVI.

21 See, for example, discussions in the following articles: Breslauer, J. (1994) 'The body politics', *Los Angeles Times*, 2 July, p. F1; Carroll, V. (1994) 'The awful art school rises once more', *The Plain Dealer*, 8 August, p. 7B; Landi, A. (1994) 'The unkindest cut', *ARTnews* 93, p. 46; No Author (1994) 'Loathsome performances', *The New Criterion*, 13/1, pp. 1–2; Rich, F. (1994) 'The gay card', *New York Times*, 26 June, p. A17; Rich, F. (1994) 'Trail of lies', *New York Times*, 17 July, p. A17; Robles, J. J. (1994) 'Disturbing viewers is one of the things art can do', *Star Tribune*, 3 April, p. 21A; Schemo, Đ. J. (1994) 'Endowment ends program helping individual artists', *New York Times*, 3 November, p. C19; Trescott, J. (1994) 'NEA takes modest cut', *Washington Post*, 24 June, p. B1; Wilson, S. (1994) 'Artist's grim performance stirs senators to act foolishly', *Arizona Republic*, 22 July, p. A2.

22 See, for example, the biographical accounts given in Brantley, B. (1994) 'A little infamy goes a long way', *New York Times*, 29 October, p. A13; Tillotson, K. (1994) 'Rituals are essence of artist's performance', *Star Tribune*, 1 November, p. 4A.

23 Athey (1997: 436) commented: 'every scene has a continual polarization of filth and glitz'. For example in the final part of the trilogy, Athey features in one scene having jewellery pulled from his anus. He is also given an enema and gagged until he vomits. The piece culminates in Athey and two others being 'buried' on stage (they are encased in black plastic body bags and dropped onto the stage; dirt is then shovelled onto them).

24 For a review of one performance of the work, see Cash (1995: 100).

25 See also the photographic work of Catherine Opie, whose *Self-Portraits* series shows her tattooed body and her arms pierced with dozens of hypodermic needles, very much in the style of Athey. Opie in fact performed in Athey's troupe as part of the cast of *Deliverance*, and took a series of photographs of Athey, called *Polaroids*. A critic commented on one of the photographs thus:

I think my favorite image from that show was one of Athey in the role of Saint Sebastian, which shows his fully tattooed body suspended from scaffolding, with spinal tap needles (with feathers) throughout his body, going through 2–1/2 inches of flesh. His face is bleeding from a removed crown of thorns, and his scrotum is enlarged with saline solution. It's an incredibly powerful, heretical image of queer sexuality with Athey in the role of Christian martyr. It's also a difficult image to look at.

(Reilly 2001: 84)

Opie has stated that she is surprised her work on Athey did not lead to public criticism:

I was surprised when nothing came down about the show. I thought it might be shut down. I was shocked that it got no press. Maybe if the images had been shown at the New Museum of Contemporary Art or at the Brooklyn Museum it would have gotten slammed. Everyone's scared to death to take that work on. It terrifies them.

(quoted in Reilly 2001: 85)

26 On Stelarc's suspension pieces, see McEvilley (1984); Waterlow (1991). On Stelarc's work more generally, see Jonson (1994); Koplos (1995). See also Stelarc's website at www.stelarc.va.com.au.
27 Quoted in Johnson, P. C. (1997) '*Lustmord* horrifies but intrigues', *Houston Chronicle*, 11 July, p. 1.
28 Holzer and Athey also share an affinity for the use of blood in their work. Holzer's artworks have foregrounded blood – both metaphorically (as a familial relationship, as a consequence of injury, illness or death) and literally (as a medium for her artwork).
29 On Holzer's work generally, see Auping (1992); Danto (1994); Ferguson (1986); Joselit (1990); Pejic (1990); Siegel (1985); Varnedoe and Gopnik (1993); Waldman (1997).
30 *Lustmord* thus initially existed in this magazine supplement. Once a year, thirty pages of the magazine supplement are dedicated to the work of one artist: Anselm Kiefer and Jeff Koons have previously published works in this way. *Lustmord* has since then been developed into an installation, which has been shown in many locations, including the Barbara Gladstone Gallery in New York City in 1986, at the Adelaide Festival at the University of South Australia Art Museum in 1998, and at the National Gallery of Australia in Canberra as part of the *Read My Lips: Jenny Holzer, Barbara Kruger, Cindy Sherman* exhibition in 1998.
31 It appears in some works by Otto Dix. In its English translation as 'lust murder', the term dates from the 1880s. For a feminist reading of such killings, see Cameron and Frazer (1987).
32 Holzer states:

I wrote it from reading first-person accounts and also reports written by the United Nations, Amnesty International and news services [about Bosnia]. And I should also say, I wrote it about women at large; it wasn't only about the situation in Bosnia. This sort of stuff goes on everywhere all of the time and I was able to draw on things that I know and have experienced and that other people have told me. It's not an alien subject.

(quoted in Ruf 1997: 111)

Holzer, along with a number of other artists, had been working with clothes designer Liz Claiborne to develop a series of artworks about domestic violence: see Simon (1994: 80–1).

33 Some commentators have suggested that Holzer selected this archaic term deliberately to provide another referent for the work, that of Germany's own violent history:

> A feminist reading might suggest that if Holzer's invocation of the female body is taken to be metaphorical then her critique against masculine violence would target both women and land (the former being literal rape victims, the land – often gendered feminine – the eternal victim of the rape of war).
>
> (No Author 1995: 22)

34 See the comments in No Author (1995); Weir (1998); and as reported in Ruf (1997: 113); Smolik (1997).
35 *Lustmord* was installed as part of the exhibition *Read My Lips: Jenny Holzer, Barbara Kruger, Cindy Sherman*, at the National Gallery of Australia, Canberra, 6 June to 9 August 1998.
36 Johnson, P. C. (1997) '*Lustmord* horrifies but intrigues', *Houston Chronicle*, 11 July, p. 1.
37 Holzer states that the observer can be

> a companion or family member who is trying to deal with the aftermath. It can be a person who has to remove the body. Death is not a clean affair, especially when it happens violently. There's always someone left at the end who has to do the dirty work.

> However, significantly, whoever this 'observer' actually is, it is key that for Holzer the observer is someone 'left behind' (in Kammerung and Holzer 1997: 122).

38 I am indebted to the analysis of *Lustmord*'s linguistic and grammatical devices in Volkart (1997).
39 Quoted in Johnson, P. C. (1997) '*Lustmord* horrifies but intrigues', *Houston Chronicle*, 11 July, p. 1.
40 Various accounts of the history of such 'body art' can be found in Adams (1996); Badovinac (1998); Dorment, R. (1995) 'Look at me: I'm a work of art', *Daily Telegraph*, 19 June, p. 21; Goldberg (1988); Jones (1998); Phelan (1993); Walker (1999); Weintraub et al. (1996). On aesthetics, wounding and trauma, see also McHugh (1999).
41 See Lesser (1993) on the oscillation between position of victim and position of killer in film and photography.

6 All that remains: image in a place of ruin

1 I'm greatly indebted to Richard Sherwin for reading this chapter. Richard sent me an email of such generosity, compassion and thoughtfulness that I include it here, in its entirety, with his permission. It offers a parallel narrative of the event, and of the imperatives of mourning and memory in the wake of trauma.

> Hi Alison, forgive me for the delay in getting back to you on your chapter, 'All That Remains'. I read it, with great interest, then put it aside. I knew I would have to read it again. Still too close for an objective saying of what occurred, what is left, what it means. I am close to this matter: a witness, not ten blocks away at the time of occurrence – at once a subject (what is this experience?), an object (you were there?), and something strangely in between, a sort of historian (I happened to have my camcorder with me that morning and recorded images, sounds, the frenzy of it all and, as I would only later perceive, the deadliness). More: this semester in my Visual Persuasion seminar I had

students work on two 9/11 related projects: their midterm was a visual piece of demonstrative evidence relating to the Victims' Compensation Fund, and their final was a movie made for a civic group client intent on avoiding the loss of Libeskind's vision amid over-commercialization in the rebuilding process. And, indeed, now we are suspended in the moment between vision and greed, Libeskind and developer Larry Silverstein together with Silverstein's architect, the politically savvy David Childs of Skidmore Owens & Merrill.

So from this multiplicity of entanglements and vantage points I come to respond to your writing.

The greatest obstacle to reading about something one has directly experienced as traumatic is resistance. The survivor says, 'this is my experience'. It is not public, not for sale, not open to aestheticization. the survivor is protective of the unutterable as if it were his or her own kin. (Even as I walked out of Tribeca that day into adjoining neighborhoods I felt my face had become inscrutable to others, those off site who could never know, could not really imagine what had just transpired. I imagine veterans walking away from a war scene experience this. In your wonderfully economical phrase, truly it is having 'seen too much'. In the extreme, Primo Levi, battling against the utter loneliness of exile from the sayable, the imaginable. In some small measure, from that day's experience I could glean more about such exile.)

Your writing is careful and kind. At only two moments of reading was I stopped by what struck me as an unnatural utterance. First, Slavoj Žižek (pp. 124–5). That brilliant thinker, whose work I admire, seemed here to cross the invisible line toward clueless profundity. I could not stomach his lofty words. In this context, they struck me (with almost literal force) as redolent with the narcissism of bloodless intellection. ('Be not so glib, my friend', I wanted to say.) That aside, I was stopped by the dissonance in the phrase 'witnessing history'. Though I know what you meant, for me the experience of 'witnessing' lacked abstraction. The distance necessary to characterize the experience in any way, including its 'historic' aspect, was simply unavailable. I suspect that only a less immersed observer could speak in this way.

Of the things I most loved in the piece: your reference to the 'sense of ethical demand involved in witnessing'. Yes. But what exactly is demanded of the witness here? We know how Bush and his gang of warriors quickly corrupted this ethical impulse with childlike talk about good and evil, the wounded giant's response to unacceptable humiliation, the impulse to lash out, to declare friends and enemies, and to annihilate the latter. Now, every time that I hear the phrase 'bad guys' I involuntarily shudder.

Yet there was a purer ethical moment in the immediate aftermath of 9/11. People opened up to one another. Strangers felt deeply for others; many spoke with a surprising eloquence about intimate feelings, vulnerabilities, pain. People bonded. The great need and corresponding response that the shared injury gave rise to, on the largest scale I have ever witnessed: compassion. An almost unthinkable human response, perhaps not wholly unlike the unthinking response of firemen and police officers who rushed into death. After, in the midst of post-traumatic mourning, before thoughts of rebuilding and commemoration arose, a surge of common humanity – wounded, vulnerable, in perpetual danger of aloneness – New Yorkers rallied to relieve the weight of our common condition, so rarely spoken of.

My friend, Jack Saul, a psychologist who specializes in trauma, said he had seen it before. In Kosovo, and elsewhere. 'It's a biological response,' he told me at the time. 'Comes in a highly predictable sequence of responses to trauma. It passes as suddenly as it arrives'. He was right. Yet, was this mass mutual compassion (this common mutual reassurance) less significant for its biological predictability and transience? Is this not laid bare the moment's authentic ethical response to what occurred?

I fear, having begun my response, a flood gate threatens to open. So a few more restrained, fragmentary observations and I am done. I agree that seeing can be traumatic. Images can wound and heal.

Yet, the experience, off screen, remains apart, different in some inexplicable way. Image always approximates more the simulacrum, or at least risks falling into that abyss of pseudo-memory, pseudo-experience . . . When the first tower fell, I saw an absolute absence: the space the tower had just before filled. Dumb disbelief greeted that absence (a *de trop* of emptiness) . . . Filling the void, Libeskind's poignant, unsurpassable insight: the bathtub should be left, exposed. Eloquent embodiment and symbol. Yet, that commemorative si[gh]t[e] is already lost from view, covered over (in cement) and built over (for the PATH train that now runs 30 feet above). A transgressive passage captures denial – manifest in a quest for false renormalization, quite notable in the exquisitely rendered, aridly beautiful – placeless, faceless, painless – memorials offered recently to the public. The memorial business threatens to overtake Libeskind's vision. The enduring tribute threatens to become a mall: our own cultural gravesite, memorial to a collective incapacity to accept the reality of suffering and death. And if it is precisely this tragic reality that is the bedrock of our authentic ethical response to trauma, is not 'business as usual', the chimera of false immortality, eternal commerce, infinite fungibility, that best embodies the proverbial 'death in life' – nullifying the ethical?

Forgive me these reflections which your recollection has evoked. Many thanks for the gentle beauty of your account. I hope that something amid these musings is of interest to you.

2 There is now an ever-expanding literature on September 11th. As a small selection, see Baudrillard (2002); Borradori (2003); Carroll (2002); Chomsky (2002); Scraton (2002); Strawson (2002); Virilio (2002); Žižek (2002). Both Habermas and Derrida, in their dialogues with Giovanna Borradori on terrorism and September 11th, comment on where they were at the time of the attacks and in the next weeks of the immediate aftermath (see Borradori 2003).

3 It is ironic that I was watching *The West Wing*, with its narrative of American democracy and ethical government. *The West Wing* also became the first television drama to engage with the events of September 11th by creating a special 'didactic' episode (entitled 'Isaac and Ishmael') dealing with terrorism and America's potential responses to terrorism. The news anchor for Australia's Channel Nine described the experience of waiting to broadcast the story:

> We wanted to go live to air but programming decided to stay with *The West Wing*. At this stage the story was just ballooning. It seemed like ages until *The West Wing* finished, probably around 25 minutes – in TV terms that's an eternity'.
> (quoted in Mangan, J., Hamer, M. and Das, S. (2003) 'September 11 remembered', *The Age*, 11 September, p. 7)

In the face of the media fervour surrounding the event and its intensely visual and 'live' nature, it seems incredible to me – and somewhat embarrassing – that I missed the immediate televisual coverage.

4 Walker, S. (2002) 'That day was a blur of horror; those that follow seem worse', *The Age*, *9:11 One Year On*, 11 September, pp. 6–7.

5 Quoted in Hochman, D. (2003) 'Tough guise', *The Age*, *A2*, 9 August, p. 5.

6 Lane, A. (2001) 'This is not a movie', *The New Yorker*, 24 September, pp. 79–80, at p. 79.

7 Walker, S. (2002) 'That day was a blur of horror; those that follow seem worse', *The Age, 9:11 One Year On*, 11 September, pp. 6–7, at p. 7.

8 Similar figures were identified among the planes' passengers and the Pentagon staff: for example, 'the four-year-old girl who was flying with her mother. The three-year-old boy who was flying with his parents', in Doyle, B. (2002) 'Prayer for the dead', *The Age, Insight*, 7 September, p. 4. Some were named as victims who were not physically at or near the site of the attacks: these 'victims by association' were often identified as the children whose mothers were pregnant on September 11th and whose fathers had died that day, or the pregnant women who had miscarried on or after September 11th.

9 Carney, S. (2002) 'What were you watching on TV when the planes crashed?', *The Age, Insight*, 7 September, p. 7.

10 Taken from, respectively, Hertzberg, H. (2001) 'Tuesday and after', *The New Yorker*, 24 September, pp. 27–8; Sontag, S. (2001) 'Tuesday and after', *The New Yorker*, 24 September, p. 32.

11 For example, one journalist wrote of 'a long-time neighbour' who 'hadn't been able to sleep since she saw what happened in New York': Carney, S. (2002) 'What were you watching on TV when the planes crashed?', *The Age, Insight*, 7 September, p. 7.

12 I am grateful to the work of Eduardo Cadava for drawing my attention to this point. See Cadava (1997: 145, n. 63).

13 No Author (2002) 'The Index', *The Age, 9:11 One Year On*, 11 September, p. 16. As one psychoanalyst commented: '[On September 11th] many thousands of people were traumatized, at all degrees of intensity, and to degrees of transience or permanence that we will not know about for a long time'. See Young-Bruehl (2003: 9). Franklin recounts the story of one woman journalist who reported from Ground Zero in the immediate aftermath and then volunteered at the site. Months after returning to work, 'she simply fell apart', and committed suicide. See Franklin, R. (2002) 'It started out as such a beautiful day . . .', *Sunday Age, Agenda*, 8 September, p. 4.

14 An environmental assessment of the site by the United States Geological Survey found that the dust contained primarily particles of glass fibres, gypsum, concrete and paper. Trace levels of asbestos were found in the airborne dust, while high levels of asbestos were found coating the site debris. See the online report at http://pubs.usgs.gov/of/2001/ofr-01/0429.

15 The actor Sarah Jessica Parker, quoted in S. Singer (2002) 'Manhattan rhapsody', *Vogue Australia*, April, pp. 142–7, at p. 146.

16 See Bird (2003). Many of those who lived nearby installed industrial air filters in their apartments to minimize the risk of respiratory illness. Rescue workers have suffered various illnesses attributable to working at Ground Zero during the aftermath of the attacks, and there was a sharp increase in the incidence of diseases such as asthma, bronchitis, sinusitis and eye problems in New York in the aftermath of the attacks. Elevated levels of mercury have been found in the blood of a number of police officers working at the site, and the dust's main components (glass fibres, gypsum, concrete and paper) contain a number of known or suspected carcinogens as well as substances implicated in various eye, skin and respiratory diseases. Tips on dust removal for apartment dwellers can be found on the website of the Federal Emergency Management Agency, at www.fema.gov/diz01/d1391n24.shtm, and on air purifiers at www.fema.gov/diz01/d1391n132.shtm. The question of whether the air near Ground Zero was safe to breathe is debated by two characters in *25th Hour* (2002, dir. Spike Lee).

17 McCourt, F. (2002) 'An island of guilt, revenge, love . . . and one great grey hole', *The Age, Insight*, 7 September, p. 2.

18 Thomson, A. (2002) 'New York remembers', *Sunday Age, Agenda*, 10 March, p. 4.

19 The blue clarity of the sky recurs in innumerable accounts of September 11th: there was 'a sky of warm and peerless blue', according to Franklin, R. (2002) 'It started out as such a beautiful day . . . ', *Sunday Age*, *Agenda*, 8 September, p. 4; 'the day began with what airline pilots call "severe clear": seemingly infinite visibility', in Remnick, D. (2001) 'September 11, 2001', *The New Yorker*, 24 September, pp. 54–74, at p. 54.

20 The process of retrieval of body parts continued long after the official rescue and salvage operation ended. Franklin describes how plumbers working on the rooftop water tank of an apartment building near Ground Zero found a rib and a vertebra, almost one year after the attacks. See Franklin, R. (2002) 'It started out as such a beautiful day . . . ', *Sunday Age*, *Agenda*, 8 September, p. 4.

21 By mid-January 2002 (four months after the attacks), workers had discovered 2,900 body parts, around 30 per day. See Riley, M. (2002) 'A weary army sifts a mountain of heartbreaks', *The Age*, 16 January, p. 8. By September 2003, 1,521 people had been identified as having died at the World Trade Centre (785 through DNA matching). See Thrush, G. (2003) 'WTC doc consumed with identifying the dead', *New York Newsday*, 10 September, online edition. The rubble also contained larger items: pieces of plane engine, remnants of the sculptures that adorned the corporate offices in the towers, girders, bicycles, office furniture. See Leith, S. (2002) 'Rush to grab "sacred relics" of Ground Zero', *The Age*, 31 January, p. 8.

22 As summed up by one letter writer: 'Ground Zero is a cemetery'. Quoted in Overington, C. (2002) 'Lights, cameras, souvenirs, action', *The Age*, 11 March, p. 13.

23 One family had put off holding a memorial service for their son, a firefighter, in the hope that something of his remains would be found at Ground Zero. Finally, just before the second anniversary of September 11th, they acknowledged that no such remains would be found. A vial containing approximately two teaspoons of blood donated before his death was located at a local bone marrow clinic: his family buried this in lieu of any other remains. See No Author (2003) 'With the last drop of blood, New York heroes close September 11', *The Age*, 10 September, p. 1.

24 Some of the thousands of 'missing' posters that appeared on New York City walls after September 11th are documented in George et al. (2002). The process of oscillation between hope and despair is represented in Mira Nair's contribution to Alain Brigand's (2002) portmanteau collection of short films, *11'09'01* (released in the United States with the title *September 11*). Note that without any body parts it is not possible to have a funeral for the lost one; only a memorial service can be held.

25 The abject relation of the survivor/spectator to a relic or trace of the lost beloved is one of the dynamics set in motion by Jenny Holzer's artwork, *Lustmord*: see my detailed discussion in Chapter 5.

26 For example, one woman attending the memorial event in September 2003 said: 'I'm here for my son. He's down there. We've never gotten anything back'. Quoted in No Author (2003) 'A nation remembers and looks to a brighter future', *The Age*, 12 September, p. 14.

27 See No Author (2003) 'One family's grief', *The Age*, 11 September, p. 6.

28 On New York's skyline, and the specific role of the skyscraper within it, see Damisch (2001), Chapters 6 and 7.

29 In Meyerowitz, J. (2001) 'Looking south', *The New Yorker*, 24 September, pp. 48–53, at p. 48.

30 McCourt, F. (2002) 'An island of guilt, revenge, love . . . and one great grey hole', *The Age*, *Insight*, 7 September, p. 2.

31 Rushdie, S. (2002) 'New York needs a towering memorial, emitting hope forever', *The Age*, 12 August, p. 11.

32 The speed of the buildings' collapse will undoubtedly have contributed to the sense of trauma sustained by witnesses – that such massive towers could be reduced to rubble in such a short time. Goldberger comments that a conventional demolition of the World Trade Centre would have seen its dismantling in two years. See Goldberger, P. (2001) 'Building plans', *The New Yorker*, 24 September, pp. 76–8, at p. 78.

33 And to what does the name 'Ground Zero' refer? Ground Zero was the term first used to identify the epicentre of the detonation of the first atomic bomb in New Mexico. It was then used for the same purpose in Hiroshima and Nagasaki. For a discussion of September 11th's connections to the atomic bomb, see Davis (2003).

34 The relative lack of images of Ground Zero (as opposed to images of the World Trade Center) supports this – it is as if screen images would confirm Ground Zero's existence and the World Trade Centre's loss. The exception is *25th Hour* (2002, dir. Spike Lee), which incorporates images of Ground Zero into its narrative of individual loss, betrayal and bereavement. On *25th Hour* and its relation to September 11th, see Taubin (2003).

35 Forgey, B. (2002) 'Mound urged as terror memorial', *The Age*, 9 March, p. 20.

36 From a letter to the *New York Times*, quoted in Overington, C. (2002) 'Lights, cameras, souvenirs, action', *The Age*, 11 March, p. 13.

37 From another letter to the *New York Times*, and quoted in Overington, C. (2002) 'Lights, cameras, souvenirs, action', *The Age*, 11 March, p. 13.

38 As with all crimes, the victims are to be commemorated, and not the criminals. It would be utterly impossible for any memorial to include the hijackers of the planes. In fact, the Lower Manhattan Development Corporation, in its call for entries for the World Trade Center Site Memorial Competition (to design a memorial within and around the selected site design by Daniel Libeskind for the redevelopment of the area), provides a list of Frequently Asked Questions and their relevant answers for the information of entrants. Under the subheading 'Recognition of Victims' is found the question 'Does the number of victims of the September 11th attacks (3,016) include the terrorists?' and the answer 'No'. See the online guidelines at www.renewnyc.com/Memorial/competition. A comparable example is provided by the Vietnam Memorial in Washington DC, designed by Maya Lin, which features the names of the American dead, without reference to the Viet Cong victims of the war. Artist and sculptor Chris Burden, whose work is discussed in detail in Chapter 5, created an artwork entitled *The Other Vietnam Memorial*, which takes the form of twelve sheets of copper inscribed with the names of the Viet Cong dead.

39 Phantoms both architectural and human. Relatives of the dead frequently described the distress of going to Ground Zero and seeing, in that great gaping space, their loss made literal. In one account, a woman, when asked if she had visited Ground Zero, said: 'I did a few times just a few weeks after they fell. You want to run into the rubble, thinking "somewhere under there is my husband", and then the reality hits you like a ton': Deblase, M. (2002) 'The widow', *The Sunday Age, Agenda*, 8 September, p. 6.

40 The Port Authority owns Ground Zero. It had initially demanded that rebuilding primarily involve office and retail space (along the lines of the original World Trade Centre); however, once the LMDC's campaign to commission an architecturally and functionally varied design was taken up enthusiastically by the public, the Port Authority had to soften its views. Note that both the two 'finalists' provided office and retail space in their designs, but confined it as secondary to the public spaces such as museums and cultural centers. See Goldberger (2003) for a detailed discussion of this aspect of the rebuilding process.

41 A 'public dialogue' was instituted by the LMDC, involving liaison with the families of victims, a detailed and substantial website, outreach through leafleting

and flyer distribution, public hearings, public forums and information sessions (some with web simulcast). The process is described in LMDC (2003: 1). Over 5,200 designs were submitted to the LMDC – resulting in what the LMDC called 'the largest design competition in history'. Proposals were assessed by a thirteen-member jury comprising artists, architects, a victim's relative, a resident of the area, local and state government representatives. The winning design, 'Reflecting Absence' by Michael Arad and Peter Walker, was selected in January 2004. The key motif in the design is that of the void, of absence. The designers described the memorial thus:

> a space that resonates with the feelings of loss and absence that were generated by the destruction of the World Trade center . . . It is located in a field of trees that is interrupted by two large voids containing recessed pools. The pools and the ramps that surround them encompass the footprints of the twin towers. A cascade of water . . . feeds the pools with a continuous stream. They are large voids, open and visible reminders of the absence.

See the Team Statement for the winning design on the LMDC's website at www.renewnyc.com/plan_des_dev/wtc_site/new_design_plans/memorial/memorial_statement.asp.

42 The nine designs were exhibited to the public over a six-week period: over 100,000 people visited the exhibition and 8,000 completed comments cards on the designs. A video was produced featuring the nine designs, and distributed to the public through the library system in New York City. Comments were solicited through the LMDC's website, and over 4,000 were submitted. As a result of this lengthy and wide-ranging system of garnering public opinion, it became apparent that the problems with most of the nine designs identified in the public response related to the aesthetic impact of the proposed buildings: the LMDC summarized these in relation to the various designs as 'buildings too massive', 'buildings inappropriate for the Lower Manhattan skyline', 'did not provide a bold enough skyline', 'buildings overwhelmed the site and were too futuristic'. See discussion of designs in LMDC (2003: 7–8).

43 Of the seven unsuccessful designs, it is worth noting that the design proposed by Norman Foster still received a great deal of public affirmation. As Goldberger comments on the Foster design, it involved

> a pair of seventeen-hundred-foot towers based on triangular forms. They united the jingoistic and the avant-garde. You could like them if you felt that rebuilding the twin towers was the right thing to do, and you could like them if you believed that the site deserved a serious piece of contemporary architecture.
>
> (in Goldberger 2003: 78)

44 Viñoly is a native of Uruguay who emigrated to the United States in 1979. The THINK team also involved Japanese architect Shigeru Ban, and Frederic Schwartz and Ken Smith of New York.

45 From the THINK Team Design Statement, downloaded 17 March 2003, published on the LMDC website, at www.renewnyc.com/plan_des_dev/wtc_site/new_design_plans.

46 As discussed in LMDC (2003: 5).

47 Rushdie, S. (2002) 'New York needs a towering memorial, emitting hope forever', *The Age*, 12 August, p. 11.

48 Between levels 70 and 110, around the height that the planes struck the towers of the World Trade Center. I'm grateful to Nina Philadelphoff-Puren for pointing this out to me.

49 From the THINK Team Design Statement, downloaded 17 March 2003, published on the LMDC website, at www.renewnyc.com/plan_des_dev/wtc_site/new_design_plans. All quotations are taken from this text.

50 From the Studio Daniel Libeskind Design Statement, downloaded 17 March 2003, published on the LMDC website, at www.renewnyc.com/plan_des_dev/wtc_site/new_design_plans. All quotations are taken from this text.

51 Libeskind also had to change some of the structural aspects of his plan: his desire to leave the entire slurry wall exposed had to be modified (since although the wall held on September 11th it was estimated that it could not hold, unsupported, indefinitely). Ever pragmatic, the Port Authority also wanted to use the below ground area for purposes such as providing parking for tour buses. To do so, the slurry walls would need to be reinforced, and some of the below ground area covered. In the revised proposal, the wall was to be exposed to a depth of 30 feet, with one section, 300 feet in length, exposed all the way to bedrock. In 2003, Libeskind was also required to modify a major aspect of his design: plans for the 'Freedom Tower', the 1,776 foot building that would be the tallest in the world, were rejected by the site owner, Larry Silverstein. Silverstein selected an architect of his own, David Childs, to redesign the proposed tower. After several weeks of protracted negotiations and dispute, the two architects agreed to develop a new plan, as joint architects, with Childs taking primary responsibility for the tower. The dispute is described in Neuman, W. (2003) 'Madhouse: Ground Zero tower designers at war', *New York Post*, 11 December, p. 1; Levy, J. (2003) 'WTC architects reach agreement on Freedom Tower', *New York Sun*, 16 December, p. 3'; Editorial (2003) 'Rising above Ground Zero', *New York Times*, 20 December p. A18.

52 Day, N. (2003) 'Libeskind design not just pie in the sky', *The Age, The Culture*, 8 January, p. 6.

53 Day notes that it is used in Melbourne's war memorial, the Shrine of Remembrance: see Day, N. (2003) 'Libeskind design not just pie in the sky', *The Age, The Culture*, 8 January, p. 6.

54 In early February 2003, a poll on the website of a local New York City news channel, New York 1, showed that 21 per cent of voters preferred Libeskind's design to that of the THINK team; 14 per cent of the voters preferred the THINK design to that of Libeskind; while 64 per cent did not like either of them. See Goldberger (2003: 78).

55 Arad and Walker's winning design for the memorial space within the redeveloped site also moves downwards:

> Bordering each pool [of water] is a pair of ramps that lead down to the memorial spaces. Descending into the memorial, visitors are removed from the sights and sounds of the city and immersed in a cool darkness . . . At the bottom of their descent, they find themselves behind a thin curtain of water, staring out at an enormous pool . . . Standing there at the water's edge, looking at a pool of water that is flowing away into an abyss, a visitor to the site can sense that what is beyond this curtain of water . . . is inaccessible.
> (from the Team Statement on the LMDC website at www.renewnyc.com)

56 Arad and Walker's design for the memorial, which moves only downwards, was criticized by some in exactly these terms: see, for example, 'Davidson, J. (2004) 'Still hoping for some poetry', *Newsday*, 7 January, p. A4. However, where Libeskind balanced empty gravespace with a perpendicular extension into the sky, Arad and Walker attempt to dispel the tension of the downwards move into the ground by means of a different device – that of continuous movement. Movement is provided within the memorial by means of two devices: first, and literally, by the

perpetually running water that flows through the series of pools; second, and metaphorically, by a 'continuous ribbon of names . . . in random arrangement', detailing those who died in the attacks (Team Statement on LMDC website).

57 Much has been written about the astonishing design proposed by Libeskind and built in 1997. See, for example, Müller (1997) and Schneider (1997). For a detailed and nuanced reading of Libeskind's design in the context of contemporary art and architecture on the Holocaust, see J. E. Young (2000).

58 Libeskind, quoted in J. E. Young (2000: 164–5).

59 James Young notes that Derrida questions the relation between the void and place, and states that there are in fact two kinds of void in Libeskind's design for the Jewish Museum (the fragmented design of the structure itself and an abyssal void into which no-one can enter). Young glosses Derrida's 'anxious question' as follows:

> one refers literally to the absence left behind by a murdered people, an absence that must be marked . . . The other kind of void is that sealed off place, which nobody can know. It is present but unknowable; it is like deep memory that gives shape and meaning to the surrounding present but remains hidden in and of itself.
>
> (J. E. Young 2000: 178)

Derrida's anxiety is elaborated in full in Derrida (1997). Young's comments could well apply to the design for Ground Zero, which acknowledges the need to mark the absence of those who died, while deploying the bathtub space as embodiment of a void that still remains hidden, closed to the living. Similarly, Libeskind's own intentions for the Jewish Museum design would seem to extend towards his proposal for rebuilding at Ground Zero: of the Berlin project he has commented:

> Absence . . . serves as a way of binding in depth, and in a totally different manner, the shared hopes of people. This is a conception which does not reduce the museum or architecture to a detached memorial or memorable detachment.
>
> (Libeskind 1997: 34)

60 Derrida goes on: 'Walled up, walled in because silence is not exterior to language' (1992: 14). To borrow from Derrida's comments – which are made in relation to law and justice – we might say that Libeskind exposes the walled-up void which is secreted as the pain and passion of architecture. For an elaboration of Derrida's argument, see McVeigh et al. (2001).

61 These and other examples can be seen in photographs taken on and after September 11th by hundreds of individuals, exhibited in a storefront in SoHo and later published as *Here is New York: a Democracy of Photographs* (George et al. 2002). See also the photographs from *The September 11 Photo Project* edited by Feldschuh (2002).

62 Initially, relatives asked journalists to print information about the missing in the hope that this might provoke news of their survival or details of their actual demise. Later, the series developed a memorial function for grieving relatives, and a means of translating the awful means of the loved one's death into a remembrance of their life. See the discussion of the series by the Metropolitan Editor of the *New York Times* in Riley, M. (2001) 'In portraits, the living reclaim their dead', *The Age*, Agenda, 4 November, p. 5. The informational sketches provided brief flashes of colour and texture in place of the numb impersonality of an individual's name. To that extent the Portraits provided a very different memorial than the list of names on the fence at Ground Zero (a list typical of most civic memorials). On

the gap between the name and identity in the context of the memorial, see Franses (2001).

63 See Barry, D. (2002) 'Minutes of silence and shafts of light recall New York's dark day', *New York Times*, 12 March, p. 1.

64 No Author (2001) 'Filling the void', *New York Times Magazine*, 23 September, online edition.

65 No Author (2001) 'Filling the void', *New York Times Magazine*, 23 September, online edition. In the end, the memorial was a joint initiative by John Bennett, Gustavo Bonevardi, Julian LaVerdiere, Paul Marabtz and Richard Nash-Gould. See their website at www.creativetime.org/towers/main.html.

66 In Overington, C. (2002) 'Let there be light: New York marks a dark day', *The Age*, 13 March, p. 10. Responses to the memorial were almost uniformly positive: see, for example, the letters to the *New York Times* ('Beams of blue, soaring to the sky'), 13 March 2002, online edition. The initiative was not free from criticism, however:

> CBS's decision to show a commemorative documentary [*9/11*, by the French filmmakers Jules and Gédeon Naudet] has divided New Yorkers, but so has the plan to beam towers of light into the sky. The tribute offends some survivors who say the emphasis should be on the loss of people, not buildings. To placate these critics, the designers agreed to a change of name, from 'Towers of Light' to 'Tribute in Light'. The beams will . . . shine from dusk till 11pm, for 32 days. Then they will go out.
>
> (in Overington, C. (2002) 'Lights, cameras, souvenirs, action', *The Age*, 11 March, p. 13)

Others found viewing the memorial a powerfully positive experience: 'the twin beams of light that were briefly projected into the night sky as a temporary memorial came closer to the fragility of our imaginings and touched upon the transformative potential of art' (Bird 2003: 93).

67 No Author (2001) 'Filling the void', *New York Times Magazine*, 23 September, online edition.

68 The opening credit sequence of Spike Lee's film *25th Hour* is devoted to the twin beams of light against a midnight blue sky. The temporary and evanescent nature of the Tribute in Light as a memorial fits Lee's intention in the film to depict the central character's last 24 hours of 'ordinary' life before beginning a seven-year prison sentence. The protagonist spends the entire film awaiting the profound loss of this ordinary life, against the backdrop of New York City's losses on September 11th.

69 Images of the towers were cut from both *Spider-man* and *Zoolander*. The cinematic release of *Collateral Damage* (whose plot features a firefighter seeking revenge on a terrorist who killed his wife and child in a bombing attack) was delayed five months. Allusions and references to airport security and Osama bin Laden were cut from the television shows *Will and Grace* and *Family Guy*. Scenes of a terrorist blowing up a plane were edited out of the American broadcast of *24*, while an episode of *The Simpsons* which depicted scenes at the World Trade Center was pulled from broadcast, as was an entire *Law and Order* mini-series because it focused on a terrorist attack on New York.

70 See, for example, the series *Sex and the City* and *The Sopranos*.

71 As noted above, there has been a considerable reluctance to create fictional images of Ground Zero, with, at time of writing, *25th Hour* being the only cinematic or televisual production which includes shots of Ground Zero. Less 'cinematic' cultural media than film and television drama have attempted some representations of the event and its implications. See for example Joyce Maynard's

novel *The Usual Rules* (2003), and the art of Gordon Bennett, discussed in McLean (2003).

72 The website http://groundzero.nyc.ny.us/photos/ is one such example.

73 A sign on a nearby fence reads: 'The regulations of the Port Authority of New York and New Jersey for this location PROHIBIT . . . defacing, marking or damaging property.' The memorial graffiti at Ground Zero provides an instance of individuals writing on walls without their messages being seen as damage or defacement (in contrast to the dominant public discourse on graffiti discussed in Chapter 3).

74 As memorial devices, the graffiti walls and collages of images provide immediate and satisfying means for survivors, relatives and visitors to participate in the process of memory and mourning. However, any formal memorial would be unlikely to incorporate similar devices into its construction. Although most memorials acknowledge the identities of the victims by incorporating the names of the lost, civic memorials tend to opt for an aesthetic austerity as opposed to the jumble of colour and imagery that arises out of the accumulations of individual contributions. Rachel Whiteread's Holocaust memorial in Vienna is one civic memorial which elects not to feature the names of the missing or dead: on Whiteread's memorial design, see Storr (1997); J. E. Young (2000). The memorial installed at the site of Oklahoma City's Murrah Building after the 1995 bombing by Timothy McVeigh selected a design that featured 168 empty, lighted chairs, one for each person killed in the blast (see Linenthal 2002). At time of writing, the plaques on fences surrounding Ground Zero feature printed lists of those killed in the attacks.

Bibliography

Adams, P. (1996) *The Emptiness of the Image*, London: Routledge.

Agamben, G. (1993) *Infancy and History: Essays on the Destruction of Experience*, London: Verso.

Amor, M. (1995) 'Felix Gonzalez-Torres: towards a postmodern sublimity', *Third Text*, 30: 67–78.

Athey, R. (1997) 'Deliverance', in J. Oppenheimer and H. Reckitt (eds) *Acting on AIDS: Sex, Drugs and Politics*, London: Serpent's Tail.

Attorney-General's Department (New South Wales) (1996) *Review of the 'Homosexual Advance Defence' Discussion Paper*, Sydney: Criminal Law Division, Attorney-General's Department.

Aukeman, A. (1995) 'Coming together and letting go', *Art News*, 959.

Ault, J. et al. (eds) (1999) *Art Matters: How the Culture Wars Changed America*, New York: New York University Press.

Auping, M. (1992) *Jenny Holzer*, New York: Universe.

Austin, J. (1996) 'Re-writing New York City', in G. Marcus (ed.) *Connected: Engagements with Media*, Chicago: University of Chicago Press.

Austin, J. (1998) 'Knowing their place: local knowledge, social prestige and the writing formation in New York City', in J. Austin and M. N. Willard (eds) *Generations of Youth*, New York: New York University Press.

Avgikos, J. (1991) 'This is my body', *Artforum*, 6: 79–83.

Avgikos, J. (1994) 'Jenny Holzer', *Artforum*, 38(September): 102.

Badovinac, Z. (1998) *Body and the East: From the 1960s to the Present*, Cambridge, MA: MIT Press.

Bal, M. (1999) *Quoting Caravaggio: Contemporary Art, Preposterous History*, Chicago, IL: University of Chicago Press.

Barrie, D. (1991) 'The scene of the crime', in B. Hoffman and R. Storr (eds) *Censorship I*, special issue of *Art Journal*, 50(3): 29–32.

Baudrillard, J. (2002) *The Spirit of Terrorism*, London: Verso.

Beal, G. (1990) 'But is it art? the Mapplethorpe/Serrano controversy', *Apollo*, 345: 317–21.

Beck, U. (1992) *Risk Society*, London: Sage.

Bird, J. (2003) 'The mote in God's eye: 9/11, then and now', *Journal of Visual Culture*, 2(1): 83–97.

Bois, Y.-A., Buchloh, B., Foster, H., Hollier, D., Krauss, R. and Molesworth, H. (1994) 'The politics of the signifier II: a conversation on the *Informe* and the abject', *October*, 67: 3–21.

Bolton, R. (ed.) (1992) *Culture Wars: Documents from the Recent Controversies in the Arts*, New York: New Press.

Borradori, G. (2003) *Philosophy in a Time of Terror: Dialogues with Jürgen Habermas and Jacques Derrida*, Chicago, IL: University of Chicago Press.

Brittain, D. (1997) 'Sophy Rickett', *Creative Camera*, April/May: 32–3.

Burrough, B. and Helyar, J. (1990) *Barbarians at the Gates: The Fall of RJR Nabisco*, New York: HarperCollins.

Cadava, E. (1997) *Words of Light: Theses on the Photography of History*, Princeton, NJ: Princeton University Press.

Cameron, D. and Frazer, L. (1987) *The Lust to Kill*, Cambridge: Polity Press.

Carmilly, M. (1986) *Fear of Art: Censorship and Freedom of Expression in Art*, New York: Bowker Press.

Carr, C. (1993) *On Edge: Performance at the End of the Twentieth Century*, Hanover, NH and London: University Press of New England.

Carroll, J. (2002) *Terror: A Meditation on the Meaning of September 11*, Melbourne: Scribe.

Cash, S. (1995) 'Ron Athey at P.S.122', *Art in America*, 83(February): 99–100.

Cash, S. and Ebony, D. (1998) 'Works attacked at Dallas museum', *Art in America*, 86(5): 144.

Castleman, C. (1982) *Getting Up: Subway Graffiti in New York*, Cambridge, MA: MIT Press.

Cembalest, R. (1990) 'The obscenity trial', *ARTNews*, 89(10): 136–41.

Chalfant, H. and Prigoff, J. (1987) *Spraycan Art*, London: Thames & Hudson.

Childs, E. C. (ed.) (1997) *Suspended License: Censorship and the Visual Arts*, Seattle, WA: University of Washington Press.

Chomsky, N. (2002) *September 11*, Sydney: Allen & Unwin.

Coetzee, J. M. (2003) *Waiting for the Barbarians*, New York: Viking.

Coleman, A. D. (1993) 'Child minders', *British Journal of Photography*, 22 April: 28–9.

Collings, M. (1997) *Blimey! From Bohemia to Britpop: The London Artworld from Francis Bacon to Damien Hirst*, London: 21 Publishing.

Collins, A. (1995) 'Hip hop graffiti culture (HHGC): addressing social and cultural aspects', online at www.graffiti.nsw.gov.au/HHGC.htm.

Cooper, M. and Chalfant, H. (1984) *Subway Art*, New York: Holt, Rinehart & Wilson.

Cordess, C. and Trucan, M. (1993) 'Art vandalism', *British Journal of Criminology*, 33(1): 95–102.

Corris, M. (1997) 'Damien Hirst and the ends of British art', *Art/Text*, 58 (August–October): 64–71.

Cossman, B. (1995) *Censorship and the Arts*, Toronto: Ontario Association of Art Galleries.

Cresswell, T. (1996) *In Place/Out of Place*, Minneapolis, MN: University of Minnesota Press.

Damisch, H. (2001) *Skyline: The Narcissistic City*, Stanford, CA: Stanford University Press.

Danto, A. (1994) 'Jenny Holzer', in his *Embodied Meanings*, New York: Farrar Strauss Giroux.

Davis, W. A. (2003) 'Death's dream kingdom: the American psyche after 9–11', *Journal for the Psychoanalysis of Culture and Society*, 8(1): 127–36.

Dawson, B. (2003) *Street Graphics New York*, New York: Thames & Hudson.

De Certeau, M. (1985) 'Practices of space', in M. Blonsky (ed.) *On Signs*, Baltimore, MD: Johns Hopkins University Press.

Demos, T. J. (1995) 'The aesthetics of mourning', *Flash Art (International)*, 184: 65–7.

Derrida, J. (1992) 'Force of law: the "mystical foundation of authority"', in D. Cornell, M. Rosenfeld and D. G. Carlson (eds) *Deconstruction and the Possibility of Justice*, New York: Routledge.

Derrida, J. (1997) 'Jacques Derrida on "between the lines"', in D. Libeskind (ed.) *Radix-matrix: Architecture and Writings*, Munich: Prestel-Verlag.

Devereaux, M. (1993) 'Protected space: politics, censorship and the arts', *Journal of Aesthetics and Art Criticism*, 51(2): 207–15.

Donoghue, D. (2003) *Speaking of Beauty*, New Haven, CT: Yale University Press.

Dornberg, J. (1988) 'Deliberate malice', *Art News*, 87(8): 63.

Douglas, M. (1966) *Purity and Danger: An Analysis of Concepts of Pollution and Taboo*, London: Routledge and Kegan Paul.

Douzinas, C., Goodrich, P. and Hachamovitch, Y. (eds) *Politics, Postmodernity and Critical Legal Studies: The Legality of the Contingent*, London: Routledge.

Douzinas, C. and Nead, L. (1999a) 'Introduction', in their *Law and the Image: The Authority of Art and the Aesthetics of Law*, Chicago, IL: University of Chicago Press.

Douzinas, C. and Nead, L. (eds) (1999b) *Law and the Image: The Authority of Art and the Aesthetics of Law*, Chicago, IL: University of Chicago Press.

Dubin, S. (1992) *Arresting Images*, London: Routledge.

Duerksen, C. J. and Goebel, R. M. (1999) *Aesthetics, Community Character and the Law*, Chicago, IL: American Planning Association.

Dugdale, J. (1995) *Lengthening Shadows Before Nightfall*, Santa Fe, NM: Twin Palms.

Fedida, P. (2003) 'The relic and the work of mourning', *Journal of Visual Culture*, 2(1): 62–8.

Feiner, J. S. and Klein, S. M. (1982) 'Graffiti talks', *Social Policy*, 12(3): 47–53.

Feldschuh, M. (ed.) (2002) *The September 11 Photo Project*, New York: Regan.

Ferguson, B. (1986) 'Wordsmith: an interview with Jenny Holzer', *Art in America*, 74(12): 108–15, 153.

Ferrell, J. (1996) *Crimes of Style: Urban Graffiti and the Politics of Criminality*, Boston, MA: Northeastern University Press.

Fiss, O. M. (1998) *The Irony of Free Speech*, Cambridge, MA: Harvard University Press.

Fleming, J. (1997) 'Wounded walls: graffiti, grammatology and the age of Shakespeare', *Criticism*, 39(1): 1–30.

Foster, H. (1993) *Compulsive Beauty*, Cambridge, MA: MIT Press.

Foster, H. (1996) 'Obscene, abject, traumatic', *October*, 78: 107–24.

Foucault, M. (1998) 'What is an author?', in J. D. Faubion (ed.) *Aesthetics, Method and Epistemology: Essential Works by Michel Foucault, 1954–1984*, New York: New Press.

Franses, R. (2001) 'Mourning and melancholia', *Journal for the Psychoanalysis of Culture and Society*, 6(1): 97–104.

Frascina, F. (2003) '*The New York Times*, Norman Rockwell and the new patriotism', *Journal of Visual Culture*, 2(1): 100–30.

Freeland, C. (2000) *But is it Art?*, Oxford: Oxford University Press.

Friedman, R. D. (1995) 'Still photographs in the flow of time', *Yale Journal of Law and the Humanities*, 7(1): 243–65.

Frohnmayer, J. (1993) *Leaving Town Alive: Confessions of an Arts Warrior*, New York: Houghton Mifflin.

Gamboni, D. (1997) *The Destruction of Art: Iconoclasm and Vandalism since the French Revolution*, New Haven, CT: Yale University Press.

Gearey, A. (2001) *Law and Aesthetics*, Oxford: Hart.

Geason, S. and Wilson, P. (1990) *Preventing Graffiti and Vandalism*, Canberra: Australian Institute of Criminology.

George, A. R., Peress, G., Shulan, M. and Traub, C. (eds) (2002) *Here is New York: A Democracy of Photographs*, New York and Zurich: Scalo.

Gibson, R. (1999) 'Crime scene', essay in catalogue for the exhibition 'Crime Scene' at the Justice and Police Museum, Sydney, 1999–2000.

Giddens, A. (1999) 'Risk and responsibility', *Modern Law Review*, 62: 1–10.

Glass, A. (1997) 'The compassionate decision-maker', *Law/Text/Culture*, 3: 162–75.

Glazer, N. (1979) 'On subway graffiti in New York', *The Public Interest*, 54 (winter): 3–11.

Goldberg, R. L. (1988) *Performance Art: From Futurism to the Present*, London: Thames & Hudson.

Goldberger, P. (2003) 'Eyes on the prize', *The New Yorker*, 10 March: 78–82.

Goldman, R. and Papson, S. (1996) *Sign Wars: The Cluttered Landscape of Advertising*, New York: Guilford Press.

Goodrich, P. (1990) *Languages of Law*, London: Weidenfeld and Nicolson.

Goodrich, P. (1992) 'The continuance of the antirrhetic', *Cardozo Studies in Law and Literature*, 4: 207–25.

Goodrich, P. (1994) '*Jani Anglorum*: signs, symptoms, slips and interpretation in law', in C. Douzinas, P. Goodrich and Y. Hachamovitch (eds) *Politics, Postmodernity and Critical Legal Studies: The Legality of the Contingent*, London: Routledge.

Goodrich, P. (1995) *Oedipus Lex: Psychoanalysis, History, Law*, Berkeley, CA and London: University of California Press.

Goodrich, P. (1996) *Law in the Courts of Love: Literature and Other Minor Jurisprudences*, New York and London: Routledge.

Gordon, M. (1996) 'Sexualizing children: thoughts on Sally Mann', *Salmagundi*, 111 (summer): 144–5.

Grimwade, C. (1998) 'Reckless sex: the discursive containment of gender, sexuality and HIV/AIDS', in A. Howe (ed.) *Sexed Crime in the News*, Sydney: Federation Press.

Gurstein, R. (1996) *The Repeal of Reticence: A History of America's Cultural and Legal Struggles over Freedom of Speech, Obscenity, Sexual Liberation and Modern Art*, New York: Hill & Wang.

Guthrie, D. (1989) 'Taboo artist: Serrano speaks', *New Art Examiner*, September: 45–6.

Hachamovitch, Y. (1994) 'In emulation of the clouds', in C. Douzinas, P. Goodrich and Y. Hachamovitch (eds) *Politics, Postmodernity and Critical Legal Studies: The Legality of the Contingent*, London: Routledge.

Hagen, C. (1991) 'Andres Serrano: after the storm', *ARTnews*, 90(7): 61–2.

Haldar, P. (1999) 'The function of ornament in Quintilian, Alberti, and Court Architecture', in C. Douzinas and L. Nead (eds) *Law and the Image: The Authority of Art and the Aesthetics of Law*, Chicago, IL: University of Chicago Press.

Hall, C. (1994) 'Sense and sensuality', *Art Review*, 46(July–August): 50–2.

Halsey, M. and Young, A. (2002) 'The meanings of graffiti and municipal Administration', *Australian and New Zealand Journal of Criminology*, 35(2): 165–86.

Handler Spitz, E. (1991) *Image and Insight*, New York: Columbia University Press.

Haver, W. (1996) *The Body of this Death: Historicity and Sociality in the Time of AIDS*, Stanford, CA: Stanford University Press.

Hermer, J. and Hunt, A. (1996) 'Official graffiti of the everyday', *Law and Society Review*, 30(3): 455–80.

Hess, E. (1991) 'No place like home', *Artforum*, October: 94–9.

Higonnet, A. (1998) *Pictures of Innocence*, London: Thames & Hudson.

Hirsch, M. (1997) *Family Frames: Photography, Narrative and Postmemory*, Cambridge, MA and London: Harvard University Press.

Hobbs, R. (1994) 'Andres Serrano: the body politic', in Institute of Contemporary Art (ed.) *Andres Serrano: Works 1983–1993*, Philadelphia, PA: Institute of Contemporary Art.

Hoffman, B. and Storr, R. (eds) (1991a) *Censorship I*, special issue of *Art Journal*, 50(3).

Hoffman, B. and Storr, R. (eds) (1991b) *Censorship II*, special issue of *Art Journal*, 50(4).

Holzer, J. (1997) *Lustmord*, Stuttgart: Kunstmuseum des Kantons Thurgau.

hooks, b. (1995) *Art on my Mind*, New York: New Press.

Howe, A. (1997) '"More folk provoke their own demise": homophobic violence and sexed excuses – rejoining the provocation law debate, courtesy of the homosexual advance defence', *Sydney Law Review*, 19: 336–65.

Howe, A. (1999) 'Reforming provocation (more or less)', *Australian Feminist Law Journal*, 12: 127–35.

Hughes, G. (1998) *Swearing: A Social History of Foul Language, Oaths and Profanity in English*, London: Penguin.

Hutchings, P. (2001) *The Criminal Spectre in Law, Literature and Aesthetics: Incriminating Subjects*, London: Routledge.

Irigaray, L. (1991) *Marine Lover of Friedrich Nietzsche*, New York: Columbia University Press.

Irigaray, L. (1993) *An Ethics of Sexual Difference*, Ithaca, NY: Cornell University Press.

Jacobson, B. (1998) *1989–1997*, Santa Fe, NM: Twin Palms.

Jarman, D. (1995a [1988]) *Chroma*, London: Vintage.

Jarman, D. (1995b) *Derek Jarman's Garden*, London: Thames & Hudson.

Jay, M. (1999) 'Must justice be blind? The challenge of images to law', in C. Douzinas and L. Nead (eds) *Law and the Image: The Authority of Art and the Aesthetics of Law*, Chicago, IL: University of Chicago Press.

Johnston, P. (1996) '"More than ordinary men gone wrong": can the law know the gay subject?', *Melbourne University Law Review*, 20: 1152–91.

Jones, A. (1998) *Body Art/Performing the Subject*, Minneapolis, MN: Minnesota University Press.

Jonson, A. (1994) 'Performance anxiety', *Art + Text*, 49(September): 22–3.

Joselit, D. (1990) 'Holzer: speaking of power', *Art in America*, 78/10: 155–7.

Julius, A. (2002) *Transgressions: The Offences of Art*, London: Thames & Hudson.

Kammerung, C. and Holzer, J. (1997) 'Interview', in J. Holzer, *Lustmord*, Stuttgart: Kunstmuseum des Kantons Thurgau.

Koch, S. (1986) 'Guilt, grace and Robert Mapplethorpe', *Art in America*, 74(11): 144–51.

Koplos, J. (1995) 'Stelarc at the kitchen', *Art in America*, 81(December): 104.

Korsmeyer, C. (1998) 'Disgust', unpublished paper, on file with author.

Kristeva, J. (1982) *The Powers of Horror: An Essay in Abjection*, New York: Columbia University Press.

Lacan, J. (1994) *Le Seminaire, Livre IV, La Relation d'objet, 1956–57* (ed. Jacques-Alain Miller), Paris: Editions du Seuil.

Lachmann, R. (1988) 'Graffiti as career and ideology', *American Journal of Sociology*, 94: 229–50.

La Placa, J. (2003) 'The right to offend', *Art Review*, December–January: 48–53.

Laplanche, J. and Pontalis, J.-B. (1986) 'Fantasy and the origin of sexuality', in V. Burgin (ed.) *Formations of Fantasy*, London and New York: Methuen.

Legendre, P. (1997) 'Introduction to the theory of the image: Narcissus and the Other in the mirror', in P. Goodrich (ed.) *Law and the Unconscious: A Legendre Reader*, New York: St Martin's Press.

Lesser, W. (1993) *Pictures at an Exhibition: An Inquiry into the Subject of Murder*, Cambridge, MA: Harvard University Press.

Levy-Leboyer, C. (ed.) (1984) *Vandalism: Behaviour and Motivations*, Amsterdam: Elsevier.

Libeskind, D. (ed.) (1997) *Radix-matrix: Architecture and Writings*, Munich: Prestel-Verlag.

Libeskind, D. (2002) 'Design statement', Lower Manhattan Development Corporation website, www.renewnyc.com/plan_des_dev/wtc_site/new_design_plans.

Linenthal, E. T. (2002) 'Up from Ground Zero: memorializing mass murder', *Christian Science Monitor*, 14 March, online at www.csmonitor.com/2002/0314/p12s03–coop.htm.

Lippard, L. (1990) 'Andres Serrano: the spirit and the letter', *Art in America*, April: 238–45.

Lombardo, P. (1994) 'Cruellement bleu', *Critical Quarterly*, 36(1): 131–3.

Lower Manhattan Development Corporation (2003) *The Public Dialogue: Innovative Design Study*, available online at www.renewnyc.com.

Lunny, A. M. (2003) 'Provocation and "homosexual" advance: masculinized subjects as threat, masculinized subjects under threat', *Social and Legal Studies*, 12(3): 311–34.

Lupton, D. (1994) *Moral Threats and Dangerous Desires*, London: RoutledgeFalmer.

Macdonald, N. (2001) *The Graffiti Subculture: Youth, Masculinity and Identity in London and New York*, Basingstoke: Palgrave Macmillan.

McEvilley, T. (1984) 'Stelarc', *Artforum*, 22(9): 81.

McEvilley, T. (1995) 'The serpent in the stone', in C. Iles (ed.) *Marina Abramovic: Objects Performance Video Sound*, Oxford: Museum of Modern Art.

McHugh, K. (1999) 'The aesthetics of wounding: trauma and self-representation', *Strategies: Journal of Theory, Culture and Politics*, 12(2): 117–26.

McKillop, S. and Vernon, J. (eds) (1991) *National Overview on Crime Prevention*, Canberra: Australian Institute of Criminology.

McLean, I. (2003) 'Illuminations or a season in hell', *Artlink*, 23(1): 36–9.

McVeigh, S., Rush, P. and Young, A. (2001) 'A judgment dwelling in law: violence and the relations of legal thought', in A. Sarat (ed.) *Law, Violence and the Possibility of Justice*, Princeton, NJ: Princeton University Press.

Maloney, M. (1997) 'Everyone a winner! Selected British art from the Saatchi Collection 1987–97', in the catalogue accompanying the 'Sensation' exhibition, London: Royal Academy of the Arts.

Manco, T. (2002) *Stencil Graffiti*, New York: Thames & Hudson.

Manderson, D. (2000) *Songs without Music: Aesthetic Dimensions of Law and Justice*, Berkeley, CA, and London: University of California Press.

Marquis, A. G. (1995) *Art Lessons from the Rise and Fall of Public Arts Funding*, New York: Basic Books.

Marr, D. (1999) *The High Price of Heaven*, St Leonards, NSW: Allen & Unwin.

Maynard, J. (2003) *The Usual Rules*, New York: St Martin's Press.

Merck, M. (1999) '"Not in a public lavatory": the prosecution of *The Romans in Britain*', in C. Douzinas and L. Nead (eds) *Law and the Image: The Authority of Art and the Aesthetics of Law*, Chicago, IL: University of Chicago Press.

Merkel, J. (1990) 'Art on trial', *Art in America*, 78(12): 41–51.

Merryman, J. H. and Elsen, A. E. (1998) *Law, Ethics and the Visual Arts*, London and Boston, MA: Kluwer Law International.

Miller, W. (1998) *The Anatomy of Disgust*, Cambridge, MA: Harvard University Press.

Minkinnen, P. (1999) *Thinking without Desire: A First Philosophy of Law*, Oxford: Hart.

Mison, R. B. (1992) 'Homophobia in manslaughter: the homosexual advance as insufficient provocation', *California Law Review*, 80: 133–78.

Mitchell, W. J. T. (1992) *The Reconfigured Eye: Visual Truth in the Post-Photographic Era*, Cambridge, MA: MIT Press.

Moran, L. J. (1996) *The Homosexual(ity) of Law*, London: Routledge.

Morgan, A. L. (1996) 'Cultural commitments: rethinking arts funding policy', *Afterimage*, 23(4): 12–5.

Morgan, S. (1987) 'Something magic', *Artforum*, 25(9): 118–23.

Müller, A. M. (1997) 'Daniel Libeskind's muses', in D. Libeskind (ed.) *Radix-matrix: Architecture and Writings*, Munich: Prestel-Verlag.

Murphy, T. (1994) 'As if: *Camera Juridica*', in C. Douzinas, P. Goodrich and Y. Hachamovitch (eds) *Politics, Postmodernity and Critical Legal Studies: The Legality of the Contingent*, London: Routledge.

Nead, L. (1999) 'Bodies of judgment: art, obscenity and the connoisseur', in C. Douzinas and L. Nead (eds) *Law and the Image: The Authority of Art and the Aesthetics of Law*, Chicago, IL: University of Chicago Press.

Neveldine, R. Burns (1998) *Bodies at Risk: Unsafe Limits in Romanticism and Postmodernism*, Albany, NY: State University of New York Press.

No Author (1995) 'Body matters', *Creative Camera*, October–November: 22.

Parkes, J.C. (1996) 'Et in Arcadia . . . Homo: sexuality and the gay sensibility in the art of Derek Jarman', in *Derek Jarman: A Portrait*, catalogue accompanying the Jarman retrospective at the Barbican, London: Barbican Art Gallery.

Peake, T. (1999) *Derek Jarman*, London: Little, Brown.

Pejic, B. (1990) 'What will become of our sensitive skin?', *Artforum*, 29(September): 130–7.

Phelan, P. (1990) 'Serrano, Mapplethorpe, the NEA, and you', *The Drama Review*, 34(1): 4–15.

Phelan, P. (1993) 'The ontology of performance: representation without reproduction', in her *Unmarked*, London: Routledge.

Phillips, S. (1999) *Wallbangin': Graffiti and Gangs in L.A.*, Chicago, IL: University of Chicago Press.

Post, R. (1998) (ed.) *Censorship and Silencing: Practices of Cultural Regulation*, Los Angeles: Getty Research Institute for the History of Art and the Humanities.

Powers, S. J. (1999) *The Art of Getting Over: Graffiti at the Millennium*, New York: St Martin's Press.

Princenthal, N. (1994) 'Felix Gonzalez Torres: multiple choice', *Art + Text*, 48: 40–3.

Pritchard, V. (1967) *English Medieval Graffiti*, Cambridge: Cambridge University Press.

Reilly, M. (2001) 'The drive to describe: a conversation with Catherine Opie', *Art Journal*, 60(2): 82–95.

Roberts, J. (1996) 'Mad for it! Philistinism, the everyday and the new British art', *Third Text*, 35(summer): 29–42.

Rollins, T. (1993) *Felix Gonzalez-Torres*, New York: ART Press.

Ruf, B. (1997) 'Tautological revelations – linguistic monuments – Trojan horses', in J. Holzer, *Lustmord*, Stuttgart: Kunstmuseum des Kantons Thurgau.

Rugoff, R. (ed.) (1997) *The Scene of the Crime*, Los Angeles: UCLA Armand Hammer Museum of Art.

Sante, L. (1992) *Evidence*, New York: Farrar, Strauss and Giroux.

Sarat, A. and Kearns, T. (eds) (1998) *Law in the Domains of Culture*, Ann Arbor, MI: University of Michigan Press.

Sarat, A. and Simon, J. (2001) 'Beyond legal realism? Cultural analysis, cultural studies, and the situation of legal scholarship', *Yale Journal of Law and the Humanities*, 13(1): 3–32.

Schama, S. (1998) 'Dept. of Acting Out: there's something about Rembrandt that attracts wackos', *New Yorker*, 24–31 August, pp. 49–50.

Schauer, F. (1998) 'The ontology of censorship', in R. Post (ed.) *Censorship and Silencing: Practices of Cultural Regulation*, Los Angeles: Getty Research Institute for the History of Art and the Humanities.

Schneider, B. (1997) 'Daniel Libeskind's architecture in the context of urban space', in D. Libeskind (ed.) *Radix-matrix: Architecture and Writings*, Munich: Prestel-Verlag.

Scholder, A. (ed.) (1999) *Fever: The Art of David Wojnarowicz*, New York: Rizzoli.

Schwartz, G. (1998) 'The destruction of art: iconoclasm and vandalism since the French Revolution', *Art in America*, 86(7): 29–33.

Schwenger, P. (1996) 'Derek Jarman and the colour of the mind's eye', *University of Toronto Quarterly*, 65(2): 419–26.

Sciorra, J. and Cooper, M. (2002) *R.I.P.: Memorial Wall Art*, London: Thames & Hudson.

Scott Bray, R. (2002) 'The eschatology of the image', PhD thesis, University of Melbourne.

Scraton, P. (ed.) (2002) *Beyond September 11th: An Anthology of Dissent*, London: Pluto Press.

Sebald, W. G. (2002) *Austerlitz*, Harmondsworth: Penguin.

Sherwin, R. (2000) *When Law Goes Pop*, Chicago, IL: University of Chicago Press.

Siegel, J. (1985) 'Jenny Holzer's language games', *Arts Magazine*, 60(December): 64–8.

Siegel, L. (1996) 'Harsh sentence for English graffiti artist', *ARTnews*, 95(6): 78.

Sill, M. (2000) 'The writing is on the wall', *SAIN Unlimited*, 2: 142–5.

Silverman, K. (2000) *World Spectators*, Stanford, CA: Stanford University Press.

Simon, J. (1994) 'No ladders, snakes: Jenny Holzer's *Lustmord*', *Parkett*, 40–41: 79–85.

Smith, P. J. (1993) '*Blue* and the outer limits', *Sight and Sound*, 3(10): 18–19.

Smolik, N. (1997) 'History inscribed on women's bodies', in J. Holzer, *Lustmord*, Stuttgart: Kunstmuseum des Kantons Thurgau.

Solnit, R. (1997) 'Sally Mann', *Creative Camera*, December–January: 38–9.

Sontag, S. (1991) *Aids and its Metaphors*, London: Penguin.

Spector, N. (1995) *Felix Gonzalez-Torres*, New York: Guggenheim Museum.

Stallabrass, J. (2000) *High Art Lite*, London: Verso.

Stallybrass, P. and White, A. (1986) *The Politics and Poetics of Transgression*, Ithaca, NY: Cornell University Press.

Stanley, L. A. (1991) 'Art and "perversion": censoring images of nude children', in B. Hoffman and R. Storr (eds) *Censorship II*, special issue of *Art Journal*, 50(4): 20–7.

Steiner, W. (1995) *The Scandal of Pleasure*, Chicago, IL: University of Chicago Press.

Steiner, W. (2001) *Venus in Exile: The Rejection of Beauty in Twentieth-Century Art*, New York: Free Press.

Stewart, S. (1988) '*Ceci Tuera Cela*: graffiti as crime and art', in J. Fekete (ed.) *Life after Postmodernism: Essays on Value*, London: Macmillan.

Storr, R. (1996) 'Setting traps for the mind and heart', *Art in America*, 84(1): 70–9.

Storr, R. (1997) 'The struggle between forgetting and remembering', *Art News*, 96(3): 127–8.

Strawson, J. (ed.) (2002) *Law After Ground Zero*, London: GlassHouse.

Stychin, C. (1995) *Law's Desire*, London: Routledge.

Sykes, J. (ed.) (1979) *Designing against Vandalism*, London: Design Council.

Taubin, A. (2003) 'Going down', *Sight & Sound*, April: 12–15.

Tiefenbrun, S. (ed.) (1998) *Law and the Arts*, Westport, CT: Greenwood Press.

Todd, M. (1972) *The Barbarians: Goths, Franks and Vandals*, London: B.T. Batsford.

Todd, S. (1995) 'Serrano's calvary', *Art & Text*, 51(May): 44–9.

Turner, G. T. (1998) 'Spencer Tunick at I-20', *Art in America*, 86(12): 90–1.

Vance, C. (1989) 'The war on culture', *Art in America*, 77: 39–45.

Varnedoe, K. and Gopnik, A. (1993) *High and Low: Modern Art, Popular Culture*, New York: Museum of Modern Art.

Vernon, J. and McKillop, S. (eds) (1989) *Preventing Juvenile Crime*, Canberra: Australian Institute of Criminology.

Virilio, P. (1986) *Speed and Politics*, New York: Semiotext(e).

Virilio, P. (1994) *The Vision Machine*, London: British Film Institute.

Virilio, P. (1997) *Open Sky*, London: Verso.

Virilio, P. (2002) *Ground Zero*, London: Verso.

Volkart, Y. (1997) 'I sing her a song about us', in J. Holzer, *Lustmord*, Stuttgart: Kunstmuseum des Kantons Thurgau.

Waldby, C. (1996) *AIDS and the Body Politic: Biomedicine and Sexual Difference*, London and New York: Routledge.

Waldman, D. (1997) *Jenny Holzer*, New York: Guggenheim Museum.

Walker, J. (1999) *Art and Outrage*, London: Pluto Press.

Wallis, B. (1991) 'Fallout from Helms amendment', *Art in America*, 77: 29.

Walsh, M. (2000) *Chris Ofili*, exhibition guide, London: Serpentine Gallery.

Waterlow, N. (1991) 'Stelarc: suspensions', *Art + Text*, 40(September): 41–50.

Watney, S. (1989) *Policing Desire*, London: Methuen.

Watney, S. (1994) 'In purgatory: the work of Felix Gonzalez-Torres', *Parkett*, 39: 38–47.

Weber, S. (1996) 'Mass mediauras, or: art, aura and media in the work of Walter Benjamin', in his *Mass Mediauras: Form Technics, Media*, Sydney: Power Institute.

Weinberg, J. (1994) 'Urination and its discontents', *Journal of Homosexuality*, 27 (1–2): 225–43.

Weintraub, L., Danto, A. and McEvilley, T. (1996) *Art on the Edge and Over: Searching for Art's Meaning in Contemporary Society*, Litchfield, CT: Art Insights.

Weir, K. (1998) *Read my Lips: Jenny Holzer, Barbara Kruger, Cindy Sherman*, Canberra: National Gallery of Australia.

White, E. B. (1949) *Here is New York*, New York: Harper & Brothers.

White, J. B. (1990) *Justice as Translation*, Chicago, IL: University of Chicago Press.

White, R. (1999) *Hanging Out: Negotiating Young People's Use of Public Space*, Barton, ACT: National Crime Prevention, Attorney-General's Department.

Wollen, P. (1997) 'Vectors of melancholy', in R. Rugoff (ed.) *The Scene of the Crime*, Los Angeles: UCLA Armand Hammer Museum of Art.

Young, A. (1990) *Femininity in Dissent*, London: Routledge.

Young, A. (1996) *Imagining Crime*, London: Sage.

Young, A. (2000) 'Aesthetic vertigo and the jurisprudence of disgust', *Law and Critique*, 11(3): 241–65.

Young, J. E. (2000) *At Memory's Edge: After-Images of the Holocaust in Contemporary Art and Architecture*, New Haven, CT, and London: Yale University Press.

Young-Bruehl, E. (2003) 'The interpretation of an architect's dream: relational trauma and its prevention', *Journal for the Psychoanalysis of Culture and Society*, 8(1): 51–61.

Zeigler, J. W. (1994) *Arts in Crisis: The National Endowment for the Arts Versus America*, Chicago, IL: a cappella books.

Žižek, S. (2002) *Welcome to the Desert of the Real*, London: Verso.

Index

Abramovic, M. 101–2
aesthetic vertigo 20, 41, 44
aesthetics 9, 10, 14; and jurisprudence 9,
    11–12, 15, 19
art: and abjection 20, 29, 36, 42–3, 44;
    bodily fluids in 21, 22, 29, 30; and
    disappearance 78, 79, 87, 88, 89, 90,
    91; and disgust 20, 21, 25, 28, 29, 32,
    34, 36, 41–4; and forensics 98–100;
    illegitimate touchings within 20,
    41–4; law's disavowal of 12, 13;
    legitimacy of 20, 26, 27, 44; as object
    of governance 8, 10, 12, 16; and
    passim
Athey, R. 100, 105–10; and
    autobiography 107–8, 109, 110, 115;
    and *4 Scenes in a Harsh Life* 108; and
    HIV 105, 107, 108; implication of
    audience 110; media representations
    of 105–7

Bal, M. 15, 144 n35
Basquiat, J.-M. 51, 55
blood: in art 88, 110, 111; in law 84–7; as
    metaphor 92
body art 115
Burden, C. 98, 100–5; critical responses
    to 104; and implication of audience
    100, 104; and injury/death 98, 100,
    102; and sculpture 100–1; and *Shoot*
    102–4

crime scene images 99–100

(de)positions, meanings of 18–19
Derrida, J. 137
disgust: and aesthetic vertigo 44; as
    response to artwork 41–4
Douzinas, C. and Nead, L. 9, 44

Dubin, S. 13, 144 n35, 149 n70
Dugdale, J. 96–7

Foster, H. 42–3

ghosts 133; *see also* phantoms
Gonzalez-Torres, F. 79, 88–90, 92, 94,
    95–6; artworks as gift 95–6; and blue
    88, 90; and rehearsal 89; and touch
    88, 90, 94, 96
Goodrich, P. 9, 93
graffiti 75–7, 121, 140; as art 50–2;
    conjoined with vandalism 56–8; and
    gangs 59–60; hip hop 52, 59, 64, 65,
    66, 68, 69, 70, 76; in New York City
    50, 61, 69, 71, 73, 77; and public
    space 71–4; represented as crime
    56–62; represented as unskilled
    55–6; represented as waste 53–6;
    slogans 52, 66–7, 68, 74, 76;
    stencils 52, 67–8; styles of writing
    64–5
graffiti writers: culture of 64–5;
    stereotypes of 62–3
Green v *R* 79–82
Ground Zero: as physical space 127–8,
    130–1; rebuilding of 131–8; and
    trauma 127–9; as wound 129, 130

Hachamovitch, Y. 12
Harvey, M. 21, 25, 34, 36–7, 41
Holocaust: memorials 117–19, 120;
    museums 119–20
Holy Virgin Mary 21, 38–39, 40, 54;
    exhibition in New York of 38–41;
    media representation of 39, 40–1;
    vandalism of 40
Holzer, J. 100, 111–12, 116; artworks of
    111, 116; *see also Lustmord*

homosexual advance defence 79–82
hooks, b. 1, 14

image: appearance of 17, 78, 93–4; and
    judgment, law's reliance on 12, 13;
    and memorials 122, 133, 138–40;
    protests about 34–5, 38–40, 47–9

Jarman, D. 79, 90–4; and blindness 91;
    and blue 91, 93; and hearing 93, 94;
    and rehearsal 91
judgment: another scene of 93–4; in art
    78–9, 87, 90, 93–4; in law 78–9, 87,
    93–4; loss of 104–5; as response to
    the other 78–9, 87, 93, 94; and *passim*

Libeskind, D. 121, 134–5, 136, 137–8
Lustmord 111–15; linguistic devices in
    112–13; meanings of 111; responses
    to 112

Mapplethorpe, R. 21, 26–8, 38; artworks
    of 27–8
Murphy, T. 11
Myra 21, 24–5, 34–7, 40, 41–2, 43–4;
    exhibition in London of 34–5; media
    representations of 34–6, 41;
    vandalism of 35, 40
Myra Hindley: media image of 24–5; and
    Moors murders 24, 37

NEA v *Finley et al.* 22–3
New Jersey 121–2

Ofili, C. 21, 38–9, 54

passion 78, 87, 90, 94; *see also* Gonzalez-
    Torres
Pell v *NGV* 28–30, 31–3
phantasy 80, 81–2, 87
phantoms 137, 139
Piss Christ 21, 22–3, 25, 29–33, 37, 38,
    39, 40, 41–4, 45, 47–8, 54; exhibition
    in Melbourne of 21, 22–3, 32–3,
    47–9; media representations of 23,
    30; vandalism of 33, 48–9

R v *Andrew and Kane* 82–84, 93
Rush, P. *see* passion

'Sensation' 24, 34–5, 38–41, 43
September 11th 2001 *see* World Trade
    Center
Serrano, A. 21, 22–3, 29–30, 32, 41, 42,
    43, 45–9, 54; and the Culture Wars
    22–3; on *Piss Christ* 29–31; *see NEA* v
    Finley et al.
Sherwin, R. 164 n1
spectatorship 13–15, 17, 18–19, 21, 28,
    31, 37, 41–2, 43, 44, 46, 49, 78, 88, 89,
    93, 94, 109, 110, 113, 114, 115, 125,
    127; *see also* witnessing, in art
Stelarc 108–9
stencils: as art 52; as political practice
    67–8; techniques of 52

tags 68–71, 76; as calligraphy 69; choice
    of 69–70; corporate 71, 73; in graffiti
    culture 68–9
trauma 110, 111, 122, 126–7, 128, 129,
    134, 135, 138, 140
Tunick, S. 1–9, 13, 15, 19, 20; artworks
    of 1, 4–5; in Melbourne 1–3; in
    New York City 5–7; *see also*
    New Jersey

urination (in art) 21, 30, 31, 53–4

witnessing, in art 100, 104, 110,
    115–16
Wojnarowicz, D. 92
World Trade Center, attacks on 122,
    123–5; as image 123–4; as media
    event 123, 125–6; memorial
    competition 131–7; and trauma
    126–7, 128, 129, 134, 135, 138;
    see also Ground Zero; trauma

X v *Commonwealth* 84–7, 93

Yang, W. 97

Žižek, S. 124, 125, 126